TOWN AND COUNTRY.

WITHIN & WITHOUT US

By JOHN S. ADAMS.

TOWN AND COUNTRY;

OR,

LIFE AT HOME AND ABROAD,

WITHOUT AND WITHIN US.

BY

JOHN S. ADAMS.

BOSTON:
PUBLISHED BY J. BUFFUM,
23 CORNHILL.
1855.

Stereotyped by
HOBART & ROBBINS,
New England Type and Stereotype Foundry,
BOSTON.

Press of Geo. C. Rand, 3 Cornhill.

CONTENTS.

TOWN AND COUNTRY.

SAVED BY KINDNESS.

"A kind word is of more value than gold or precious stones."

CHAPTER I.

"THEN you are nere!" said a stern, gruff voice, addressing a pale, sickly-looking youth, whose frame trembled and whose lip quivered as he approached one who sat at the side of a low pine table; — it was his master, a man of about forty, of athletic form, and of power sufficient to crush the feeble youth.

"Well," he continued, "if you are sure that you gave it to him, go to bed; but mind you, whisper — breathe not the secret to a living soul, on peril of your life! You may evade my grasp, but like blood I will track you through life, and add a bitter to your every cup of sweet."

The lad had no sooner left the room than a man entered, whose carelessly arranged apparel and excited appearance indicated that something of vast importance — at least, as far as he was concerned — burthened his mind.

"Harry," he said, throwing himself upon a chair, "I fear we are betrayed — discovered — completely used up."

"Discovered!" shouted the person addressed. "How? where? why?"

"It is so, friend Harry. The boy you sent made a sad error."

"Then murder the boy!" and, clutching a dagger, he motioned to leave the room, and would have done so to plunge it in the bosom of the lad, had not his informant interfered, and thus prevented him from executing so rash and cruel an act.

"What! — I *will* — *will* do it!" he shouted, endeavoring to release himself from the hands of the other.

"Never!" was the bold, unwavering response. "Move a step, and death shall be *thy* doom. Seest thou *that?*" and the speaker drew from his bosom a richly-mounted pistol.

"Doubtless thou art right," said Harry, in a more calm manner; "the excitement of the moment urged me to desperation, and, if any but you had arisen in my path, the glistening steel should have met his heart. But, Bill, how, — I am confused, my eyes swim,— tell me, how are we discovered? Must the last act in the great drama of our fortune-making be crushed in the bud? — and who dare do it?"

"If you will restrain your indignation, I will tell you."

"A hard task, yet I will try."

"That answer will not do; you must say something more positive."

"Then I say, I will."

"Enough,— the boy Sim handed the note to the kitchen-girl."

"But, Bill, think you she suspected its contents?"

"That I cannot say, but she is inquisitive, and has been known to unseal letters committed to her care, by some ingenious way she has invented. She looked uncommonly wise when she handed it to me and said, 'Mr. Bang, that's of no small importance to you.'"

"The deuce she did! I fear she deserves the halter," said Harry.

"What, with the *h* off?"

"No, there is too much *Caudleism* in her to make her worthy of that; but this is no time for our jokes. Your suspicions are too true; but how shall we act? what plans shall we adopt?"

"None, Harry, but this; — we must act as though we were the most honest men on earth, and act not as though we suspected any of suspecting us."

"O, yes, I understand you, Bill; we must not suspect anything wrong in her."

"That 's it," answered Bill, and, plunging his hand into his pocket, he drew from thence a small scrap of greasy, pocket-worn paper, and read a few words in a low whisper to his friend Harry. A nod from the latter signified his approval. He returned the mysterious memorandum to his pocket, and planting upon his head a poor, *very* poor apology for a hat, swung his body round a few times on his heel, and leaving the house, pushed open a small wicket-gate, and entered the street. He hurriedly trudged along, heaping silent curses upon the head of Harry's boy, the kitchen-girl, and sundry other feminine and masculine members of the human family not yet introduced to the reader.

Bold Bill gone, Harry sat for some considerable length of time ruminating upon the strange turn affairs had taken, and indulging in vague speculations upon whether the next would be as unfavorable; and at this point of our story we will divulge somewhat of his history.

Henry Lang had been in years past a man well-to-do in the world; he was once a merchant respected for his strict integrity and punctuality in business affairs; but by a false step, a making haste to be rich, he was ruined. The great land speculation of '37 and thereabout was the chief, and in fact the only cause of his misfortune. On one day he could boast of his thousands, and no paper held better credit than that signed or endorsed by him. The next, the bubble broke, his fortune was scattered, his riches took to themselves wings and flew away, his creditors, like vultures, flocked around and speedily devoured what little remained of his once large possessions. He was a man easily affected by such occurrences, and they deeply wounded his sensitive feelings. What should he do? He looked around upon those who once professedly loved him; but no hand was extended, no heart sympathized with him in the hour of trouble. He left his country, and with it a wife and one child, a daughter, lovely, if not in personal appearance, in highly virtuous and intellectual qualities, which, after all, will be admitted to be of more value than that which time withers and sickness destroys.

With a sad heart Mr. Lang left these and the spot of earth around which many fond recollections clustered. After twenty months of tedious wanderings, he returned, but he was a changed man; his ambitious spirit had been crushed, all his hopes had departed, and he gave himself up to the fanciful freaks of a disordered mind. Defeated in his honest endeavors to obtain a livelihood, he was now seeking out dishonest ways and means to retrieve his fallen fortune. He sought for those of a kindred spirit, nor was he long in finding such; in a short time he became acquainted, and soon after connected, with a gang of adventurous men, about six in number, who by various fraudulent means were each amassing much wealth.

"And he deserted me in this my time of need! Can it be true that he has gone? For him I would willingly have endured any privation. Did he not know that my love was strong? Could he not believe me when I said, that, as I joyed with him in his prosperity, I would mourn with him in its reverse?—that I could ever be near to comfort and console,—one with him at all times, under all circumstances?"

"Comfort yourself, dear mother!" said a calm voice. "Remember that these trials are for our good, and that the sorrows of earth are but to prepare us for the joys of heaven. Cheer up, mother! let these thoughts rejoice thy heart! Despair not, but take courage!"

With such words did the daughter administer consolation to the afflicted, when hearing that her husband had forsaken her and sailed for a foreign port. It was indeed a heavy blow, and she felt it severely. She could have endured the thought of having all her earthly possessions taken from her, — but to be deserted, to be left at such a time dependent upon the charities of the world for a subsistence, such a thought she was not prepared to withstand.

The few words of Julia having been said, a deep silence for some moments pervaded the room. She sat and gazed up into the face of her mother, whose tears bore witness to the deep anguish of her soul. The silence was interrupted by the rising of the latter, who for a few moments paced the room, and then sank helplessly into a chair. The attentive child sprang to her relief, a few neighbors were called in, she was laid upon her bed. That night a severe attack of fever came upon her; for many days her life was despaired of; but at length a ray of hope cheered the solitude of the chamber of the sick, and at the close of six weeks her health was in a great degree restored.

"Time heals all wounds," is a common saying, true in some cases, but not in all. Some wounds there are that sink deep in the heart,— their pain even time cannot remedy, but stretch far into eternity, and find their solace there. Others there are which by time are partially healed; — such was that of Mrs. Lang. During her sickness, many of the little incidents that before had troubled her passed from her mind. She now yielded submissively to her sad allotment, believing, as during her sickness she had often been told, that afflictions come but for our own good, however paradoxical such a statement might seem to be.

The kindness of a neighbor enabled her, with her daughter, to remove their place of residence. This neighbor — a lady of moderate pecuniary circumstances — furnished them with needle-work, the compensation for which enabled them to obtain supplies necessary for a comfortable living.

CHAPTER II.

For some time Mr. Henry Lang sat with his head resting upon his hands, and with them upon the table. Deep silence prevailed, broken only, at lengthy intervals, by the loud laugh following the merry jest of some passer-by, or the dismal creaking of the swing-sign of an adjacent tavern.

How long Mr. Lang might have remained in that position is not for us to determine. But it would have been much longer, had not a loud rap at the outer door awakened him from his drowsy condition.

He started at the sound, and, taking in his hand a dim-burning candle, proceeded to answer the call. Opening the door, a man closely enveloped in a large cloak and seal-skin cap, the last of which hung slouchingly about his head and face, inquired, in a gruff, ill-mannered voice, whether a person unfavorably known to the police as "Bold Bill" had been there. Harry trembled, knowing his interrogator to be one of the city watch; yet he endeavored to conceal his fears and embarrassment by a forced smile, and remarked:

"That is indeed a strange name, and one of which I have never before heard. Tell me what he has been about."

"Why do you think he has been about anything, or why think you I am acquainted with his actions?" inquired the stranger, in a stern voice, as though the supreme majesty of the law represented by him was not to be spoken lightly of.

His scrutinizing features relaxed not in the least, but he looked our hero steadfastly in the face.

"By the appearance of your dress I judge you to be a watchman, and as such I suppose you to be in search of that odd-named person on account of his being suspected of having broken the law."

"You are right," answered the officer. "I *am* a watchman! The authority invested in me is great. I trust I duly appreciate it. I guard your dwelling when you are slumbering, unconscious of what takes place around you."

"You are very kind," remarked Harry, suddenly interrupting him, and speaking rather ironically than otherwise.

The watchman continued: "Life is to me nothing unless I can employ it in doing good. Do you understand me?"

"Perfectly."

"Will you walk in?" inquired Mr. Lang, as a sudden gust of wind nearly extinguished his light.

"No, I thank you; that would be of no service to my fellow-men; and, as I am in search of the man who committed the robbery, ten minutes ago, upon Mr. Solomon Cash, the broker, I must ——"

"Robbery!" exclaimed Harry, appearing perfectly astonished at the thought. "O, the degeneracy of the nineteenth century,— the sinfulness of the age!"

"Amen!" responded the officer; and, pulling his large, loose cloak more closely about him, he made a motion to continue on in the service of his fellow-men.

"But wait, my good man," said Harry. "Am I to suppose, from what you said, that 'Bold Bill' is the perpetrator of this base crime?"

"Precisely so," was the laconic reply; and the man moved on in execution of his benevolent designs.

"He should be brought to justice," said Harry, as he turned to enter. No sooner, however, had he closed the door, than he burst forth in a loud laugh. This was soon changed to seriousness, for he became confident that his friend Bill was in danger. To shield him, if guilty, from detection, and protect him, if innocent, was now his great object. But where should he find him? That was a problem he could not solve. The boy was sleeping soundly; he must awaken him, he must go out in search of his friend.

With this intention, he dressed himself in a stout, heavy overcoat, and, locking the door hurriedly, walked up the street. On he went, as though his life depended upon whether he reached a certain square at a certain time. He looked at nothing save some far-distant object, from which, as it approached, he withdrew his eyes, and fixed them on an object yet distant. Turning a corner, a collision took place between him and another man, who appeared to be in as much haste as himself. He was about to proceed, when he who had met him so abruptly struck him very familiarly upon the shoulder, saying, as he did so, "Harry, how are you? — good luck — tin — lots of it — watch — haste."

The person thus addressed was not long in discovering who it was that spoke to him, and from his words and actions that he had reason to be in some haste. It was he for whom he was in search; and, being aware that the nature of the case demanded despatch, he cordially grasped his hand, and, without another word between them, they in a short time reached the dwelling of Mr. Lang.

"What are the facts now?" inquired Harry, after having narrated the incident that had occurred since he left, namely, the watchman's visit.

"Then you think there is no danger in my staying here?" inquired Bill.

"Not in the least," replied Harry; "for I positively asserted that you was not here, and strongly intimated that I knew no person of your name. Danger! there is none; so proceed, friend Bill,— but a little wine."

Wine is an indispensable with all rogues; it nerves to lawlessness, and induces them, when under its influence, to commit acts which in their sober moments they would scorn to perform.

The wine-glass emptied, Bill proceeded in his narrative.

"When I left here, I started intending in a direct course to go home. Musingly I walked along, cursing my fate, and several other things, too numerous to mention, and speculating upon the probable success of our scheme, till I arrived in front of the old broker's. He was just putting up his iron-clamped shutters. I was on the opposite side, at some distance, yet not so far but that I plainly saw him enter and pack snugly away in his little black trunk divers articles of apparently great worth. I carelessly jingled the last change in my pocket, of value about a dollar or so; and the thought of soon being minus cash nerved me to the determination of robbing the broker. Thus resolved, I hid myself behind a pile of boxes that seemed placed there on purpose, till I heard the bolt spring, and saw the broker, with the trunk beneath his arm, walk away. As he entered that dark passage, 'Fogg-lane,' I pulled my cap down over my face, and dogged him, keeping the middle of the passage; and, seeing a favorable opportunity, I sprang upon him from behind, and snatched the box; then left him to his fate.

"I ran off as fast as my legs, urged on by the cry of 'stop thief,' would carry me. Notwithstanding the speed at which I ran, I found the crowd bearing down upon me; and, my hope almost failing, I had resolved to give in and suffer the consequences, when, seeing a dark lane, I ran into it, then dodged behind a pump. The crowd ran on; I found I had escaped. Now, Harry, a friendly shake in honor of my good luck."

"As you say," answered Harry, "and it is my humble opinion you are not entirely free from change."

"Really, Harry, I don't know what the box contains; however, 't is confounded heavy. It is full of gold or iron."

"My face for a scrubber, if small change is n't pretty much the contents; the fourpences and dimes lie pretty near together, friend Bill." "But," continued Harry, "'t is best to secrete yourself, box and all, till the law dogs are silenced. If they come here, I will throw them a bone; but hark! —"

The two remained silent; for the sound of approaching footsteps momentarily grew more distinct. It sounded nearer, and now was in front of the door.

"To the closet," whispered Harry; and in a moment Mr. Lang was the only occupant of the room. He was right in his supposition; for the door opened, and the same man, in the same cloak, with the same consequential air, accompanied by others, entered abruptly, and interrogated Harry rather closely. "Positively, I know nothing about him," said Mr. Lang. This declaration seemed to have a wonderful effect upon each of the officers. They gazed steadfastly at him, then at each other, and their features indicated their belief in what he said.

"Benevolent as I am," said the officer, "I must require a strict search; — not that we suspect him to be on your premises, noble sir, but my duty demands it."

The officer, having thus far declared what he thought to be his duty, proceeded to its performance by pushing open the doors through which egress could be had to the street, and all others. As chance would have it, the right door was by them unobserved. But where was the fugitive? He had been hurried into a closet. It was not after the manner of most closets. It was about three feet square, at one side of which was a door communicating with the cellar, through which any person might pass, and from thence into the street. He could not stand long and listen to the loud converse of those without. He felt himself in danger if he remained, and determined upon leaving the closet. So, having passed into the cellar, he entered the street.

The night was dark; the hour late, and no persons stirring. Softly he crept beneath the window, and, perceiving none in the room but Harry, softly tapped the glass. Mr. Lang raised his arm, by which signal Bill understood that he was aware of his having left the closet. Then through back lanes, seldom pedestrianated, and narrow passages, he wended his way, with his stolen treasure closely held beneath the loose folds of his jacket. He passed on, till, reaching a dark street, he beheld a dim light in a low oyster-cellar; he entered. A black fellow was the proprietor, cook, &c. Bill asked for lodgings.

"Well, massa, dem I 'ave; but I always take pay in advance from gemmen."

Bill asked the price.

"Wall, 'tis fourpance on a chest, and threepance on de floor."

Mr. Bang availed himself of the best accommodations, and accepted the chest. He stretched himself upon it, having settled the bill, but slept little. His mind was continually roaming. Now he imagined himself in the closet, with scarcely room to breathe, and an officer's hand on the latch; now groping along untraversed paths, till, falling into some hole, he awoke from his revery.

'T was near the dawn of day when, from his house, accompanied by the boy, Mr. Lang passed out in search of Bill. A light rain was falling, and in perspective he saw a dull, drizzly sort of a day,—a bad air for a low-spirited individual. The "blues" are contagious on such a day. Yet he strove to keep his spirits up, and to make the best of a bad job.

As he passed by the office of the broker, he perceived a

crowd, and many anxious inquiries were heard respecting the robbery. It appeared the broker had received but little injury, and was as busy as any one in endeavoring to find out the rogue. Harry put on as bold a face as possible, and inquired of the broker the circumstances, which he very minutely narrated.

"Have you any suspicions of any one?" inquired Mr. Lang.

"Of no one," was the brief response.

"It would be very sad if the rascal could not be found," continued Mr. Lang. "The gallows is too good for one who would make such a cowardly attack, and treat with such baseness one who never harmed his fellow."

"I am of your opinion," answered the broker; and the two, having thus fully expressed their opinion, parted.

Mr. Lang was not much troubled in finding his companion. He entered the cellar just as the latter had arisen from his *chesty* couch, and a cordial grasp of the hand bore witness that friends had met.

Both were aware that the place in which they were was not of very good repute, and made all possible haste to remove. But, to effect this successfully, it was necessary that Mr. Lang should have a change of dress.

He was making this change when half a dozen men unexpectedly entered. "You are my prisoner," said one, catching hold of Mr. Lang by the coat-collar. "Tropes, secure the other."

They were now both in custody, and the officers, after a little search, discovered the broken box, and arrested the black man.

"For what am I arrested?" inquired Mr. Lang.

"That you will soon know," was the reply.

"But I demand an answer now. I will not move a step till I get it."

"What! what 's that?" said a stout, rough-looking man, striking the prisoner, and treating him more like a dog than what he was.

"I demand an answer to my inquiry. For what am I arrested?"

"He 's a dangerous man," remarked another of the officers; "it 's best to put him in irons;" whereupon he drew from a capacious pocket a pair of rusty manacles. Mr. Lang, and his two fellows in trouble, found it best to coolly submit, and did so. Five minutes passed, and the cold walls of a prison enclosed them.

CHAPTER III.

Daylight breaks, and the dwellers upon a thousand hills rejoice in the first rays of the morning sun.

"Didst thou ever hear that promise, 'God will provide'? inquired a pale, yet beautiful girl, as she bent over the form of a feverish woman, in a small, yet neatly-furnished room.

"Yes," was the reply; "and he who allows not a sparrow to fall unnoticed, shall he not much more care for us? Yes, Julia, God will provide. My soul, trust thou in God!"

It was Mrs. Lang. The good lady who had befriended her was suddenly taken ill, and as suddenly died. Mrs. Lang, with her daughter, left the house, and, hiring a small room at an exorbitant rent, endeavored, by the use of her needle, to live. She labored hard; the morning's first light found her at her task, and midnight's silent hour often found her there. The daughter too was there; together they labored, and together shared the joys and sorrows of a worse than widowed and orphaned state. Naturally of a feeble constitution, Mrs. Lang could not long bear up under that labor, and fell. Then that daughter was as a ministering angel, attending and watching over her, and anticipating her every want. Long was she obliged to labor to provide the necessaries of life; often working hard, and receiving but ten to fifteen cents a day for that which, if paid for as it should be, would have brought her a dollar. It was after receiving her small pittance and having returned to her home, that the words at the commencement of this chapter fell from her lips. Her mother, with deep solicitude, inquired her success.

"He says he can get those duck trousers made for three cents, and that, if I will not make them for that, he can give me no more work. You know, mother, that I work eighteen hours of the twenty-four, and can but just make two pair,— that would be but *six cents a day.*"

"My child," said the mother, rising with unusual strength, "refuse such a slavish offer. Let him not, in order to enrich himself, by degrees take *your* life. Death's arrows have now near reached you. Do not thus wear out your life. Let us die!"

She would have said more; but, exhausted by the effort, she sank back upon her pillow. Then came the inquiry, "Didst thou ever hear that promise, 'God will provide'?"

The question had been put, and the answer given, when a slight rap at the door was heard. Julia opened it; a small package was hastily thrust into her hand, and the bearer of it hasted away. It was a white packet, bound with white ribbon, and with these words, "Julia Lang," legibly written upon it. She opened it; a note fell upon the floor; she picked it up, and read as follows:

"Enclosed you will find four five-dollar bills. You are in want; use them, and, when gone, the same unknown hand will grant you more.

"Let me break now a secret to you which I believe it is my duty to divulge. You will recollect that your father mysteriously abandoned you. He is now in this city, in ——

street jail, awaiting his trial. I am confident that he is innocent, and will be honorably acquitted; and I am as confident that it needs but your presence and your kind entreaty to bring him back once again to his family and friends. I have spoken to him, but my words have had no effect except when I spoke of his family. Then I could see how hard he strove to conceal a tear, and that I had found a tender chord, that needed but your touch to cause it to work out a reformatory resolution.

"I write because Mr. Lang was a friend of mine in his days of prosperity. I know he has no heart for dishonesty; but, thinking himself deserted by those who should cling to him, he madly resolved to give himself up, and follow where fate should lead. Yours, truly,

"CHARLES B——.

"N. B. Others have also spoken with him; but their appeals have been in vain. If you will be at the corner of L—— avenue and W—— street, at three o'clock to-day, a carriage will be in readiness to convey you to his presence. C. B."

Anxiously did Mrs. Lang watch the features of her child as she stood perusing the letter; and as she sat down with it unfolded, apparently in deep thought, her inquisitiveness increased. She inquired — she was told all. "Go," said she to her daughter, "and may the blessings of Heaven attend you!"

Julia stood wondering. She had doubted before; she feared it might be the scheme of some base intriguer; but now her doubts vanished, and hope cheered her on.

Long seemed the intervening hours, and many were the predictions made concerning the success of her mission; yet she determined to go, in the spirit of Martin Luther, though every stone in the prison should arise to persecute her.

The appointed hour came, and, letter in hand, she left her room, and repaired to the spot. There she found a carriage; and the driver, who, it appeared, was acquainted with her, inquired whether she desired to go to —— street jail. Replying in the affirmative, she entered, and the carriage drove off. When she had reached the street, and came in full view of the prison, her timidity almost overcame her; but, recollecting the object she had in view, she resisted a desire that involuntarily arose to return.

"Is the warden in?" inquired the driver of the gate-keeper.

"He is; — another feast for the lion, eh?" and the keeper, who had more self-assurance than manners, having laughed at his own nonsense, pulled a bell-cord, and the warden appeared.

"The gentleman who came this morning to see Mr. Lang wished me to bring this young lady here, and introduce her to you as Mr. Lang's daughter." Having said this, the hackman let down the steps, and aided her out. The gate-keeper retired into a sort of sentry-box, and amused himself by peeping over the window-curtain, laughing very immoderately when anything serious was said, and sustaining a very grave appearance when anything having a shade of comicality occurred.

The warden very politely conducted Julia into his office, and soon after into the jail. It was a long building inside of a building, with two rows of cells one above the other, each numbered, and upon each door a card, upon which was written, in characters only known to the officers of the prison, the prisoner's name, crime, term of imprisonment, and general conduct whilst confined.

As Mr. Lang was waiting trial, he was not in one of these

cells, but in one of large dimensions, and containing more conveniences.

As they entered, he was seated at a small table, with pen, ink and paper, engaged in writing. He did not at first recognize his child, but in a moment sprang to her, and clasping her in his arms, said, "My child."

Such a change in him needs some explanation.

After being committed to prison, his first thought was upon the change of his condition from what it formerly was; and his first resolution was to reform. He thought of the deep plots he and his companion had laid to amass a fortune; but, supposing that the latter would be convicted, and condemned to serve a long time in confinement, he concluded that that scheme was exploded.

"Yet," thought he, "if there be none on earth I can call my friends,— if my family forsake me (yet just would it be in them should they reject my company), — of what avail would my reformation be, except to a few dogging creditors, who would jeer and scoff at me at every corner, and attempt to drive me back to my present situation? It might be some satisfaction to them to see me return; but what feelings would it arouse within me,— with what hatred would I view mankind! No; if none will utter a kind word to me, let me continue on; let the prison be my home, and the gallows my end, rather than attempt to reform while those who were once my friends stand around to drive me back by scoffing remarks!"

Such were the sincere thoughts of Mr. Lang. He would return, but none stood by to welcome him. A few had visited him, most of whom had severely reflected upon his misdeeds. They opened a dark prospect for him in the future. "Now," said they, "you must here remain; receive retribution for your evil deeds, and a sad warning to others not to follow in your steps, lest they arrive at the same goal." Was there encouragement in this? Surely not; he deemed them not the words of friendship, and he was right in his judgment.

"Why did you visit this dark prison?" inquired Mr. Lang.

"Because you are here, father!" was the artless reply.

"And could you forgive your father? How could you seek him, when he forsook you?" Mr. Lang could not make this last observation without becoming affected even to tears.

Julia seemed to take courage; new energies seemed to be imparted to her. She felt an unseen influence at her side, and a holy calmness resting upon her soul.

"Prison-walls cannot bar you from my heart, though in the worst place on earth. Though friends laugh me to scorn when I seek your presence, you are my father still, and ungrateful would I be did I not own you as such!

"In thinking of the present, I do not forget the past; I remember the days of old, the years in which we were made glad; — and you, father, when free from these walls, will you not return again to your family, and make home what it once was? To-day I will see Mr. Legrange; he wants a clerk, and, by a little persuasion, I am certain I can get you the situation. Will you not reform?"

She could say no more; yet her actions spoke louder than words could possibly do, and her imploring attitude went home to the heart of her parent. He, for the first time since the commencement of his wayward course, felt that the hand of sympathy was extended to greet him, should he make a motion to return. And why should he not grasp it? He did. There, in that prison-cell, upon his knees, he promised to repent and return.

"Pleasant residence, Miss!" said the gate-keeper, as our heroine left the yard, and then laughed as though he had committed a pun that would immortalize him from that time forth.

She noticed not his ill-mannered remark, but, reëntering the carriage, thought of nothing but the joy her mother would feel upon learning her success, till the carriage stopped and the driver let down the steps. Having related her adventure, she left her home with the intention of seeing Mr. Legrange.

Mr. Legrange was a merchant on Cadiz wharf; he was wealthy, and as benevolent as wealthy. Notices were often seen in the papers of large donations from him to worthy institutions, sometimes one and sometimes three thousand dollars. His fellow-men looked upon him as a blessing to the age. There was no aristocracy in him; he did not live like a prince in the costliest house in the city, but a small, neat tenement was pointed out as his abode. Not only was he called the "Poor Man's Friend," but his associate and companion. He did not despise the poor man, and wisely thought that to do him good he must live and be upon an equality with him.

Mr. Legrange had just opened an evening paper, when a light rap at his counting-house door induced him to lay it aside. Opening it, a young woman inquired if Mr. Legrange was in.

"That is my name," was the reply. "Good-morning, Miss Lang."

Julia was rejoiced that she was recognized. She had not spoken to Mr. Legrange since her father's failure in business; previous to that sad occurrence she had known him personally, yet she scarcely thought he would know her now.

"This is a lovely day," said Mr. Legrange, handing her a chair. "Your mother is well, I hope."

"As well as might be expected: she will recover fast, now."

"Indeed! What? Some glad news?"

"Yes, sir; father is in the city, and has reformed."

"Thank God for that!" said Mr. Legrange. "It is one of the blessings of this life to *hope* for better days."

"He has reformed," continued Miss Lang, "yet he may be led back unless he gets steady employment; and I heard that ——"

"—— that I want a clerk," said Mr. Legrange, anticipating her in her remarks; "and," continued he, "your father is just the man I want. I knew him in his better days, before a fatal misstep felled him to the ground. Miss Lang, let your father call next Tuesday; to-morrow I start on a journey, and shall not return till then."

With many sincere thanks, Julia left the room; her heart overflowed with gratitude to the Giver of all things. She saw his hand and felt his presence.

It was well that Mr. Legrange was about to leave the city, as Mr. Lang's examination was to be had the next day, and Mrs. Lang and her daughter confidently expected he would be acquitted.

The morrow came; the examination began and terminated as they had expected. William Bang was remanded back to prison to await his trial for robbery. Mr. Lang was acquitted, and, joining a company of friends whom Julia had collected, left for the residence of his family.

What a meeting was that! Angels could but weep for joy at such a scene, and drop their golden harps to wipe away their tears of gladness. Long had been their separation. What scenes had the interval disclosed! And how changed were all things! She was in health when he left, but now in sickness; yet it was not strange.

That day was the happiest he had spent for many months, and he rejoiced that an angel of light, his daughter, had sought him out. She had been, indeed, a ministering spirit of good to him, and in the happy scene then around her she found her reward,— O, how abundant!

With a light and joyous step did Henry Lang repair to the store of Mr. Legrange. The sun's rays were just peering over the house-tops, and he thought that he, like that sun, was just rising from degradation to assume new life, and put forth new energy.

We need not lengthen out our tale by narrating what there ensued. He that day commenced his clerkship, and to this day holds it. He often received liberal donations from his employer in token of his regard for him, and by way of encouraging him in his attempts to regain his lost fortune.

* * * * * *

It was on a December evening that a family circle had gathered around their fireside. The wild wind whistled furiously around, and many a poor wight lamented the hard fate that led him abroad to battle the storm. "Two years ago this night," said the man, "where was I? In an obscure house, planning out a way to injure a fellow-man! Yea, would you believe it? the very man who has since been my benefactor,— my employer!"

The door-bell rang, and the conversation was abruptly terminated.

In a few minutes none other than Mr. Legrange entered; he received a hearty welcome, and was soon engaged in conversation.

"Mr. Lang," said he, as he was about to depart, "your daughter remembers receiving an anonymous letter signed 'Charles B———.' I do not say it to please my own vanity, but I ordered my clerk to write it, and sent it by my son. I thought of you when you little thought you had a friend on earth who cared for you, and rejoice that I have been the humble instrument in effecting your reformation."

"Here," he continued, handing him a paper, "this is the deed of a house on —— street, valued at eight thousand dollars; accept it as a present from me to you and your family, and remember this, that *a kind word is of more value than gold or precious stones.* It was that which saved you, and by that you may save others. Good-evening; I will see you at the store to-morrow."

Having said this, he left, waiting not to receive the thanks that grateful hearts desired to render him.

And now, reader, our story is ended. If you have followed us thus far, neglect not to receive what we have faintly endeavored to inculcate; and ever remember, while treading life's thorny vale, that "*a kind word is of more value than gold or precious stones.*"

THE LOVE OF ELINORE.

SHE stood beside the sea-shore weeping,
While above her stars were keeping
  Vigils o'er the silent deep;
While all others, wearied, slumbered,
She the passing moments numbered,
  She a faithful watch did keep.

Him she loved had long departed,
And she wandered, broken-hearted,
  Breathing songs he loved to hear.
Friends did gather round to win her,
But the thoughts that glowed within her
  Were to her most fond and dear.

In her hand she held bright flowers,
Culled from Nature's fairest bowers;
  On her brow, from moor and heath,
Bright green leaves and flowers did cluster,
Borrowing resplendent lustre
  From the eyes that shone beneath.

Rose the whisper, "She is crazy,"
When she plucked the blooming daisy,
  Braiding it within her hair;
But they knew not what of gladness
Mingled with her notes of sadness,
  As she laid it gently there.

For her loved one, ere he started,
While she still was happy-hearted,
  Clipped a daisy from its stem,

Placed it in her hair, and told her,
Till again he should behold her,
  That should be her diadem.

At the sea-side she was roaming,
When the waves were madly foaming,
  And when all was calm and mild,
Singing songs, — she thought *he* listened, —
And each dancing wave that glistened
  Loved she as a little child.

For she thought, in every motion
Of the ceaseless, moving ocean,
  She could see a friendly hand
Stretched towards the shore imploring,
Where she stood, like one adoring,
  Beckoning to a better land.

When the sun was brightly shining,
When the daylight was declining,
  On the shore she 'd watch and wait,
Like an angel, heaven-descending,
'Mid the ranks of mortals wending,
  Searching for a missing mate.

Years passed on, and when the morning
Of a summer's day gave warning
  Of the sweets it held in store,
By the dancing waves surrounded,
Like a fairy one she bounded
  To her lover's arms once more.

Villagers thus tell the story,
And they say a light of glory
  Hovereth above the spot
Where for days and years she waited,
With a love all unabated,
  And a faith that faltered not.

There 's a stone that is uplifted,
Where the wild sea-flowers have drifted;
  Fonder words no stone e'er bore;

And the waves come up to greet them,
Seeming often to repeat them,
  While afar their echoes roar —
  " DEATHLESS LOVE OF ELINORE."

'TIS SWEET TO BE REMEMBERED.

'T IS sweet to be remembered
  In the turmoil of this life,
While toiling up its pathway,
  While mingling in its strife,
While wandering o'er earth's borders,
  Or sailing o'er its sea, —
'T is sweet to be remembered
  Wherever we may be.

What though our path be rugged,
  Though clouded be our sky,
And none we love and cherish,
  No friendly one is nigh,
To cheer us in our sorrow,
  Or share with us our lot, —
'T is sweet to be remembered,
  To know we 're not forgot.

When those we love are absent
  From our hearth-stone and our side,
With joy we learn that pleasure
  And peace with them abide;
And that, although we 're absent,
  We 're thought of day by day; —
'T is sweet to be remembered
  By those who are away.

When all our toils are ended,
 The conflict all is done,
And peace, in sweetest accents,
 Proclaims the victory won;
When hushed is all the tumult,
 When calmed is all the strife,
And we, in patience, meekly
 Await the end of life:

Then they who, when not present,
 In spirit yet were near,
And, as we toiled and struggled,
 Did whisper in our ear,
"'T is sweet to be remembered,
 And thou art not forgot,"
If fortune smile upon us,
 Shall share our happy lot.

I CALL THEE MINE.

Yes, ever such I'll call thee, will ever call thee mine,
And with the love I bear thee a wreath of poesy twine;
And when the stars are shining in their bright home of blue,
Gazing on them, thou mayest know that I like them are true.

Forget thee! no, O, never! thy heart and mine are one.
How can the man who sees its light forget the noonday sun?
Or he who feels its genial warmth forget the orb above;
Or, feeling sweet affection's power, its source — another's love?

Go, ask the child that sleepeth upon its mother's breast
Whether it loves the pillow on which its head doth rest;
Go, ask the weary mariner, when the dangerous voyage is o'er,
Whether he loves the parent's smile that meets him at the door:

But ask not if I love thee when I would call thee mine,
For words are weak to tell thee all, and I the task resign;
But send thy spirit out for love, and when it finds its goal,
'T will be encircled and embraced within my deepest soul.

THE OLD TREE AND ITS LESSON.

THERE is a story about that old tree; a biography of that old gnarled trunk and those broad-spread branches.

Listen.

Many, very many years ago,—there were forests then where now are cities, and the Indian song was borne on that breeze which now bears the sound of the Sabbath bell, and where the fire of the work-shop sends up its dense, black smoke, the white cloud from the Indian's wigwam arose,—yes, 't was many years ago, when, by the door of a rough, rude, but serviceable dwelling, a little boy sat on an old man's knee. He was a bright youth, with soft blue eyes, from which his soul looked out and smiled, and hair so beautiful that it seemed to be a dancing sunbeam rather than what it really was.

The old man had been telling him of the past; had been telling him that when he was a child he loved the forest, and the rock, and the mountain stream.

Then he handed the lad a small, very small seed, and, leading him a short distance, bade him make a small hole in the ground and place the seed within it. He did so. And the old man bent over and kissed his fair brow as he smoothed the earth above the seed's resting-place, and told him that he must water it and watch it, and it would spring up and become a fair thing in his sight.

'T was hard for the child to believe this; yet he did believe, for he knew that his friend was true.

Night came; and, as he lay on his little couch, the child

dreamed of that seed, and he had a vision of the future which passed with the shades of the night.

Morning dawned, and he hastened to water and to watch the spot where the seed was planted.

It had not come up; yet he believed the good old man, and knew that it would.

All day long he was bending over it, or talking with his aged companion about the buried seed.

A few days passed, then a little sprout burst from the ground; and the child clapped his hands, and shouted and danced.

Daily it grew fairer in the sight of the child, and rose higher and higher. And the old man led him once more to the spot, and told him that even so would the body of his little sister rise from the grave in which a short time before it had been placed, and, rising higher and higher, it would never cease to ascend.

The old man wept; but the child, with his tiny white hand, brushed away his tears, and, with child-like simplicity, said that if his sister arose she would go to God, for God was above.

Then the mourner's heart was strengthened, and the lesson he would have taught the child came from the child to him, and made his soul glad.

A few weeks passed, and the old man died.

The child wept; but, remembering the good friend's lesson, he wiped away his tears, and wept no more; for the seed had already become a beautiful plant, and every day it went upward, and he knew that, like that, his sister and his good friend would go higher and higher towards God.

Days, weeks, months, years passed away. The plant had grown till it was taller than he who had planted it.

Years fled. The child was no more there, but a young man sat beneath the shade of a tree, and held a maiden's hand in his own. Her head reclined on his breast, and her eyes upturned met the glances of his towards her, and they blended in one.

"I remember," said he, "that when I was young a good old man, who is now in heaven, led me to this spot, and bade me put a little seed in the earth. I did so. I watched the ground that held it, and soon it sprang up, touched by no hand, drawn forth, as it would seem, from its dark prison by the attractive power of the bright heaven that shone above it. See, now, what it has become! It shades and shelters us. God planted in my heart a little seed. None but he could plant it, for from him only emanates true love. It sprang up, drawn forth by the sunlight of thy soul, till now thou art shadowed and sheltered by it."

There was silence, save the rustle of the leaves as the branches bowed assent to the young man's words.

Time drove his chariot on; his sickle-wheels smote to earth many brave and strong, yet the tree stood. The winds blew fiercely among its branches; the lightning danced and quivered above and around it; the thunder muttered forth its threatenings; the torrent washed about its roots; yet it stood, grew strong and stately, and many a heart loved it for its beauty and its shade.

The roll of the drum sounded, and beneath a tree gathered crowds of stalwart men. There was the mechanic, with upturned sleeves and dusty apron; the farmer, fanning himself with a dingy straw hat; the professional man and trader, arguing the unrighteousness of "taxation without representation."

Another roll of the drum, and every head was uncovered as a young man ascended a platform erected beneath the tree.

In a soft, low voice, he began. As he proceeded, his voice grew louder, and his eloquence entranced his auditors.

"Years ago," said he, "there were an old man and a young child. And the child loved the man, and the man loved the child, and taught him a lesson. He took him by the hand, and, leading him aside, gave him a seed and told him to plant it. He did so. It sprang up. It became mighty. Independent it stood, sheltering all who came unto it. That old man went home; but here stands the child, and here the tree, great and mighty now, but the child has not forgotten the day when it was small and weak. So shall the cause we have this day espoused go on; and though, to-day, we may be few and feeble, we shall increase and grow strong, till we become an independent nation, that shall shelter all who come unto it."

The speaker ceased, and immediately the air resounded with loud shouts and huzzas.

The struggle for independence came. Victory ensued. Peace rested once more upon all the land, but not as before. It rested upon a free people. Then, beneath that same tree, gathered a mighty host; and, as oft as came the second month of summer, in the early part of it the people there assembled, and thanked God for the lesson of the old tree.

An old man lay dying. Around his bedside were his children and his children's children.

"Remove the curtain," said he. "Open the window. Raise me, and let me see the sun once more."

They did so.

"See you yonder tree? Look upon it, and listen. I was a child once, and I knew and loved an old man; and he knew me and loved me, and he led me aside, placed in my hand a tiny seed, and bade me bury it in the earth, and I did so. Night came, with its shade and its dew; day, with its sunshine and its showers. And the seed sprang up,— but the old man died. Yet, ere he went, he had taught me the lesson of that seed, which was, that those who go down to the earth like that, will arise, like that, towards heaven. You are looking upon that tree which my friend planted. Learn from it the lesson it hath taught me."

The old man's task was performed, his life finished, and the morrow's light lit the pathway of many to his grave. They stood beneath the shadow of that tree; and deeply sank the truth in every heart as the village pastor began the burial service and read, "I am the resurrection and the life."

VOICES FROM THE SPIRIT-LAND.

In the silence of the midnight,
  When the cares of day are o'er,
In my soul I hear the voices
  Of the loved ones gone before;
And they, words of comfort whispering,
  Say they 'll watch on every hand,
And my soul is cheered in hearing
  Voices from the spirit-land.

In my wanderings, oft there cometh
  Sudden stillness to my soul;
When around, above, within it
  Rapturous joys unnumbered roll.
Though around me all is tumult,
  Noise and strife on every hand,
Yet within my soul I list to
  Voices from the spirit-land.

Loved ones who have gone before me
  Whisper words of peace and joy;
Those who long since have departed
  Tell me their divine employ
Is to watch and guard my footsteps, —
  O! it is an angel band!
And I love, I love to list to
  Voices from the spirit-land.

THE BEACON-LIGHT.

DIMLY burns the beacon-light
On the mountain top to-night;
Faint as whisper ever fell,
Falls the watcher's cry, — " All 's well; "
For the clouds have met on high,
And the blast sweeps angry by;
Not a star is seen this night, —
God, preserve the beacon-light!

Lo! a man whom age doth bow
Wanders up the pathway now;
Wistfully his eye he turns
To the light that dimly burns;
And, as it less glow doth shed,
Quicker, quicker is his tread;
And he prays that through the night
God may keep the beacon-light.

Far below him, rocks and waves
Mark the place of others' graves;
Other travellers, who, like him,
Saw the beacon-light burn dim.
But *they* trusted in *their* strength
To attain the goal at length; —
This old traveller prays, to-night,
" God, preserve the beacon-light! "

Fainter, fainter is its ray, —
Shall its last gleam pass away?
Shall it be extinguished quite?
Shall it burn, though not as bright?
Fervently goes up his prayer;
Patiently he waiteth there,
Trusting Him who doeth right
To preserve the beacon-light.

Look you now! the light hath burst
Brighter than it was at first;
Now with ten-fold radiance glows,
And the traveller homeward goes.
As the clouds grow darker o'er him,
Brighter grows the light before him;
God, who doeth all things right,
Hath preserved the beacon-light.

Thus upon the path we tread
God a guiding light hath shed;
Though at times our hearts are weary,
Though the path we tread is dreary,
Though the beacon's lingering ray
Seems as if 't would pass away, —
Be *our* prayer, through all the night,
"God, preserve the beacon-light!"

Threatening clouds may gather o'er us,
Countless dangers rise before us:
If in God we seek for strength,
He will succor us at length:
He his holy light will send,
To conduct us to the end.
Trust thy God, through day and night,
He 'll preserve *thy* beacon-light.

BEAR UP.

Bear up, bear up, though Poverty may press thee,
There 's not a flower that 's crushed that does not shed,
While bowing low, its fragrance forth to bless thee,
At times, more sweet than when it raised its head;
When sunlight gathered round it,
When dews of even crowned it,
By nature nursed, and watched, and from its bounty fed

Bear up, bear up! O, never yield nor falter!
  God reigneth ever, merciful and just;
If thou despairest, go thou to his altar,
  Rest on his arm, and in his promise trust.
    There Hope, bright Hope, will meet thee;
    There Joy, bright Joy, shall greet thee;
And thou shalt rise to thrones on high from out the dust.

A WELCOME SONG TO SPRING.

Shout a welcoming to Spring!
  Hail its early buds and flowers!
It is hastening on to bring
  Unto us its joyous hours.
Birds on bough and brake are singing,
All the new-clad woods are ringing;
In the brook, see Nature flinging
  Beauties of a thousand dyes,
    As if jealous of the beauties
  Mantling the skies.

Hail to Beauty! Hail to Mirth!
  All Creation's song is gladness;
Not a creature dwells on earth
  God would have bowed down in sadness!
Everything *this* truth is preaching,
God in all his works is teaching,
As if man by them beseeching
  To be glad, for he doth bless;
    And to trust him, for he's mighty
  In his tenderness.

THE HOPE OF THE FALLEN.

CHAPTER I.

It was at the close of a beautiful autumnal day that Edward Dayton was to leave the place of his nativity. For many years he had looked forward, in joyous anticipation, to the time when he should repair to the city, and enter upon the business of life. And now that that long looked-for and wished-for day had arrived, when he was to bid an adieu to the companions of his youth, and to all the scenes of his childhood, it was well for him to cast a retrospective glance; and so he did.

Not far distant, rearing its clear white steeple far above the trees, stood the village church, up the broad, uncarpeted aisle of which he had scores of times passed; and, as the thought that he might never again enter those sacred walls came to his mind, a tear glistened in his eye that he could not rudely wipe away.

Next was the cot of the pastor. He had grown old in the service of his Master, and the frosts of nearly three-score winters rested their glory upon his head. All loved and respected him, for with them he had wept, and with them he had rejoiced. Many had fallen around him; withered age and blooming youth he had followed to the grave; yet *he* stood forth yet, and, with clear and musical voice, preached the truths of God.

An old gray building, upon whose walls the idler's knife had carved many a rude inscription, was the village school.

There, amid those carvings, were seen the rough-hewn initials of many a man now "well-to-do in the world." Some, high above the rest, seemed as captains, and almost overshadowed the diminutive ones of the little school-boy, placed scarce thirty inches from the ground.

Edward was a *pet* among the villagers. He had taken the lead in all the frolickings, and many a bright-eyed lass would miss his presence, and loud, clear laugh, at the coming "huskings."

Young and old reluctantly bade him "good-by," and, as the stage wound its circuitous way from the village, from many a heart ascended a prayer that He who ruleth over all would prosper and protect him.

"Good luck to him, God bless him!" said dame Brandon, as she entered the house. "He was always a kind, well-meant lad," she continued, "and dame Brandon knows no evil can befall him; and Emily, my dear, you must keep your eye on some of the best fruit of the orchard, for he will be delighted with it, and much the more so if he knows your bright eyes watched its growth and your hands gathered it."

These words were addressed to a girl of seventeen, who stood at an open window, in quite a pensive mood. She seemed not to hear the remark, but gazed in the direction the stage had passed.

The parents of Edward had died when he was quite young, and he, their only child, had been left to the care and protection of dame Brandon; and well had she cared for him, and been as a mother to the motherless.

"Now, Emi', don't fret! Edward won't forget you. I've known him long; he has got a heart as true as steel."

'T was not this that made her sad. She had no fears that he would forget his Emi', but another thought pressed heavily on her mind, and she said,

"But, aunty, city life is one of danger. Temptations are there we little think of, and stronger hearts than Edward's have quailed beneath their power."

"Well done!" quoth Mrs. B., looking over her glasses; "a sermon, indeed, quite good for little you. But girls are timid creatures; they start and are frightened at the least unusual sound." She assumed a more serious manner, and, raising her finger, pointing upwards, said, "But know you not there is a Power greater than that of which you speak?"

Emily seemed to be cheered by this thought. She hummed over a favorite air, and repaired to the performance of her evening duties.

Emily Brandon was a lovely creature, and of this Edward Dayton was well aware. He had spent his early days with her. His most happy hours had been passed in her company. Together they had frolicked over the green fields, and wandered by their clear streams. Hours passed as minutes when in each other's company; and, when separated, each minute seemed an hour.

Now, for the first time, they were separated; and ever and anon, as she passed about at her work, she cast a fitful glance from the window, as if it were possible he might return.

How she wished she could have gone with him, to gently chide when sinners should entice, and lead him from error's path, should gay temptation lure him therein! She was young in years, yet old in discretion; and had a heart that yearned for the good of all.

"Well, aunt," said she, "I *hope* good luck will betide him, but sad thoughts *will* come when I think of what he will have to bear up under."

"O, hush!" said the old lady; "simple girls have simple stories."

CHAPTER II.

It was a late hour in the evening that the coach entered the metropolis. Railroads were not then in vogue, and large baggage-waggons, lumbering teams and clumsy coaches, were drawn by two or more horses, over deep-rutted roads, and almost endless turnpikes.

The bells had rang their nine o'clock peal; most of the stores were closed; the busy trader and industrious mechanic had gone to their respective homes, and left their property to faithful watchers, whose muffled forms moved slowly through the streets of the great city.

Not all had left their work; for, by the green and crimson light that streamed from his window, and served to partially dissipate the darkness, it was seen that he of pestle and mortar labored on, or, wearied with his labor, had fallen asleep, but to be awakened by the call of some customer, requesting an antidote for one of the many "ills which flesh is heir to."

Other open places there were, whose appearance indicated that they were bar-rooms, for at their windows stood decanters filled with various-colored liquids. Near each of these stood a wine-glass in an inverted position, with a lemon upon it; yet, were not any of these unmistakable signs to be seen, you would know the character of the place by a rumseller's reeling sign, that made its exit, and, passing a few steps, fell into the gutter.

In addition to these other signs, were seen scattered about the windows of these places, in characters so large that he who ran might read, "Bar-room," "Egg-pop," "N. E. Rum," etc.

Those were the days of bar-room simplicities. "Saloons" were not then known. The refined names which men of the present day have attached to rum, gin and brandy, were not then in use. There were no "Wormwood-floaters" to embitter man's life, and *Jewett* had not had his "fancy."

The coach rolled on, and in a short time Edward was safely ensconced in a neatly-furnished room in a hotel known as "The Bull's Horn." It was indeed a great disadvantage to him that he came to a city in which he was a total stranger. He had no acquaintance to greet him with a friendly welcome; and the next day, as he was jostled by the crowd, and pushed aside by the hurried pedestrian, he realized what it was to be a stranger in a strange land, and an indescribable sensation came upon him, known only to those who have been placed in similar circumstances.

He looked around,—strange forms met his view. No one greeted him, no hand of friendship was held forth to welcome him. All the world seemed rushing on for something, he knew not what; and, disheartened at the apparent selfishness that pervaded society, he returned to his room, and wished for the quietness of his own sweet village, the companionship of his own dear Emi'.

The landlord of the tavern at which our hero had housed himself was a stout, burly man, and quite communicative. From him Edward learned much of importance. Mr. Blinge was his name. He was an inveterate smoker, and his *pet* was a little black pipe, dingy and old, and by not a few deemed a nuisance to "The Bull's Horn." This he held between his teeth, and, seating himself behind his bar, puffed away on the high-pressure principle.

Edward had not been many minutes in his room before Mr. Blinge entered with his pet in his mouth, hoped he did n't intrude, apologized, and wished him to walk below, saying that by so doing he might become acquainted with some "*rare souls.*"

By "below" was meant a large, square room, on the ground floor, of dimensions ample enough to hold a caucus in. By some it was called a "bar-room," by others the "sitting-room," and others the "gentlemen's parlor."

Entering, Edward encountered the gaze of about twenty individuals. Old gentlemen with specs looked beneath them, and young gentlemen with papers looked above them. A young man in white jacket and green apron was endeavoring to satisfy the craving appetites of two teamsters, who were loudly praising the landlord's brandy, and cursing the bad state of the roads in a manner worthy of "our army in Flanders."

One young man, in particular, attracted the attention of our hero. He was genteelly dressed, and possessed an air of dignity and self-command, that would obtain for him at once the good will of any. Edward was half inclined to believe his circumstances to be somewhat similar to his own. He was reading an evening paper, but, on seeing our hero enter, and judging from his manner that he was a stranger, laid it aside, and, politely addressing himself to him, inquired after his health.

The introduction over, they engaged in conversation. The young man seemed pleased in making his acquaintance, and expressed a hope that a friendship so suddenly formed might prove lasting and beneficial to each.

"I also am from the country," said he, after Edward had informed him of his history, "and, like you, am in search of employment. Looking over the evening paper, I noticed an advertisement of a concern for sale, which I thought, as I read, would be a capital chance to make a fortune, if I could find some one to invest in it with me. I will read it to you.

"'For Sale.—The stock and stand of a Confectioner, with a good business, well established. One or two young men will find this a rare opportunity to invest their money advantageously. For other particulars inquire at No. 7 Cresto-st.'

"Now, I tell you what," said the young man, before Edward had an opportunity to utter a word, "it is a fine chance. Why, Lagrange makes enough on his wines and fancy cordials to clothe and feed a regiment. Just pass there, some evening, and you will see a perfect rush. Soda-water, ice creams, and French wines, are all the rage, and Lagrange is the only man in this city that can suit the *bon ton!*"

"You half induce me to go there," said Edward. "How far is it from this place?"

"Not far, but it is too late; to-morrow morning we will go there. Here, take my card — Othro Treves is my name; you must have known my father; a member of Congress for ten years, when he died; — rather abused his health — attended parties at the capital — drank wine to excess — took a severe cold — fell ill one day, worse the next, sick the next, and died soon after. Wine is bad when excessively indulged in; so is every good thing."

Edward smiled at this running account of his new-formed acquaintance, and, bidding him "good-night," betook himself to his chamber, intending to accompany Othro to the confectioner's in the morning.

CHAPTER III.

The next morning the sun shone bright and clear in a cloudless sky, and all were made joyous by its gladsome rays.

Edward was awakened at an early hour by the departure, or preparations to depart, of the two teamsters, who, having patronized rather freely the young man in white jacket and green apron, were in a delightful mood to enjoy a joke, and were making themselves quite merry as they harnessed up their sturdy horses.

It was near nine when Othro and Edward found themselves on the way to the confectioner's. Edward was glad on account of finding one whom he thought he could trust as a friend, and congratulated himself on his good luck.

Near the head of Cresto-street might have been seen, not many years since, over the door of a large and fashionable store, a sign-board bearing this inscription: "M. Lagrange, Confectioner and Dealer in Wines and Cordials." We say it was "large and fashionable;" and those of our readers who recollect the place of which we speak will testify to the truth of our assertion.

Its large windows, filled with jars of confectionary and preserves, and with richly-ornamented bottles of wine, with the richest pies and cake strewed around, presented a showy and inviting appearance, and a temptation to indulge, too powerful to resist, by children of a larger growth than lisping infants and primary-school boys. Those who daily passed this store looked at the windows most wistfully; and this was not all, for, at their weekly reckonings, they found that several silver "bits" had disappeared very mysteriously during the previous seven days.

To this place our hero and his newly-formed acquaintance were now hastening. As they drew near, quite a bevy of ladies made their exit therefrom, engaged in loud conversation.

"Lor!" said one, "it is strange Lagrange advertised to sell out."

"Why, if I was his wife," said another, "I'd whip him into my traces, I would; an' he should n't sell out unless I was willin',—no, he should n't! Only think, Miss Fitzgabble, how handy those wines would be when one has a social soul step in!"

"O, yes," replied Miss Fitzgabble, "and those jars of lozenges! How enchantingly easy to elevate the lid upon a Sabbath morn, slip in one's hand, and subtract a few! How I should smell of sassafras, if *I* was Mrs. Lagrange!"

The ladies passed on, and were soon out of hearing. Edward and his companion entered the store, where about a dozen ladies and gentlemen were seated, discussing the fashions, forging scandal, and sipping wine.

Mr. Lagrange was actively engaged when the two entered; but, seeing them, and supposing them to have called on the business for which they actually had called, he called to one of the attendants to fill his place, and entered into conversation with Messrs. Dayton and Treves, which in due time was terminated, they agreeing to call again the next day.

First impressions are generally the most lasting. Those Edward and Othro received during their visit and subsequent conversation were favorable to the purchase.

On their return they consulted together for a long time, and finally concluded to go that day, instead of waiting till the next, and make Mr. Lagrange an offer of which they had no doubt he would accept.

Mr. Lagrange's chief object in selling out was that he might disengage himself from business. He had been a long time in it; he was getting somewhat advanced in life, and had accumulated sufficient to insure him against want, and he deemed it best to step out, and give room to the young — an example worthy of general imitation.

That the business was profitable there could be no doubt. As Othro had said, the profit on the wines was indeed immense.

On pleasant evenings the store was crowded; and, as it was filled with the young, gay, and fashionable of wealthy rank, not much difficulty was experienced in obtaining these large profits.

The return of the young men was not altogether unexpected by Mr. Lagrange. He was ready to receive them. He set before them his best wines. They drank freely, praised the wine, and extolled the store, for they thought it admirably calculated to make a fortune in.

Mr. Lagrange imparted to them all the information they desired. They made him an offer, which he accepted, after some thought; and arrangements were entered into by which Messrs. Dayton and Treves were to take possession on the morning of the following Monday.

CHAPTER IV.

No one commences business without the prospect of success. Assure a man he will not succeed, and he will be cautious of the steps he takes, if, indeed, he takes any.

If he does not expect to gain a princely fortune, he expects to earn a comfortable subsistence, and, at the same time, accumulate enough to shelter him in a rainy day, and be enabled to walk life's busy stage in comfort and respectability, and, as occasion may demand, relieve the wants of his less fortunate brethren.

For this all hope, yet the experience of thousands shows that few, very few, ever realize it. On the contrary, disappointment, in its thousand malignant forms, starts up on every hand; yet they struggle on, and in imagination see more prosperous days in the future. Thus they hope against hope, till the green sod covers their bodies, and they leave their places to others, whilst the tale is told in these few words: "They lived and died."

The next Monday the citizens were notified, by the removal of his old sign, that Mr. Lagrange had retired from business. During the day, many of Mr. Lagrange's customers came in, that they might become acquainted with the successors of their old friend. To these Messrs. Dayton and Treves were introduced, and from them received promise of support.

A colored man, who had been for a long time in the employ of Mr. Lagrange, was retained in the employ of the store. Ralph Orton was his name. He having been for a long time in the store, and during that time having had free access to the wines, had formed an appetite for them, in consequence of which he was often intoxicated.

His inebriation was periodical, and not of that kind whose subjects are held in continual thraldom; yet, to use his own words, "when he was drunk, he *was* drunk, and no mistake." He obeyed the old injunction of "what is worth doing is worth doing well," and as long as he got drunk he got well drunk.

He had ofttimes been reasoned with in his days of soberness, and had often promised to *reform;* but so many around him drank that he could not resist the temptation to drink also, and therefore broke his promise. This habit had so fastened itself upon him, that, like one in the coil of the serpent, the more he strove to escape the closer it held him.

If there is any one habit to which if a man becomes attached he will find more difficulty to escape from than another, it is that of *intemperance;* yet all habits are so one with our nature that the care taken to guard against the adoption of evil ones cannot be too great.

Behold that man! He was tempted,—he yielded. He has surrendered a noble estate, and squandered a large fortune. Once he had riches and friends; his eye sparkled with the fire of ambition; hope and joy beamed in each feature of his manly countenance, and all bespoke for him a long life and happy death. Look at him now! without a penny in his pocket, a wretched outcast, almost dead with starvation. Habit worked the change—an evil habit.

Perchance some one in pity may bestow a small sum upon him. Utterly regardless of the fact that his wife and children are at home shivering over a few expiring embers that give no warmth, without a crumb to appease their hunger, and although he himself a moment before believed that if aid did not come speedily he must perish, he hastens to the nearest groggery, and, laying down his money, calls for that which has brought upon him and his such woe.

If there is any scene upon earth over which demons joy, it must be when that rumseller takes *that* money.

This propensity of Ralph's was a serious objection to him as a servant; yet, in every other respect, he was all that could be desired. He was honest, faithful and obliging, and, knowing as they did that he was well acquainted with the trade of the city, and could go directly to the houses of Mr. Lagrange's customers, Messrs. Dayton and Treves were induced to have him remain.

At the end of a month, Edward found himself in prosperous circumstances, and wrote to his old village friends of the fact. They, as a matter in course, were overjoyed in the reception of such intelligence, and no one more so than Emily Lawton.

Edward had entered into a business in which temptations of a peculiar nature gathered about him. Like nearly every one in those days, he had no scruples against the use of wine. He thought no danger was associated with its use; and, as an objection against that would clash with the interests of his own pecuniary affairs, he would be the last to raise it.

In dealing forth to others, how strong came the temptation to deal it to himself! Othro drank, and pronounced a certain kind of wine a great luxury. Edward could not (or, at least, so he thought) do otherwise; and so he drank, and pronounced the same judgment upon it.

"What say you for an evening at the theatre?" said Othro, one evening, as they were passing from their place of business, having left it in care of their servants. "At the Gladiate the play is 'Hamlet,' and Mr. Figaro, from the old Drury, appears."

Edward had been educated in strict puritanic style, and had been taught to consider the theatre as a den of iniquity.

It is not our purpose to defend or oppose this opinion. It was his, and he freely expressed it. In fact, his partner knew it to be such before making the request.

"I suppose," said Mr. Treves, "you oppose the theatre on account of the intoxicating drinks sold there. Now, I am for a social drop occasionally. Edward, a glass of pure '*Cogniac*,' a nice cigar, and a seat in front of a grate of blazing coal, and I'll be joyful."

"You may be joyful, then," replied Mr. Dayton; "but your joy might be changed to grief, and your buoyancy of spirit be turned to sadness of heart."

"Indeed, Edward! Quite a lecture, I declare! Been studying theology, eh?"

"Not so; you are mistaken, Othro," said he. "There," he continued, pointing to a reeling sot that passed them, "ask that man where he first went for joy, and he may tell you of the theatre, or of social glasses of brandy, cigars, and such like."

They had now arrived in front of the "Gladiate," a massive stone structure, most brilliantly illuminated. Long rows of carriages stood in front, and crowds of the gay and fashionable were flocking in.

All was activity. Hackmen snapped their whips. Boys, ragged and dirty, were waiting for the time when "checks" would circulate, and, in fact, were in much need of *checks*, but those of a different nature from those they so eagerly looked for.

Anon, the crowd gathered closer; and the prospect of a fight put the boys in hysterics of delight, and their rags into great commotion. To their sorrow, it was but the shadow of a "row"; and they kicked and cuffed each other, in order to express their grief.

A large poster announced in flaming characters that that night was the last but two of Mr. Figaro's appearance, and that other engagements would prevent him from prolonging his stay, however much the public might desire him to do so; whilst, if the truth had been told, the public would have known that a printer was that moment "working off" other posters, announcing a reëngagement of Mr. Figaro for two weeks.

"Will you enter?" inquired Othro. Edward desired to be excused, and they parted; one entering the theatre, the other repairing to his home.

CHAPTER V.

The "tavern" at which our hero boarded was of the country, or, rather, the *colony* order of architecture,—for piece had been added to piece, until what was once a small shed was now quite an extensive edifice.

As was the case with all taverns in those days, so also with this,—the bar-room was its most prominent feature. Mr. Blinge, the landlord, not only smoked, but was an inveterate lover of raw whiskey, which often caused him to perform strange antics. The fact that he *loved* whiskey was not strange, for in those days all drank. The aged drank his morning, noon and evening potations, because he had always done so; the young, because his father did; and the lisping one reached forth its hands, and in childish accents called for the "*thugar*," and the mother, unwilling to deny it that which she believed could not harm it, gave.

Those were the days when seed was being sown, and now the harvesting is in progress. Vain were it for us to attempt its description; you will see it in ruined families, where are gathered blasted hopes, withered expectations, and pangs, deep pangs of untold sorrow.

The child indulged has become a man, yet scarce worthy of the name; for a habit has been formed that has sunken him below the brute, and he lives not a help, but a burden, not a blessing, but a curse, to his fellow-men.

Although Edward was opposed to the use of intoxicating drinks, his business led him to associate with those who held opposite opinions.

Among the boarders was one, a bold, drinking, independent sort of a man, who went against all innovations upon old customs with a fury worthy of a subject of hydrophobia.

His name was "Pump." Barrel, or bottle, would have been more in accordance with his character; but, as the old Pump had not foresight enough to see into the future, he did not know that he was inappropriately naming his son.

Every *Pump* must have its handle, on the same principle that "every dog must have his day." The handle to the Pump in question was a long one; 't was "Onendago."

"Onendago Pump" was written with red ink on the blank leaf of a "Universal Songster" he carried in his pocket.

Dago, as he was called, lived on appearances; that is, he acted the *gentleman* outwardly, but the beggar inwardly. He robbed his stomach to clothe his back: howbeit, his good outside appearance often got for him a good dinner.

By the aid of the tailor and the barber, he wore nice cloth and curled hair; and, being blessed with a smooth, oily voice, was enabled, by being invited to dinner here and to supper there, to live quite easy.

Edward had just seated himself, when a loud rap on the door was heard, and in a moment Mr. Onendago Pump, with two bottles, entered. With a low bow, he inquired as to our hero's health, and proposed spending an evening in his company.

"Ever hear me relate an incident of the last war?" said he, as he seated himself, and placed his two bottles upon the side-table.

"Never," replied Edward.

"Well, Butler was our captain, and a regular man he; right up and down good fellow,— better man never held sword or gave an order. Well, we were quartered at — I don't remember where — history tells. We led a lazy life; no red coats to fire at. One of the men came home, one night, three sheets in the wind, and the fourth bound round his head; awful patriotic was he, and made a noise, and swore he'd shoot every man for the good of his country. Well, Captain Butler heard of it, and the next day all hands were called. We formed a ring; Simon Twigg, he who was drunk the day before, stood within it, and then and there Captain Butler, who belonged to the Humane Society, and never ordered a man to be flogged, lectured him half an hour. Well, that lecture did Mr. Dago Pump immense good, and ever since I have n't drank anything stronger than brandy.

"Never a man died of brandy!" said Mr. Pump, with much emphasis. "Brandy 's the word!" and, without saying more, he produced a cork-screw, and with it opened a bottle.

A couple of glasses soon made their appearance. "Now, you will take a glass with me," said Dago; "it is the pure Cogniac, quality one, letter A."

"Drink, now," said he, pushing a glass towards him. "Wine is used by the temperance society. They'll use *brandy* soon. Ah, they can't do without their wine, and *we* can't do without our brandy! They want to bind us in a free country, what my father bled and almost died for,— bind us to drink cold water!" said Mr. Pump, sneeringly. "Let 'em try it! I go for freedom of the press,— universal, everlasting, unbounded freedom!"

When this patriotic bubble had exploded and the mist cleared away, he sang a bacchanalian song, which he wished every *free man* in the world would commit to memory. "What is the difference," said he, "between this and wine?

Neither will hurt a man; it is your rum-drinking, gin-guzzling topers that are harmed;—anything will harm them. Who ever heard of a genteel wine or brandy drinker becoming a pest to society? Who ever heard of such an one rolling in the mire? No; such men are able to take care of themselves. Away with the pledge!"

"Perhaps you are right," replied Edward; "yet we should be careful. Although all around me drink, I have until this moment abstained from the use of brandy; but now, at your request, I partake of it. Remember, if I, by this act, am led into habits of intemperance, *if I meet a drunkard's grave, the blame will rest upon you.*"

"Ha, ha, ha! Well done! So be it! I'll shoulder the blame, if a respectable man like you falls by brandy."

Edward drank the contents of a glass, and, placing it upon the table, said "We must be careful!"

"True!" said Mr. Pump, as he again filled the glass; "we cannot be too much so. We must avoid rum and gin as we would a viper! How I abhor the very name of *rum!* O, Mr. Dayton, think of the misery it has brought upon man! I had a sister once, a beautiful, kind-hearted creature. She was married to an industrious man; all was fair, prospects bright. By degrees he got into bad company; he forgot his home, loved rum more than that, became dissipated, died, and filled a drunkard's grave! She, poor creature, went into a fever, became delirious, raved day after day, and, heaping curses upon him who sold her husband rum, died. Since then, I have looked upon rum as a curse; but brandy,—it is a gentle stimulant, a healthy beverage, a fine drink, and *it* can do no harm."

Onendago swallowed the contents of his glass, and Edward, who, having taken the first, found it very easy to take the second, did the same. Yet his conscience smote him; he *felt* that he was doing wrong.

Like the innocent, unthinking bird, who, charmed by the serpent's glistening eyes, falls an easy prey to its crushing embrace, was he at that moment. He the bird, unconscious of the danger behind the charm.

This is no fictitious tale. Would to Heaven it contained less of truth! The world has seen many men like "Mr. Pump," and many have through their instrumentality fallen; many not to rise till ages shall have obliterated all memory of the past, with all its unnatural loves! Whilst others, having struggled on for years, have at length seen a feeble ray of light penetrating the dark clouds that overshadowed their path, which light continued to increase, till, in all its beauty, the star of temperance shone forth, by which they strove ever after to be guided.

It was near midnight when Mr. Pump left. The two had become quite sociable, and Mr. Pump saw the effect of his brandy in the unusual gayety of Edward.

The latter was not lost to reflection; and now that he was alone, thoughts of home, his business, and many other matters, came confusedly into his mind.

Letters he had received of warning and advice. He took them in his hands, looked over their contents, and with feelings of sadness, and somewhat of remorse, thought of his ways.

A bundle of old letters! A circle of loved friends! How alike! There is that's pleasant, yet sad, in these. How vividly they present to our view the past! The writers, some, perhaps, are dead; others are far away. Yet, dead or alive, near or far distant, we seem to be with them as we read their thoughts traced out on the sheet before us.

As Edward read here and there a letter, it *did* seem as though his friends stood beside him, and spoke words of advice which conscience whispered should be heeded. *Love* was the theme of not a few, yet all warned him to flee from evil. He returned the parcel, and, as he did so, he pledged himself that if he drank any it should be with moderation: and that, as soon as he felt its ruinous effects, to abstain altogether.

The next morning Othro was late at the store; yet, when he arrived, he was full of praise of the play.

"Figaro acted Hamlet to a charm," said he; "and Fanny Lightfoot danced like a fairy. But two nights more! Now, Edward, if you do not wish to offend me, and that exceedingly, say you will go with me to-morrow night."

CHAPTER VI.

Three years had elapsed since the events of the last chapter. Edward had often visited his native village, and, as the results of these visits, Emily Lawton became Mrs. Dayton; and she, with Mrs. Brandon, was removed to an elegantly furnished house in the city. Yet, with all its elegance, Mrs. Brandon, who had been accustomed to rural simplicity, did not feel happy except when in her own room, which Edward had ordered to be furnished in a style answering her own wishes.

Messrs. Dayton and Treves had been highly successful in their business operations; and, enjoying as they did the patronage of the *élite* of the city, they, with but little stretch of their imaginative powers, could see a fortune at no great distance.

Becoming acquainted with a large number of persons of wealth, they were present at very many of the winter entertainments; and, being invited to drink, they had not courage to refuse, and did not wish to act so ungenteel and uncivil. Others drank; and some loved their rum, and would have it. Edward had taken many steps since the events of our last chapter; yet, thought he, "I drink moderately."

There was to be a great party. A musical prodigy, in the shape of a child of ten years, had arrived, and the leaders of fashion had agreed upon having a grand entertainment on the occasion.

Great was the activity and bustle displayed, and in no place more than at the store of Dayton and Treves. As ill-luck would have it, Ralph had been absent a week on one of his drunken sprees, and his employers were obliged to procure another to fill his place.

The event was to take place at the house of a distinguished city officer; and, as Messrs. Dayton and Treves were to provide refreshment, their time was fully occupied.

The papers were filled with predictions concerning it; and the editors, happy fellows, were in ecstasies of joy on account of having been invited to attend. Nor were Messrs. Dayton and Treves forgotten; but lengthy eulogies upon their abilities to perform the duty assigned them occupied prominent places, and "steamboat disasters," "horrid murders," and "dreadful accidents," were obliged to make room for these.

In the course of human events the evening came. Hacks were in demand, and the rattling of wheels and the falling of carriage-steps were heard till near midnight.

The chief object of attraction was a small boy, who had attained considerable proficiency in musical knowledge, not of any particular instrument, but anything and everything; consequently a large assortment of instruments had been collected, upon which he played. As music had called them together, it was the employment of the evening, and the hour of midnight had passed when they were summoned to the tables.

Those gentlemen who desired had an apartment to themselves, where wine and cigars circulated freely. Some, in a short time, became excited; whilst others, upon whom the same cause had a different effect, became stupid. One poor fellow, whose bloated countenance told a sad tale, lay almost senseless; another sat dreamingly over his half-filled glass, whilst another excited the risibilities of not a few by his ineffectual attempts to light his cigar.

Our hero, like his companions, was a little overcome by too frequent potations from the bottle. It was a sad sight to a reflective mind. The majority were young men, whose eyes had been blinded to the danger they were in, by adhering to a foolish and injurious custom.

As hour passed hour, they became more excited, until a high state of enthusiasm existed.

* * * * * *

All the ladies had retired, except one, and she strove hard to conceal her rising sorrow by forced smiles; yet she could not restrain her feelings,— her heart seemed bursting with grief. In vain did officious servants seek to know the cause. To the inquiries of the lady of the house she made no reply. She dare not reveal the secret which pierced her very soul; but, burying her face in her hands, seemed resolved upon not being comforted. Finally, yielding to the persuasive influence of Mrs. Venet, she expressed her fears that Edward had tarried too long at the bowl.

Mrs. Venet tried to comfort her by saying that, if what she so much feared *was true*, yet it was nothing uncommon; and mentioned several men, and not a few ladies, who had been carried away in a senseless condition.

These words did not comfort her; on the contrary, they increased her fears, and led her to believe that there was more danger at such parties than there was generally thought to be; and the fact that Edward had often attended such parties increased her sorrow, for she knew not but that he had been among that number of whom Mrs. Venet spoke.

Imagination brought to her view troubles and trials as her

future lot; and last, not least, the thought of Edward's temperament, and of how easily he might be led astray, rested heavily upon her heart. Mrs. Venet at length left her, and repaired to the gentleman's apartment, in order to learn the cause of his delay.

She knocked at the door.

"Who in the devil 's there, with that thundering racket?" inquired a loud voice.

"It is Mrs. Venet," replied the lady.

"O, it is, is it? Well, madam, Dayton the confectioner, and a dozen jovial souls, are having a rare time here. Put that down in your memorandum-book, and leave us to our meditations."

"Yes, and these to profit and loss," said another, and the breaking of glasses was heard.

"If Mr. Dayton is within, tell him his lady is waiting for him," said Mrs. Venet.

"Ed, your wife 's waiting," said one of the party.

"Then, friends, I — I — I must go," said the inebriated man, who, though badly intoxicated, had not wholly forgotten her.

His companions endeavored to have him remain, but in vain. He unbolted the door, and, leaving, closed it upon them.

Mrs. Venet, who was standing without, laid hold of his coat, and, knowing the excited state of Mrs. Dayton, and fearing that the appearance of her husband would be too much for her to bear, endeavored to induce him not to enter the room, or, at least, to wait until he had recovered from the effects of his drinking.

He appeared rational for a while, but, suddenly breaking away, shouted, "Emily, where are you?"

The sound of his voice resounded through the building,

and his drunken companions, hearing it, made the building echo with their boisterous laughter.

He ran through the entries gazing wildly around, and loudly calling for his wife.

The servants, hearing the tumult, hastened to the spot; but neither they nor Mrs. Venet could induce him to become quiet.

The latter, finding she could have no influence upon him, repaired to the room in which she left Mrs. Dayton, and found her senseless upon the floor, and to all appearances dead. She had heard his wild cries, and what she had so much feared she then knew to be true.

Mrs. Venet rang for the servants, and ordered some restoratives. These were soon obtained, and by their free use she had nearly recovered, when her husband rushed into the room.

Upon seeing his wife, the raging lion became as docile as a lamb. A sudden change came over him; he seemed to realize the truth, and it sent an arrow to his soul.

Again the injured wife fainted, and again the restoratives were faithfully applied; but it was evident that if Mr. Dayton remained in her presence it would be difficult to restore her, and the man who before would not be approached was led quietly away. In a short time Mrs. Dayton became sensible, and her first words were to inquire after Edward. Being told, she was induced to lie down, and, if possible, enjoy a little sleep; but sleep she could not. Her mind became almost delirious, and fears were entertained by her attendants that she would lose her reason.

The effects of Edward's carousal were entirely dissipated by the sudden realization of the truth.

To Mrs. Dayton this was an hour of the deepest sorrow. She looked back upon the past, and saw happiness; in the future nothing but misery seemed to await her. Yet a change came over her; she thanked God for his past mercies, and wisely trusted him for their continuance. She implored pardon for past ingratitude, and prayed that she might be more grateful in future, and that, having tasted of the cup of sorrow, she might not drink the bitter draught.

CHAPTER VII.

The next morning Edward repented of his crime, and in his inmost soul felt it to be such,—a crime of deepest dye.

Emily wept as she bent over him.

"Cease thy tears," said he, "and forgive; it is but that word, spoken by thee, that can send peace to my soul. Yet what peace can I expect? I have wronged thee!"—and the wretched man wept like a child.

New thoughts continually sprang into existence,—the days of his youth, the bliss of home, and his present situation. He felt disgraced;—how should he redeem his character?

"O, that the grave would hide me," continued Edward, "and that in death I might forget this crime! But no! I cannot forget it; it will cling to me through life, and the future ——"

He would have said more, but the strong emotions of his soul choked his utterance.

He arose and paced the room in agony of feeling which pen cannot describe. Suddenly halting, he gazed steadfastly upon the face of his wife. It was deadly pale, and a tear dimmed the usual lustre of her eye.

"Comfort thyself," said he; "no further evil shall come upon thee. It shall never be said *you* are a drunkard's wife,—no, no, no, never!"

"Let us, then, forget the past," said Mrs. Dayton.

"What! forget those days when I had not tasted? O,

misery indeed, if I cannot retain their remembrance!'" said Edward.

"Not so, Edward; we would remember those, but forget the evil that has befallen us,—all will be well."

"Do you—can you forgive?"

"God will forgive; and shall not I?"

"Then let this be a pledge of the future;" and, taking her hand in his, he said, "I resolve to walk in the path of right, and never more to wander, God being my witness and my strength."

"'T is well thou hast pledged thyself," said she; "but know thou the tempter is on every side. Should the wine-cup touch thy lips, dash it aside, and proclaim yourself a pledged man."

"I will!" was the response, and, taking a pen, he boldly placed his name to the following pledge:

"PLEDGE.—We pledge ourselves to abstain from the use of all intoxicating drinks, except the moderate use of *wine, beer* and *cider.*"

Such was the pledge to which he affixed his name, and such the pledge by which men of those days endeavored to stay the tide of intemperance. Did not every man who signed that pledge himself to become a moderate drinker; and is not every moderate drinker pledged to become a drunkard? What a pledge! Yet we should not blame the men of former years for pursuing a course which they conscientiously thought to be right. That was the first step. It was well as far as it led; but it paused at the threshold of the ark of safety, and there its disciples fell. They had not seen, as have men of late years, the ruinous tendency of such a course; and knew not, as we now do, that total abstinence is the only sure course.

The pledge Edward had signed was no preventive in his

case. He had tasted; in fact, he had become a lover of strong drink; and the temptation of having it constantly beside him, and daily dealing it out to others, was too strong for him to resist. When he drank, he *did* think, as Emily had bade him, that he was a pledged man; but that pledge permitted him to drink *wine*. The remedy such a pledge applied was of no avail. It failed to reach the fountain-head, and strove to stop the stream by placing slight resistances in its way.

A long time must elapse before a man can know the heart of his fellow-man, if, indeed, it can ever be known; and it was not until Edward had become addicted to habits of intemperance that he discovered the professed friendship of Mr. Treves to be insincere. Words of warning seldom came from his lips. What cared he if Edward did fall? Such being the case, the business would come into his own hands; and such "a consummation devoutly to be wished" it was very evident that if Edward did not soon reform was not far distant.

Now Emily Dayton began to experience anxious days and sleepless nights, and Mrs. Brandon begged of Edward to reform. Often he would do so. He would sign that pledge; but it was like an attempt to stay a torrent with a straw. That pledge! 't was nothing! yea, worse than nothing!

* * * * * *

Six months of sorrowing passed, and what a change we behold! Experience has shown to Edward that the use of brandy *is* dangerous, and good dame Brandon has been led to believe that there are temptations in the city which she little thought of.

Edward, driven from his business, revels in bar-rooms, and riots at midnight; whilst the patient, uncomplaining, enduring Emily, forced by creditors from her former home, finds shelter from the storm in a small tenement; where, by the aid of her needle, she is enabled to support herself and aged aunt, whilst a prattling infant plays at her side, and, laughing in its childish sports, thinks not of the sorrows it was born to encounter, and knows not the sad feelings of its mother's wounded heart.

CHAPTER VIII.

In a low, damp, dark cellar, behold a man washing the glasses of a groggery. His ragged dress and uncombed hair, his shabby and dirty appearance, do not prevent us from seeing indications of his once having been in better circumstances, and that nature never designed that he should be where he now is.

Having rinsed a few cracked tumblers, he sat down beside a red-hot cylinder stove, and, bending over till his head rested upon his hands, he, in a half-audible voice, talked to himself.

"Here 't is, eighteen forty — some years since I saw that Dayton cove; eh, gone by the board? The daily papers say he was up for a common drunkard; but, being first time, was lectured and sent home. Plaguy poor home his, I reckon! Wonder if the lecture did him as much good as Old Batter's did me. Ah! he liked that brandy, and said I should bear the blame if he was ruined; but he an't that yet. Here I am, ten times worse off than he is, and *I* an't ruined. No! Mr. Dago Pump is a man yet. Well, well! what shall I say? — business awful dull, and it 's damp and dark here; I feel cold 'side of this red-faced stove."

Mr. Onendago Pump poked the fire, and continued to do so till a ragged little boy, without shoes, stockings or cap, came down the slippery steps, and asked for "two cents' worth of rum, and one cent's worth of crackers."

The proprietor of this subterraneous establishment threw aside an old wire that served as a poker, and demanded payment in advance. The child handed him the three cents, received his rum and crackers, and left.

Mr. Pump, who for a long time had lived on appearances, could do so no longer; for, persisting in his opinion that brandy could not hurt him, he drank so much that *bad* soon supplanted *good* appearances, and his company was soon discarded.

Mr. Blinge would not have him about his premises, although the one drank as much as the other, and a great similarity existed between them.

He was turned out of the tavern, and, having purchased four shillings' worth of brandy, commenced business in the cellar we have alluded to, replenishing his stock by daily applying to a neighboring pump; and, for every gill of brandy he drew from the tap, poured a gill of water in at the bung, and thus kept up a stock in trade.

In a short time, a collection of drinking loafers met daily at his place, and Dago Pump could see no difference between his respectability as proprietor of a bar-room, and his who, being owner of thousands, fitted up "oyster saloons," which places had suddenly sprung up in all large cities.

Edward had fallen; he had become what was termed a "common drunkard." His wife wept tears of anguish; she entreated; she begged him to reform. She prayed to Heaven for its aid; yet week passed week, month followed month, on Time's unending course, and she was a drunkard's wife still. All friends had forsaken her. Friends! shall we call them such? No; they did not deserve the name. Their friendship only had an existence when fortune smiled; when a frown mantled its countenance, or a cloud intervened, they fled. Yet God was raising up friends for her, and from a class of society from whom she little expected aid. God was working, in his mysterious way, a deliverance. He had heard the prayers that for many long years had gone up to his throne from thousands of wretched families; and, moved to pity, he was to show them that he was a God of mercy.

Othro Treves — where is he? Not in that elegant store; it long since passed into other hands. Has he made his fortune, and retired? Such we might suppose to be the case, did we not know that he trusted to moderate drinking. Man might as well trust a leaky vessel to bear him across the ocean, as to trust that.

The clock struck twelve.

"'T is midnight," said a female voice, "and he has not come. God send repentance to his heart! Hope has almost failed me; yet I *will* hope on."

"Another glass of brandy for me," said a man, addressing Mr. Dago Pump.

"And rum for me," said another.

"Gin with a hot poker in it for me," said the third; and Mr. Pump poured out the poisons.

Half a dozen men stood in front of some rough boards that served as a "bar."

One of these — a tall, well-formed man — gazed fixedly upon the glasses, seemingly in deep thought.

"*Stop!*" he suddenly exclaimed. Mr. Pump nearly dropped the bottle. It was as an electric shock to him: an ashy paleness came over his face. "Stop!" he again exclaimed. All eyes were fixed upon him. Some tried to laugh, but could not. Dago set down the bottle, and the glasses, half filled, stood upon the bench before him.

"I have been thinking," said he who had caused this strange effect, "is it right for us to drink that? It does us no good; it brings upon us much evil; that 's what I 've been a-thinking while 't was being poured out."

"So have I," exclaimed another.

"And I," said a third. "I would have been worth fifty

thousand dollars, this day, had I never touched stuff like that. I tell you what, coveys, *let 's come out.*"

"Hurra!" shouted yet another; "I 've spent a good fortune in rum-shops. That 's what I say; let 's come out."

"Yes," said the first speaker, "let us come out. We have been *in* long enough;—in the gutter, in the grog-shop, in misery, in disgrace, in poverty, in jail, and in ruin. I say, let us come out, out of all these."

"Amen!" responded all.

"Let us come out," he continued; "but what can temperance folks do? I have signed the pledge, and signed, and signed, but I cannot keep it. I had no friends; temperance folks never came to me. I have often thought that, if a friend would reach forth his hand, and help me from the gutter when I have lain there, I would do anything for such a friend. But when I am drunk they laugh at and jeer me. Boys stone and cuff me, and men stand by and laugh at their hellish sport. Yes, those calling themselves 'friends of temperance' would laugh at me, and say, 'Miserable fool, nothing can save him! When such are dead, we can train up a generation of temperate people.' I am kicked and cuffed about like a dog, and not a hand is extended to relieve me. When I first tasted, I told him who gave it me the blame should rest on him if I fell. Where *he* is now, I know not; but, wherever he is, I know his is a miserable existence. Years have passed since then, and here I am, a miserable drunkard. My wife—where is she? and my good old aunt—where is she? At home in that comfortless room, weeping over *my* fall, and praying for *my* reform. Brothers, let us arise; let us determine to be men—free men!"

"It is done," said one and all; and the keeper of the cellar dashed bottle after bottle against the wall.

"Yes, let us renounce these habits; they are hard to renounce; temptation is hard to resist."

"The present pledge is not safe for us," said the keeper of the cellar, as he took a demijohn of liquor up the steps, and emptied it in the gutter.

"Then let us have one of our own," said the first speaker. "Let it be called '*The Hope of the Fallen;*' for we are indeed fallen, and this, our last refuge from more fearful evils, is our only hope. May it not disappoint us! May we cling to it as the drowning man grasps the rope thrown out for his rescue! And not for us alone shall this hope exist. Let us go to every unfortunate in our land, and speak kindly to him. Ah, my friends, we know the value of a kind word. Let us lift him from the gutter, place him upon his feet, and say, 'Stand up! I myself also am a man.'"

Having said this, he sent out for pen, ink and paper, and a pledge was carefully drawn up, of which the following is a copy:

"We, whose names are hereunto affixed, knowing by sad experience that the use of wine, beer, cider, rum, brandy, gin, and *all* kinds of intoxicating drinks, is hurtful to man, beast and reptile, do hereby pledge ourselves most solemnly to abstain now, henceforth, and forever, from the use of them in whatever shape they may be presented; to neither eat, drink, touch, taste, nor handle them; and in every place, and on every occasion, to use our influence in inducing others to do the same."

The speaker was the first to place his name to this document; and the keeper of the cellar started when he read the name of "Edward Dayton."

"Is it possible!" said he, and, grasping his hand, he shook it most heartily.

Edward was as much astonished as he. Such a change had taken place that they could not at first recognize each other.

"Yes," said Edward, "you tempted me to drink. I forgive. I now tempt *you* to sign this pledge."

No words were required to induce all present to sign.

They all spake of their past lives, related the sorrows they had felt, the misery they had endured; and such was the interest manifested by each in listening to these plain, unvarnished tales, that they resolved upon meeting in that same place the next night.

The next day, the report spread like wild-fire about the city that drunkards themselves were reforming. Many doubted, and would not believe such to be the case.

"*They* are past reforming," said public opinion; "let them die; let us take care of the young."

CHAPTER IX.

They met in the same place the next night, but the next they did not. Their numbers had so increased that the cellar would not contain them; and they engaged a large hall, and gave public notice that a meeting would be held at which reformed drunkards would speak. Those who before doubted did so no more; yet from many the sneering, cold-hearted remark was heard, "They will not hold on."

At the hour appointed, hundreds thronged to the place, and hundreds departed, being unable to gain admittance. That night, nearly *five hundred* signed the new pledge, and new additions were made daily.

It had a power which no previous pledge had possessed; a power, with God's aid, to bring man from the lowest depths of woe, place him on his feet, and tell him, "Sin no more."

The new society increased in numbers. In other cities the same feeling arose, and societies of the same kind were formed. The papers were filled with accounts of their meetings, and the cause spread, to the astonishment and grateful admiration of all.

Days of prosperity gladdened the heart of Edward. Joy took the place of sorrow in his family. He, like his thousands of brethren, had been snatched as a brand from the burning, and stood forth a living monument to the truth that there was a hope for the fallen.

Twelve years have passed since that ever-memorable night. Millions have become better men, and yet the pledge remains to exert its influence, and who can doubt that God directs its course?

'T is sending joy to the mourning, and many a wounded heart it heals. Is there a power that can exceed this? Is there another pledge that has effected as much good?

Let us, then, push on the car. Let our influence be such as will advance, and not retard, its progress. Let us do this, and ere long we may rejoice together, and earth hold a grand jubilee, and all men shall testify that the Pledge is the "hope of the fallen."

THOUGHTS THAT COME FROM LONG AGO.

There are moments in our life
When are hushed its sounds of strife;
When, from busy toil set free,
Mind goes back the past to see:
Memory, with its mighty powers,
Brings to view our childhood hours;
Once again we romp and play,
As we did in youth's bright day;
And, with never-ceasing flow,
Come the hours of Long Ago.

Oft, when passions round us throng,
And our steps incline to wrong,
Memory brings a friend to view,
In each line and feature true;
Though he long hath left us here,
Then his presence seemeth near,
And with sweet, persuasive voice,
Leads us from an evil choice; —
Thus, when we astray would go,
Come restraints from Long Ago.

Oft, when troubled and perplexed,
Worn in heart and sorely vexed,
Almost sinking 'neath our load,
Famishing on life's high road,—
Darkness, doubt, and dark despair
Leading us we know not where, —
How hath sweet remembrance caught
From the past some happy thought!
And, refreshed, we on would go,
Cheered with hopes from Long Ago.

What a store-house, filled with gems
Of more worth than diadems,
Each hath 'neath his own control,
From which to refresh his soul!
Let us, then, each action weigh,
Some good deed perform each day,
That in future we may find
Happy thoughts to bring to mind;
For, with ever ceaseless flow,
Thoughts will come from Long Ago.

DETERMINED TO BE RICH.

Rise up early, sit up late,
  Be thou unto Avarice sold;
Watch thou well at Mammon's gate,
  Just to gain a little gold.

Crush thy brother neath thy feet,
  Till each manly thought is flown;
Hear not, though he loud entreat,
  Be thou deaf to every moan.

Wield the lash, and hush the cry,
  Let thy conscience now be seared;
Pile thy glittering gems on high,
  Till thy golden god is reared.

Then before its sparkling shrine
  Bend the neck and bow the knee;
Victor thou, all wealth is thine,
  Yet, what doth it profit thee?

THE HEAVEN SENT, HEAVEN RETURNED.

Pure as an infant's heart that sin ne'er touched,
That guilt had ne'er polluted; and she seemed
Most like an angel that had missed its way
On some kind mission Heaven had bade it go.
Her eye beamed bright with beauty; and innocence,
Its dulcet notes breathed forth in every word,
Was seen in every motion that she made.
Her form was faultless, and her golden hair
In long luxuriant tresses floated o'er
Her shoulders, that as alabaster shone.
Her very look seemed to impart a sense
Of matchless purity to all it met.
I saw her in the crowd, yet none were there
That seemed so pure as she; and every eye
That met her eye's mild glance shrank back abashed,
It spake such innocence.
One day she slept, —
How calm and motionless! I watched her sleep
Till evening; then, until the sun arose;
And then, would have awakened her, — but friends
Whispered in my ear she would not wake
Within that body more, for it was dead,
And she, now clothed in immortality,
Would know no more of change, nor know a care.
And when I felt that truth, methought I saw
A bright angelic throng, in robes of white,
Bear forth her spirit to the throne of God;
And I heard music, such as comes to us
Oft in our dreams, as from some unseen life,
And holy voices chanting heavenly songs,
And harps and voices blending in one hymn,
Eternal hymn of highest praise to God
For all the good the Heaven-sent one had done
Since first it left the heavenly fold of souls,
To live on earth, and show to lower man
How pure and holy, joyous and serene,
They may and shall assuredly become

When all the laws that God through Nature speaks
Are kept unbroken! * * *

* * * She had now returned,
And heaven resounded with angelic songs.
Before me lay the cold, unmoving form;
Above me lived the joyous, happy one!
And who should sorrow? Sure, not I; not she;
Not any one! For death, — there was no death, —
But that which men called death was life more real
Than heart had e'er conceived or words expressed!

FLOWERS, BRIGHT FLOWERS!

Flowers from the wild-wood,
  Flowers, bright flowers!
Springing in desert spot,
Where man dwelleth not, —
  Flowers, bright flowers,
Cheering the traveller's lot.

Given to one and all,
  Flowers, bright flowers!
When man neglecteth thee,
When he rejecteth thee,
  Flowers, bright flowers,
God's hand protecteth thee!

Remnants of paradise,
  Flowers, bright flowers!
Tinged with a heavenly hue,
Reflecting its azure blue,
  Flowers, bright flowers,
Brightest earth ever knew!

Cheering the desolate,
  Flowers, bright flowers!
Coming with fragrance fraught,
From Heaven's own breezes caught,
  Flowers, bright flowers,
Teachers of holy thought!

Borne to the curtained room,
  Flowers, bright flowers!
Where the sick longs for light,
Then, for the shades of night,
  Flowers, bright flowers,
Gladdening the wearied sight!

High on the mountain-top,
  Flowers, bright flowers!
Low in sequestered vale,
On cliff, mid rock, in dale,
  Flowers, bright flowers,
Ye do prevail!

FORGET ME NOT.

Forget *me* not when other lips
  Shall whisper love to thee;
Forget me not when others twine
  Their chaplets for thy brow;
Forget *me* not, for I am thine,
  Forever onward true as now,
As long as time shall be.

There may be words thou mayest doubt,
  But when *I* tell thee "I am thine,"
Believe the heart's assurance true,
  In sorrow and in mirth
Forever it doth turn to you,
  Confiding, trusting in thy worth.
Thou wilt, I know, be mine.

WHAT IS TRUTH?

Long, long ago, one whose life had been one of goodness — whose every act had been that of charity and good will — was persecuted, hated and maligned! He came with new hopes. He held up a light, whose rays penetrated far into the future, and disclosed a full and glorious immortality to the long doubting, troubled soul of man.

He professed to commune with angels! He had healed the sick; he had given sight to the blind; caused the lame to walk; opened prison-doors, and had preached the Gospel to the poor. Those he chose for his companions were from humble rank. Their minds had not become enslaved to any creed; not wedded to any of the fashionable and popular forms of the day, nor immovably fixed to any of the dogmas of the schools. He chose such because their minds were free and natural; "and they forsook all and followed him."

Among the rulers, the wealthy and the powerful, but few believed in him, or in the works he performed. To them he was an impostor. In speaking of his labors some cant phrase fell from their wise lips, synonymous with the "it is all a humbug" of our day. His healing of the sick was denied; or, if admitted, was said to be some lucky circumstance of fate. His opening of the eyes of the blind was to them a mere illusion; the supposed cure, only an operation of the imagination.

All his good deeds were underrated; and those who, having seen with their own eyes, and heard with their own ears, were honest enough to believe and openly declare their belief, were looked upon by the influential and those in high places as most egregiously deceived and imposed upon.

But, notwithstanding the opposition, men did believe; and in one day three thousand acknowledged their belief in the sincerity of the teacher, and in the doctrines which he taught.

Impressed deeply with the reality and divinity of his mission,— looking to God as his father, and to all mankind as his brethren,— Jesus continued his way. To the scoffs and jeers of the rabble, he replied in meekness and love; and amid the proud and lofty he walked humbly, ever conscious of the presence of an angelic power, which would silence the loudest, and render powerless the might of human strength.

He spoke as one having authority. He condemned the formalism of their worship; declared a faith that went deeper than exterior rites and ceremonies; and spoke with an independence and fearlessness such deep and soul-searching truths, that the people took up stones to stone him, and the priests and the rulers held council together against him.

At length the excited populace, beholding their cherished faith undermined, and the new teacher day by day inculcating doctrines opposed to those of Moses and the prophets, determined to take his life, and thus terminate his labors and put a stop to his heresies.

They watched his every movement. They stood by and caught the words as they fell from his lips, hoping thus to get something by which to form an accusation against him. In this they failed. Though what he said was contrary to their time-worn dogmas, yet nothing came from his lips but sentiments of the purest love, the injunctions of reason and justice, and the language of humanity. Failing in this plan to ensnare him, justice was set aside, and force called in to their aid.

See him now before a great tribunal, and Pilate, troubled in soul, compelled to say, "I find no fault in this man."

Urged to action by the mad crowd around him, balancing his decision between justice, the prisoner's release, and injustice, the call to crucify him, he knows not what to do. In an agony of thought, which pen cannot describe or human words portray, he delays his irrevocable doom.

In the mean time, the persecutors grow impatient; and louder than ever, from the chief priests and the supporters of royalty, goes up the infamous shout, "Crucify him, crucify him!" At this moment, the undecided, fearful Pilate casts a searching glance about him. As he beholds the passionate people, eager for the blood of one man, and he innocent, and sees, standing in their midst, the meek and lowly Jesus, calm as an evening zephyr over Judea's plains, from whose eye flows the gentle love of an infinite divinity,— his face beaming in sympathy with every attribute of goodness, faith and humanity,— all this, too, before his mad, unjust accusers, from whose eyes flash in mingled rays the venom of scorn and hate,— his mind grows strong with a sense of right. His feelings will not longer be restrained, and, unconscious of his position, forgetting for the moment the dignity of his office, he exclaims, with the most emphatic earnestness, "WHAT IS TRUTH?"

Eighteen hundred years have intervened between that day and this; and now the same inquiry is heard, and often with the same earnestness as then. Men ask, and often ask in vain, "what is truth?" and yet the great problem to millions remains unsolved.

Generations pass on, and leave to others the great question for them to ask, and they, in turn, to leave unanswered. The child, ere it can speak in words, looks from its wistful eye, "What is truth?" Youth comes, and all the emotions of the soul are awakened. It arises from the playfulness of childhood, forgets its little games, and, finding itself an actor in the drama of life, looks over the long programme of parts from which it is to choose its own, and anxiously inquires "What is truth?" Manhood feels the importance of the question; and Age, though conscious of its near approach to the world of revealed truth, repeats it.

The present is an era of thought. Men begin to assume a spirit of independence, and to look less upon human authority, and more upon that light which lighteth every man that cometh into the world. And it is well that it is so. It is well that we begin to look upon liberty in another light than a mere absence of iron bonds upon our hands and feet; that we begin to discern that

> "He is a freeman whom the truth makes free,
> And all are slaves beside."

We are pressing on to know the truth. We have grown weary of darkness, and are seeking the light. We should remember, in our researches, that, to find out truth, we must not be pledged to any form, any opinion, or any creed, however old or dearly cherished such limitations may have been with ourselves or others. We must come to the task like little children, ready to learn. We must leave our beliefs behind us. We must not bring them, and attempt to adapt our discoveries in the realms of eternal truth to them; but we must build up the structure with the material we find in the universe of God; and then, when reared, if we find that in doing so we have a stone from our old temple nicely adjusted in the new, very well;—let it remain, and thank God for it.

Men have trusted too much in the views of past ages, and taken for truth many an error, because some one back in by-gone ages introduced it as such, and it has been believed in and held most sacred.

Let our course be our own course, and not that of others. Let us seek for truth as truth. Let us be honest and press on, trusting in God the rewarder of all, who will bless all our efforts to ascertain his truths, and our duty to him, to our fellow-men, and to ourselves.

THE HOMESTEAD VISIT.

He had wandered far and long, and when, on his return to the scenes of his early life, he came in full view of the old house, in which and around which those scenes were clustered, he threw down his oaken staff, raised his hands, and clapped them like a child. Then a tear would roll down his face; then a smile illumine it; then he would dance with joy. As he approached the building, he observed that the door was open; and the large, hospitable-looking room was so inviting, and there being no one present, he entered, and indulged in thoughts like these:

I STAND where I have stood before:
  The same roof is above me,
But they who were are here no more,
  For me to love, or love me.
I listen, and I seem to hear
  A favorite voice to greet me;
But yet I know that none are near,
  Save stranger forms, to meet me.

I 'll sit me down, — for I have not
  Sat here since first I started
To run life's race, — and on this spot
  Will muse of the departed.
Then I was young, and on my brow
  The rays of hope were shining;
But Time hath there his imprint now,
  That tells of life's declining.

How great the change! — though I can see
  Full many a thing I cherished —
Yet, since beneath yon old oak tree
  I stood, how much hath perished.
Here is the same old oaken floor,
  And there the same rough ceiling
Each telling of the scenes of yore,
  Each former joys revealing.

But, friends of youth — they all have fled;
  Some yet on earth do love us;
While others, passed beyond the dead,
  Live guardian ones above us.
Yet, o'er us all one powerful hand
  Is raised to guard forever,
And all, ere long, one happy band
  Be joined, no more to sever.

I 've trimmed my sail on every sea
  Where crested waves are swelling;
Yet oft my heart turned back to thee,
  My childhood's humble dwelling.
I 've not forgot my youthful days,
  The home that was my mother's,
When listening to the words of praise
  That were bestowed on others.

See, yonder, through the window-pane,
  The rock on which I rested;
And on that green how oft I 've lain —
  What memories *there* are vested!
The place where once a sister's hand
  I held — none loved I fonder;
But she 's now with an angel band,
  Whilst I a pilgrim wander.

There was a pretty, blue-eyed girl,
  A good old farmer's daughter;
We used the little stones to hurl,
  And watch them skip the water.
We 'd range among the forest trees,
  To gather woodland flowers;
And then each other's fancy please
  In building floral bowers.

Within this room, how many a time
  I 've listened to a story,
And heard grandfather sing his rhyme
  'Bout Continental glory!

And oft I 'd shoulder his old staff,
  And march as proud as any,
Till the old gentleman would laugh,
  And bless me with a penny.

Hark! 't is a footstep that I hear;
  A stranger is approaching;
I must away — were I found here
  I should be thought encroaching.

* * * * * * * *

One last, last look — my old, old home!
  One memory more of childhood!
I 'll not forget, where'er I roam,
  This homestead and the wild-wood.

THE MARINER'S SONG.

O THE sea, the sea! I love the sea!
For nothing on earth seems half as free
As its crested waves; they mount on high,
And seem to sport with the star-gemmed sky.
Talk as you will of the land and shore;
Give me the sea, and I ask no more.

I love to float on the ocean deep,
To be by its motion rocked to sleep;
Or to sit for hours and watch the spray,
Marking the course of our outward way,
While upward far in a cloudless sky
With a shriek the wild bird passeth by.

And when above are the threatening clouds,
And the wild wind whistles 'mid the shrouds,
Our masts bend low till they kiss the wave,
As beckoning one from its ocean cave,

Then hurra for the sea! I love its foam,
And over it like a bird would roam.

There is that 's dear in a mountain home,
With dog and gun 'mid the woods to roam;
And city life hath a thousand joys,
That quiver amid its ceaseless noise;
Yet nothing on land can give to me
Such joy as that of the pathless sea.

When morning comes, and the sun's first rays
All around our gallant topmast plays,
My heart bounds forth with rapturous glee,
O, then, 't is then that I love the sea!
Talk as you will of the land and shore;
Give me the sea, and I ask no more!

LOVE'S LAST WORDS.

They knew that she was going
To holier, better spheres,
Yet they could not stay the flowing
Of their tears;
And they bent above in sorrow,
Like mourners o'er a tomb,
For they knew that on the morrow
There 'd be gloom.

There was one among the number
Who had watched the dying's breath,
With an eye that would not slumber
Until death.
There, as he bent above her,
He whispered in her ear
How fondly he did love her,
Her most dear.

"One word, 't will comfort send me,
When early spring appears,
And o'er thy grave I bend me
In my tears.
A single word now spoken
Shall be kept in Memory's shrine,
Where the dearest treasured token
Shall be thine."

She pressed his hand — she knew him —
With the fervor of a child;
And, looking fondly to him,
Sweetly smiled.
And, smiling thus, she started
For her glorious home above,
And her last breath, as it parted,
Whispered "*Love*."

LIGHT IN DARKNESS.

Sometimes my heart complaineth
And moans in bitter sighs;
And dreams no hope remaineth,
No more its sun will rise.

But yet I know God liveth,
And will do all things well;
And that to me he giveth
More good than tongue can tell.

And though above me linger
At times dark Sorrow's shroud,
I see Faith's upraised finger
Point far beyond the cloud.

MT. VERNON, AND THE TOMB OF WASHINGTON.

The heat of noon had passed, and the trees began to cast their evening shadows, when, in company with a friend, I seated myself in a carriage, and drove off in the direction of Mount Vernon. We crossed the long bridge, and found ourselves in the old State of Virginia.

It was a delightful afternoon; one just suited to the purpose to which we had devoted it. The trees were clad in fresh, green foliage, and the farms and gardens were blooming into early life. To myself, no season appears so beautiful as that of spring. All seasons to me are bright and glorious, but there is a charm about spring that captivates the soul. Then Nature weaves her drapery, and bends over the placid lake to jewel herself, as the maiden bends before her mirror to deck her pure white brow with diamonds and rubies. All is life, all animation, all clothed with hope; all tending upward, onward to the bright future.

> "The trees are full of crimson buds, the woods are full of birds,
> And the waters flow to music, like a tune with pleasant words."

In about one hour we reached the city of Alexandria. Between this place and Washington a steamboat plies, going and returning four times a day. The road from Washington to Alexandria is about decent; but the road from thence to Mount Vernon is in the worst possible condition,—so bad, in fact, that we dismounted and walked a considerable distance, it being far less tiresome to walk than to ride. The road winds in a very circuitous route through a dense forest, the lofty trees of which, rising upon either hand, cast their deep shadows upon us. The place, that would otherwise have been gloomy, was enlivened by the variable songs of the mocking-birds, and the notes of their more beautiful-plumed though less melodious companions.

Occasionally we passed the hut of a negro, and met a loaded team from some Virginian farm, drawn by three or four ill-looking, yet strong and serviceable horses. These teams were managed by negroes,— never less than two, and in some cases by three or four, or, as in one instance, by an entire family, man, wife and children, seated on their loads, whistling and singing, where also sat a large black-and-white mastiff. Long after we passed and they had receded from our view, we could distinctly hear their melodious voices singing their simple yet expressive songs, occasionally interrupted by a "*gee, yawh, shau,*" as they urged on their dilatory steeds.

The homes of the negroes were in some cases built of stone; mostly, however, of boards, put loosely together, and in some instances of large logs, the crevices being filled with mud, which, the sun and wind having hardened, were white-washed, presenting a very strong though not very beautiful appearance, the architecture of which was neither Grecian nor Roman, but evidently from "original designs" by a not very fastidious or accomplished artist.

Groups of women and children were about these houses; some seated on the grass, in the shade of the tall trees; others standing in the doors, all unemployed and apparently having nothing to do but to talk, and this they appeared to engage in with a hearty good will.

We continued our way over stones, up steep, deep-rutted hills, covered partly with branches and brambles, and down as steep declivities, through ponds and brooks, now and then cheered by the *pleasing* prospect of a long road, evidently designed to illustrate the "*ups* and *downs* of life."

After a tiresome journey, partly walked, partly ridden, which was somewhat relieved of its tediousness by the romantic and beautiful scenery through which we passed, we came in view of Mount Vernon.

An old, infirm, yet good, sociable negro met us at the gate, and told us that there was another road to the Mount, but that it was not as good as the one we came over, and also that there was a private road, which was not as good as either of the others! We smiled, threw out a hint about aërial navigation. He smiled also, and, thinking we doubted his word, said, "Indeed, it is not as good; I would n't tell you a lie about it." Mercy on pilgrims to Mount Vernon! If you ever go there, reader, do provide yourself with a conscience that can't be shaken out of you.

Having been kindly furnished with a letter from Mr. Seaton, the editor of the *Intelligencer*, and Mayor of Washington city, to the proprietor of the estate, we inquired whether he was at home, and with pleasure learned that he was.

We passed into what we deemed an almost sacred enclosure, so linked is it with the history of our country, and the glorious days that gave birth to a nation's freedom. It seemed as though we had entered an aviary, so many and so various the birds that floated in the air around us, and filled it with the rich melody of their songs.

At a short distance stood a beautiful deer, as if transfixed to the spot, his large, black, lustrous eyes turned towards us, his ears erect, till, suddenly starting, he darted away, and leaped down the steep hill-side to the water's brink.

The house I need not describe, as most persons are acquainted with its appearance, from seeing the numerous engraved representations of it. It shows many evidences of age and decay. Time is having his own way with it, as the hand that would defend it from his ravages, and improve its looks, is kept back, that it may remain as nearly as possible in the same condition as when occupied by our first president. We entered and passed through several rooms, endeavoring to allay our curiosity by asking more questions than our attendant could conveniently answer and retain his senses.

We saw the massive key of that old French prison-house, the Bastile, presented to General Washington by that friend of freedom and humanity, General Lafayette, soon after the destruction of that monument of terror. We noticed that depredations had been committed by visitors upon the costly marble fire-frame, which was a gift to Washington.

Mr. Washington being called to the farm, we availed ourselves of the services of the old negro before mentioned, who led us around the estate. On our way to the tomb, we passed through what we judged to be a kitchen. The floor was brick, and a fireplace occupied nearly all of one side of the room; one of those old-fashioned contrivances which were in vogue in those days when people went more for comfort than appearance. Half a score of negroes were in the room, who gazed at us as we entered, covered with dust and dirt, the real *free soil* of Virginia. They seemed to think our intentions more of a warlike than a peaceable nature. We soon inclined them to the latter belief, however, by gently patting a curly-headed urchin upon the head, and distributing a few pennies among the crowd.

Five minutes' walk, and we were at the tomb.

"There is the old General," said the aged negro, as he touched lightly the sarcophagus with his cane; "that, yonder, is his wife," pointing to a similar one at the left.

Silently I stood and gazed at the marble coffin that held the mortal remains of him whom, when he lived, all people loved, and the memory of whom, now that he has passed from our material vision, all people revere. A few branches of cypress lay upon it, and at its base a few withered flowers.

The sarcophagus that holds the dust of Washington is placed upon a low pedestal, formed of brick. A brick wall is at the sides, and an iron slat fence or gateway in front. Over this gateway a white stone is set in the brick-work, and bears this inscription:

WITHIN THIS ENCLOSURE ARE
THE REMAINS
OF
GENERAL GEORGE WASHINGTON.

Short, indeed, but how full of food for thought!

"General George Washington!" He needs no long and fulsome epitaph carved in marble to tell his worth. Did his memory depend upon that alone, the marble would crumble into dust, mingle with his, and his name pass away with the stone that man vainly thought would preserve it. No; his monument is a world made free, and his memory as lasting as immortal mind. Wherever the light of freedom shall penetrate, it will bear on its every glistening ray his cherished name; and whenever and wherever men shall struggle with oppression, it shall inspire them with vigor, and cheer them on to victory.

Marble will perish, and monuments of adamant will crumble to dust; but the memory of Washington will live as long as there is a heart to love, or a mind to cherish a recollection of goodness.

"He was a good old man," said the negro, "and he has gone to his rest."

"We are all going," he continued, after a pause. I thought a tear stole down his wrinkled face; but he turned his back to me, and left me to my own reflections.

Deep silence was about us. We heard not even the notes

of a bird. Not a zephyr moved the air, not a rustling leaf was there. In front, far below, lay the Potomac. Not a breath of wind moved the surface of its waters, but calmly, peacefully, undisturbed, the river moved on, as though conscious of the spot it was passing. On its glassy surface were reflected the branches that bent over and kissed it as it flowed, and the last rays of a declining sun tinted with their golden light the hills on the opposite shore.

I stood at the tomb of Washington: on my right stood a distinguished Indian chief; on my left, "Uncle Josh," the old African, of three-score years and ten. We represented three races of the human family, and we each were there with the same feelings of love, honor, and respect to departed worth.

Night was hastening on. I clambered up the embankment, and plucked a few green leaves from a branch that hung over the tomb; gazed once more, and yet again, within the enclosure; then turned away, and hastened to overtake my companions, who were far in advance.

If our country is ever called to pass through another struggle, may God, in his wisdom, raise up for it another Washington!

The sun had passed the horizon, and the cool evening air, laden with the fragrance of shrubbery and flowers, gathered about us. A lively squirrel sprang across our path; a belated bird flew by; and, amid the pleasant, quiet scenes of rural life, we wended our way homeward.

FREEDOM'S GATHERING.

I SEEMED to live beyond the present time;
   Methought it was when all the world was free,
And myriad numbers, from each distant clime,
   Came up to hold their annual jubilee.
From distant China, Afric's sunburnt shore,
   From Greenland's icebergs, Russia's broad domain,
They came as men whom fetters bound no more,
   And trod New England's valley, hill, and plain.
They met to hold a jubilee, for all
Were free from error's chain, and from the oppressor's thrall.

Word had gone forth that slavery's power was done;
   The cry like wild-fire through the nations ran;
Russia's tame serf, and Afric's sable son,
   Threw off their chains — each felt himself a man.
Thrones that had stood for ages were no more;
   Man ceased to suffer; tyrants ceased to reign;
And all throughout the world, from shore to shore,
   Were loosed from slavery's fetter and its chain;
And those who once were slaves came up as free,
Unto New England's soil, to keep their jubilee.

New England! 't was a fitting place, for it
   Had sent its rays upon them, as a star
Beams from the glorious heaven on slaves who sit
   In chains, to lure them where free seraphs are;
The light it had shed on them made them start
   From their deep lethargy, then look and see
That they of Freedom's boon might have a part,
   Their nation glorious as New England be.
And then like men they struggled till they won,
And Freedom's high-born light shone as a noonday sun.

Men gathered there who were men; nobly they
   Had long and faithful fought 'gainst error's night,

And now they saw the sunlight of that day
 They long had hoped to see, when truth and right
Should triumph o'er the world, and all should hold
 This truth self-evident, that fellow-men,
In God's own image made, should not be sold
 Nor stalled as cattle in a market-pen.
Praises they sang, and thanks they gave to God,
That he had loosed the chain, and broke the oppressor's rod.

They gazed o'er all the past; their vision's eye
 Beheld how men in former years had groaned,
When Hope's own flame burned dim, and no light nigh
 Shone to disperse the darkness; when enthroned
Sat boasting Ignorance, and 'neath its sway
 Grim Superstition held its lurid lamp,
That only darkened the obstructed way
 In which man groped and wandered, till the damp,
Cold, cheerless gateway of an opening tomb
Met his extended hand, and sealed his final doom.

Perchance *one* mind, illumined from above,
 Did strive to burst the heavy bonds it wore,
Pierce through the clouds of error, and, in love
 With its new mission, upward seek to soar.
Upon it shone truth's faintest, feeblest ray;
 It would be free; but tyrants saw and crushed
Man's first attempt to cast his chains away,
 The first aspirings of his nature hushed.
Thus back from men was Freedom's genius driven,
And Slavery's chains in ten-fold strength were riven.

In gazing o'er the past, 't was this they saw —
 How Evil long had triumphed; but to-day
Man bowed to nothing but God's righteous law,
 And Truth maintained its undisputed sway.
Right conquered might; and of this they were proud,
 As they beheld all nations drawing near, —
Men from all lands, a vast, unnumbered crowd,
 While in their eyes full many a sparkling tear
Trembled a while, then from its cell did start,
Witness to the deep joys of an o'erflowing heart.

There came up those who 'd crouched beneath the lash,
Had bowed beneath the chains they scarce could bear,
Till Freedom's lightning on their minds did flash,
And roused them as a lion in his lair
Is roused when foes invade it, then, with strength
Near superhuman, one bold effort made
To break their cruel bondage, till at length
Beneath their feet they saw their fetters laid.
'T was then they lifted their freed hands on high,
And peans loud and long resounded through the sky.

Up, up they came, and still the bannered host
Far in the distance met my wondering eye;
On hill and dale, on all New England's coast,
White banners waved beneath a cloudless sky.
The aged sire leaned on his oaken staff,
Manhood stood up in all its strength and pride,
And youth came dancing with a joyous laugh,
With woman, lovely woman, at their side;
Bright eyes, glad hearts, and joyous souls, were there,
Free as the light that shone, unfettered as the air.

The mind, that spark of Deity within
That hath its nurture from a higher world,
No longer bound by tyranny and sin,
Beheld its highest, noblest powers unfurled.
No more did Error bind it to its creed,
Or Superstition strive to blind its sight;
It followed only where God's truth did lead,
And trusted him to guide its course aright.
The inner as the outer man was free,
And both united held this glorious jubilee.

* * * * * * *

—— 'T was all a vision, and it passed away,
As dreams depart; yet it did leave behind
Its deep impressions, thoughts that fain would stay
And hold communion with the tireless mind.
I wished that it were real; alas! I heard
The clank of Slavery's fetters rend the air;

And feelings of my heart were deeply stirred,
When I beheld my brethren, who dare
Proclaim all "equal," yet in chains of steel
Bind men, who, like themselves, can pain and pleasure feel.

God in his wisdom meant all should be free,
All equal: each a brother unto man.
Presumptuous mortal! who His great decree
Durst strive to change to suit *thy* selfish plan!
Know thou that his fixed purpose will be done,
Though thou arrayest all thy puny strength
In war against it! *All* who feel the sun
Shall own his goodness, and be *free* at length.
God cares for mortals, though he reigns on high;
Freedom is His own cause, and it shall *never* die!

My country! if my heart one wish doth hold,
For thee and for thy good, it is that thou
No more permit thy children to be sold!
Forbid that they as slaves to man shall bow!
For them our fathers nobly fought and bled;
For them they poured their life-blood forth as rain;
Shall it in foreign lands of us be said,
We bind our *brothers* with a galling chain?
While the Old World is struggling to be free,
America! shall this foul charge be laid to thee?

We all may err; may oft be led astray;
Let him who 'd free the slave be careful he
Is not a slave himself to some fond way
He would adopt to set his brother free!
All seek one end; for all one good would gain;
Then, on as brothers, hand in hand proceed!
Paths that seem intricate will all be plain,
If we but follow where God's truth would lead.
Trust Him for strength in darkness and in light;
His word will cheer us on, — His presence give us might.

SONG OF THE BIRD.

On the topmost branch of the highest tree
I sit and sing, I am free! I am free!
When the lightnings flash, when the thunders roar,
I plume my wings and away I soar!
But soon on the branch of a lofty tree
Gayly I sing, I am free! I am free!

A huntsman he came by my nest one day,
And thought that with gun my song he would stay;
But I left my nest when he thought me there,
And I roamed about in my native air.
Then, when he was gone, on the highest tree
Gayly I sung, I am free! I am free!

It is I, 't is I, that at dawn of day
Go to meet the sun at its earliest ray.
I love its heat; so I cheer it along
With chirping notes and melodious song;
And all the day on the highest tree
Gayly I sing, I am free! I am free!

When the dusky shades of the night appear,
In my nest on high I have naught to fear;
Sweetly I slumber till dawning of day,
Then to the East, for the sun, I 'm away,
Till, borne on its rays to the highest tree,
Gayly I sing, I am free! I am free!

O, I love my nest, and my nest loves me!
It rocks like a bark on the dancing sea;
Gently it bows when I wish to retire;
When in, it rises higher and higher.
O, I love my nest, and I love the tree,
Home and the haunt of the bird that is free!

I CHANGE BUT IN DYING.

I CHANGE but in dying, — I am faithful till death!
I will guard thee with care from pollution's foul breath;
I promise that ne'er in neglect thou shalt pine;
I change but in dying, — say, wilt thou be mine?

I come not with riches; good fortune ne'er blest me;
Yet one of less worth hath often carest me;
The light of true love o'er thy pathway shall shine;
I change but in dying, — say, wilt thou be mine?

I change but in dying, — no holier vow
From lips mortal e'er came than I breathe to thee now;
It comes from a heart with love for thee sighing;
Believe me, 't is true, — I change but in dying!

HE IS THY BROTHER.

Go, break the chains that bind the slave;
  Go, set the captive free;
For Slavery's banners ne'er should wave,
  And slaves should never be.

Yet not in anger. Hasty words
  Should not to thee belong.
They will not loose a single link,
  But bind them yet more strong.

O, while ye think to him in chains
  A brother's rights are due,
Remember him who binds those chains!
  He is thy brother, too!

THE WINE-DEALER'S CLERK.

CHAPTER I.

"WILL you sign the pledge?" asked one young man of another.

"No!" was the ready response; and, after a moment's pause, "You are wrong, and I am right. You wish to deprive me of a social glass, free companionship with those I love, life's best enjoyments, and to live bound down to the contracted limits of a temperance-pledge. — *Me* sign! No! Go ask leave of the soaring eagle to clip his wings; of the oriole to tarnish his bright plumage; of the bounding deer to fetter his free limbs,— but do not ask *me* to sign a pledge!"

The young men parted. Each went his way; one to his counting-room, the other to his home.

The proprietors of the store with which the former was connected had been for a number of years busily engaged in the importation, adulteration and sale of wines and brandies. From the cellar to the attic of their large warehouse, pipes, puncheons, and barrels of the slow poison were deposited, with innumerable bottles of wine, reputed to be old as a century, if not older. A box or two of Flemish pipes relieved the sameness of the scene,— barrels on barrels.

From the counting-room of the establishment a large number of young men had gone forth to become either wholesale or retail dealers in the death-drugged merchandise. The ill-success which attended these, and the lamentable end to which they arrived, would have been singular and mysterious, had it followed in the wake of any other business. But, as it was, effect followed cause, and such is the law of nature.

One, a young man of promise in days gone-by, recently became the inmate of an alms-house in a distant city; another, urged to madness by frequent potations, died as the fool dieth; and a third, who had been the centre light of a social circle, as he felt the chill of death come upon him, called all his friends near, and said to them, "Deal not, deal not in the arrows of death, lest those arrows pierce thine own heart at last!"

All these facts were known to the public; yet they countenanced the traffic in which Messrs. Laneville & Co. were engaged. They were merchants, they were wealthy; for these reasons, it would seem, the many-headed public looked up to them with a feeling bordering on reverence, somewhat awed by their presence, as though wealth had made them worthy, while many a less rich but ten-fold more honest man walked in the shadow of the mighty Magog, unseen,— uncared for, if seen. Messrs. Laneville & Co. knew that the law was against their business; they knew, also, that public opinion, if not actually in favor of it, willingly countenanced it.

Perchance the cry of some unfortunate widow might at times reach their ears; but it was speedily hushed by the charmed music of the falling dollar, as it was exchanged for their foul poison. Forgetting they were men, they acted as demons, and continued to deal forth their liquid death, and to supply the thousand streams of the city with the *cause* of the crime it was obliged to punish, and the pauperism it was obliged to support.

The "Vincennes" had just arrived at the wharf as James entered the store. It had been the custom of the owners, on the annual arrival of this vessel, to have a party on board.

On this occasion, they made the usual arrangements for the festivity. Cards of invitation were speedily written, and distributed among members of the city government, editors, clergymen, and other influential persons. James was free to invite such of his friends as he chose, and in doing so the question arose whether he should ask George Alverton to be present. It was known to him that George was a teetotaller, and had that morning invited him to sign the pledge. He knew that at the entertainment wine would circulate. He knew that some would indulge rather freely, and that the maintenance of a perfect equilibrium by such would be very difficult. Suppose he, himself,— that is, James,— should be among these last mentioned, and that, too, before his friend George; would it not demolish his favorite argument, which he had a thousand times advanced, that he knew *right* from *wrong*,— when to drink and when to stop drinking? yet, thought he, I may not indulge too freely. Yes; I *will* maintain my position, and show by practice what I teach by preaching. Besides, it would be very impolite, as well as uncourteous, in me, not to invite one whose character I value so highly as his,— one whose friendship I so much esteem. I will invite him. He shall be present, and shall see that I can keep sober without being pledged to do so.

CHAPTER II.

George Alverton was the son of a nobleman. Start not, republican reader, for we mean not a stiff-starched branch of English nobility, but one of America's noblemen,— and hers are nature's! He was a hard-working mechanic; one of God's noblest works,— an honest man! Americans know not, as yet, the titled honors of the Old World; and none, save a few, whose birth-place nature must have mistook, would introduce into a republican country the passwords of a monarchical one.

"An invite for you," said the laughing Josephine, as George entered at dusk. "And ten to one it 's from that black-eyed Kate, who is bewitching all the young men within a twenty-mile circuit with her loving glances — eh? A match, ten to one!"

"Always gay," said George, as he turned half aside to avoid the mischievous look of his sister; "but, by the way, Jos, to be serious, an invite did you say? How do you know that?"

"O, by the way 't is folded; we girls have a way of knowing a love-letter from bills of exchange, and an invitation from bills of lading. Just look at it; see how pretty 't is enveloped, how handsomely directed,—*George Alverton, Esq., Present.* It 's no use, George; you need n't look so serious. You are a captured one, and when a bird 's in a net he may as well lie still as flutter!"

Josephine handed the note to her brother, slyly winking as she did so, as much as to say,

"The marriage-bells are ringing, love."

George, observing the superscription, was convinced that it was from James Clifton, and remarked,

"Don't be too hasty; it is from James; the direction must be wrong; it was doubtless intended for you. Look out, Jos; *you* may be the captured one, after all!"

Josephine was not to be thus thrown from her ground; so, turning to her brother with a laugh, she said,

"For me! Well, if so 't is so; but I judge from what I see. Notwithstanding your insinuation that James writes to no one but myself, I 'll venture a bright gold dollar that this is for yourself, even though it be from James. Open the budget, and prove the truth of what I say."

George untied the white ribbon that bound it, and, opening the envelope, found an invitation to a gentleman's party to be held that evening on board the "Vincennes." Josephine laughed merrily over what she deemed her brother's defeat, and George as heartily over what he deemed his victory. He was advised to go; not, however, without an accompanying hint of its being a dry affair, as ladies were to be excluded. Josephine was puzzled to know the reason of their exclusiveness, and what festivity was to be engaged in of which they could not partake.

"I scarcely know what to do," said George, "as wines will be circulated, and I shall be asked, a dozen times or more, to drink of them."

"Go, by all means," said his sister; "stand your own ground, be firm, be resolute, refuse if asked to partake; but do so in a manner that, while it shows a determination to resist temptation, will not offend, but rather induce him you respect to think whether it will not be best for him also to refuse."

"I will. I am aware of the situation in which James is placed. He has a generous, a noble heart, that needs but to know the right to do it. I will go; and if by example, persuasion or otherwise, I can prevail upon him to sign the pledge, I will do so, and thank God for it. I will speak to him kindly, and in reason. Others will drink, if he does not; others will fall, if he escapes; and such examples are the most convincing arguments that can be used to prove that an unpledged man, in these days of temptation, is unsafe, and unmindful of his best and dearest interests."

CHAPTER III.

Notwithstanding the short interval between the reception of the cards and the hour of festivity, the time appointed saw a goodly number assembled in the well-furnished, richly-decorated cabins of the ship.

It was evident that some individuals had been busy as bees, for all was clean and in the best of order. Wreaths of evergreen and national flags decorated the vessel, and bouquets of bright and fragrant flowers, conspicuously arranged, loaded the air with their sweet perfumes. There were card-tables and cards, scores of well-filled decanters, and glasses almost without number. At one end of the cabin stood a table filled with fruits of the most costly kind. There were oranges fresh from the land that gave them growth, and other products of sunny Italy and the islands beyond the seas. The captain was as lively as a lark, and as talkative as wit and wine could make him. He spoke of his quick voyage, praised his ship till praise seemed too poor to do its duty, boasted of its good qualities, said there was not a better craft afloat, and finished his eulogy by wishing success to all on board, and washing it down with a glass of Madeira, which, he said, was *the* stuff, for he made it himself from grapes on the island.

Messrs. Laneville & Co. were in high glee. They drank and played cards with men worth millions; spoke of the inclemency of the season, and expressed great surprise that so much poverty and wretchedness existed, with one breath, and with the next extolled the wines and administered justice to the eatables. Editors were there who had that morning written long "leaders" about the oppression of the poor by the rich, and longer ones about the inconsistencies of their contemporaries, who ate and drank, and dreamt not of inconsistency in themselves, though they guided the press with temperance reins, and harnessed themselves with those who tarried long at the wine.

James drank quite often, and George as often admonished him of his danger. But the admonitions of a young man had but little if any influence, counteracted as they were by the example of the rich and the great about him. There was Alderman Zemp, who was a temperance man in the world, but a wine-drinker in a ship's cabin. He had voted for stringent laws against the sale of liquors, and had had his name emblazoned on the pages of every professedly temperance paper as a philanthropist and a righteous man; and on the pages of every anti-temperance publication, as a foe to freedom, and an enemy to the rights of humanity. But he drank; yes, he had asked James to take a glass of the water of Italy, as he called it. Clergymen, so called, disgraced themselves, and gave the scoffers food for merriment. Judges who that day might have sentenced some unfortunate to imprisonment for drinking, drank with a gusto equalled only by lawyers who would talk an hour in court to prove a man discreditable evidence because he was known to visit barrooms! It was the influence of these, and such like, that made James drink, and caused the labor of George to prove all unavailing. It is the example of the rich that impedes the progress of temperance, — they who loll on damask sofas, sip their iced champagnes and brandies, and never get "drunk," though they are sometimes "indisposed."

The clock struck twelve, then one, and the morning hours advanced, light-foot messengers of the coming day. The gay and the jocund laugh was hushed, and the notes that told of festive mirth were silenced. Nature, either fatigued by exertion or stupefied by wine, had sank to repose; and those who had lingered too long and indulged too freely were lying on the cabin-floor helpless. George retired at a seasonable hour. James remained, and fell, as others, before the enchanting wine-cup's power!

CHAPTER IV.

The next morning George called at the store of Laneville & Co. No one was in save a small lad, who, to his inquiry, replied that all were sick. The youth was a short, porpoise-shaped lad, who appeared quite independent for his age and station, and told George that he had better call the next day, as the folks would n't be down. In an instant George suspected the cause of their absence. Though he knew James would be mortified to be seen, yet he determined upon visiting him, thinking it a favorable opportunity to submit to him the expediency of taking that step which he had urged upon him on the morning previous.

Conscious of being engaged in an act of duty, he ascended the steps that led to the door of the house. He rang; a servant-girl answered his call.

"Holloa!" shouted a voice at the head of the stairs. "Who 's there?—what cow 's got into my pasture now? Another glass, friends,—*once* more! Now drink, 'Death to the temperance cause, and ill-luck to fanatics!' Holloa! down below,—come aloft!"

"Hush! be quiet," said a female voice, in a whisper. "James, do respect yourself."

"Hush! who says hush? My soul 's in arms; come on, John Duff! bring liquor here, and cursed be he who says, I 've had enough!"

The closing of a door put an end to this extemporaneous address. George stood like a statue; he knew not which course to take,—whether to go up to his friend's room, or go down to the street. He soon determined, and sent word that he wished to speak to James. In a moment the latter was again to be heard declaiming disconnected sentences on all manner of subjects, until, learning the wish of George, he shouted,

"Yes, tell him to come up and revel in the groves of Madeira, or dance with peasant-girls at the grape-gatherings in Sicily! Yes, George, up here, and see how a man can live a temperance life without signing the pledge, and be as independent as he pleases!"

As George entered, James grasped his hand,—swung him round rather familiarly, and pushed him towards a chair.

The furniture and all that was in the room was in the greatest confusion, not excepting James Clifton himself. There was a boot-jack and a vase of flowers side by side on the mantel; a pair of boots on the centre-table, with two or three annuals on them, as though to keep them from being blown away; a nice hat stood on the hearth filled with coal-ashes, while an inkstand upside down on a pile of linen bosoms had left an impression not easily effaced; the paintings that were in the room were turned face towards the wall,—some freak of James', as though ashamed to have them see the performances.

"Now, George," said Mr. Clifton, "you can be convinced of the truth of my doctrine. I did n't sign the pledge, and I 'm as sober, sober as a brandy-smasher! You recollect what a great poet says,—

'Drink till the *moon* goes down.'

I can improve that; I say,—

'Drink till *yourselves* go down.'

What an age this is, when temperance fanatics dance through the world to smash decanters, and make one pledge himself to be a *fool!* Independence is my motto! I go for independence now, independence forever, and as much longer as possible. Who says I am not right? Deluded mortals, who wink at sin, and kick at brandies! Magnificent monstrosities, making manliness moonshine; metaphysical Moors murdering Munchausen —"

"But hold, James," said George, interrupting him in his remarks; "keep within bounds,— let us reason." It was not with much hope of success that George asked his friend to "reason," for his condition was one not in the least degree favorable to such a performance.

"Reason?" exclaimed James. "I'm not a reasonable,— reasoning, I mean,— I'm not a reasoning being! Go ask the pigs to reason!"

Notwithstanding all this, George seemed inclined to argument, for he immediately said,

"Don't you see the ill effects of last night's indulgence in the confusion around you, and feel them in your own mind and body?"

"Now you talk like a man. Let us send the 'Jamestown' to Ireland with bread and butter. 'T is a vote! passed unanimously by both houses of Congress. We'll fire a full broadside of gingerbread at the old Green Isle, and teach the people to eat for a living."

This rambling from the inquiry George had made induced him to relinquish all hope of influencing him at that time. He saw how he had fallen; and he needed no prophet's ken to behold his future course, unless he turned from the path he was now so enthusiastically following.

Seeing that no good could be effected by his remaining, George arose to depart, when James caught his arm, and told him not to be in such haste.

"I want you to take a glass of wine;" and, ringing the bell, a servant was at the door before Mr. Alverton had an opportunity to say or do anything.

"You know I don't drink wines," said George; "why do you ask me?"

"Don't drink?"

"You look surprised, but you know I do not."

"Everybody drinks."

"Not all, if I am one of that extensive number."

"Well, my employer sells liquors, my minister drinks his wine, and my friends all drink, except you; and you are a sort of nondescript, a sort of back-action member of human society, a perfect ginger-cake without any ginger in it. Say, got a pledge in your pocket? *I* have; here it is:" and he pulled forth a slip of paper, on which he had written some half-legible lines.

"See how you like it;—it is what is called the Independent Pledge. I'll read it.

"'We the undersigned, believing the use of wines and other liquors beneficial to ourselves in general, and the dealers in particular, pledge ourselves to act as we please in all matters of politics and phrenology.'"

The servant, who yet stood at the door waiting orders, burst forth into a loud laugh, as the reading of this was finished, while George, though inwardly sorrowing over the situation of his friend, could not refrain from smiling at his ridiculous appearance and doings. There was a good humor running through the method of his madness, that made him far from being disagreeable.

Mr. Alverton passed to the door, and, motioning the servant aside, entreated her not to bring him wine.

"Well, sir, that be's just as he says," said she, in a loud voice, and in a manner that convinced Mr. Alverton that she cared not as to what might follow.

"Good!" shouted James. "Why, she's my confidential; she's as true to me as a book. Sal, bring up two decanters of that best."

The girl laughed, and bounded out of the room to do as he requested.

The wine came; a long talk ensued, as unmeaning and useless as that we have above related, and George left with a heavy heart, promising to call on the morrow.

As he entered the street, and the cool, fresh air of an autumn morning greeted him, he felt somewhat revived, and, quickening his step, he soon reached his home. He dare not mention his adventure to Josephine, though he wanted to. She was the betrothed of James. In one month they were to be married! Dark and frowning were the clouds that gathered in their blackness over the mind of George, as he mused on what had been and what was to be. Should he tell her all? It was his duty. Should he shrink from the performance of his duty? No.

CHAPTER V.

"Never!" exclaimed the young lady, as she wiped her eyes, and a smile of joy and hope burst through her tears. "George, I know he will not go too far,— O, no! As an eagle may touch the earth, yet, soaring again, float in its own element in the light of the sun, so may he, though he has this once fallen, soar upward, and higher than ever, planning not another descent so low."

"I hope it may be so," said George.

"And why not hope? You know each has an opinion of his own, but that opinion may be changed. Though he now opposes the pledge, and the cause of which it is the representative, yet he may think differently, and may, through your influence, become one of its most zealous advocates. Don't mention to him that I know of his act," exclaimed Josephine, springing to catch the arm of her brother, as he opened the door to leave.

She was answered in the negative, and in the examination of a few articles that were being prepared for her bridal-day she gradually forgot all unpleasant misgivings, and nothing but happiness could she see before her.

It was not until the next day that George had an opportunity of seeing his friend. He then met him at the store, and James laughed over the doings of the day previous as a "good joke," as he called them. On that occasion, as on several subsequent ones, he urged him to sign and become a total-abstinent; but, with such influences as those which surrounded him, it was not strange that these efforts proved ineffectual.

Weeks passed, and the hour of marriage drew nigh. The festivity was to be one of unusual splendor and gayety. For a long time had preparations been in progress.

It was painful for George to refer to a matter which he would not have spoken of had it not so much concerned the welfare of a sister whom he loved as his own self. When he mentioned the circumstances attending the party on board the "Vincennes," she, in the fulness of her love, excused James, and brought up a host of arguments to prove the impossibility of a reöccurrence of any similar event.

Love is stronger than death; and, mastering all things, overlooks or decreases the evil and enlarges the goodness of its object. It was so in this case. Josephine's attachment to James led her to sacrifice all other feelings and opinions to her deep affection for him, and made her willing to stand by him or fall with him, as the vine to the tree, bright and fresh, though the once sturdy oak lies fallen and blighted.

The evening came, and with it many a bright and joyous heart to the home of George Alverton. A more beautiful bride never pronounced the bridal-vow than she who there, encircled with bright eyes and smiling faces, gave all to James Clifton. And when it was over, when they joined the bright galaxy that were about them and mingled with others in the festive mirth of the hour, a life of joy and social comfort was predicted for the hearts which that night were made one! Music was there with its charms, Terpsichore with her graceful motions, and everything from commencement to close was conducted in so happy and agreeable a manner, that not a few young folks, as they rode home, agreed to go through the same performance at their earliest convenience.

After the usual "calls" had been attended and a few weeks had elapsed, James and his young wife located themselves in a dwelling-house, which was furnished in an elegant though not in an extravagant manner. He was to continue with Messrs. Laneville & Co. They reposed the utmost confidence in him, and considered him the best judge of liquors in the city. On the day of his marriage they increased his salary one third, so that his income was by no means to be complained of. It was such as to enable him to live well, and to lay aside quite a large amount quarterly. His prospects were good, and no young man ever had better hopes of success.

We cannot close this chapter without referring again to the fact that he dealt in that which made widows of wives, orphans of children, and sent down the stream of life a rivulet of death. This fact was like a cloud hanging over his path; and, though it was but as a speck far up in sky, who could tell what it might become?

CHAPTER VI.

For a year the young couple were most happy. The moments flew too quickly by; so laden were they with joy, they would have them endure forever. "Little Jim" was a smart one, if he was n't as old as his father, and the handsomest piece of furniture in the house! Nobody doubted that; at least, it would n't have been well for them to have expressed their doubts in a very audible manner, if they held any.

Tasting, trying and judging of liquors, led to a loving, sipping and drinking of them. We may hate temperance, but it is certain we cannot hate a good without loving a bad thing. In offering for sale an article of food or beverage, the influence of our using it ourselves, or not using it, goes a great ways towards our disposing of it, or our not disposing of it. James knew this, and acted accordingly. He always had the best of liquors in his house, as it was often the case that, after selling a man a large amount, he invited him home to dine. They, in turn, invited him out in the evening, and it was often a late hour when he returned. At home the presence of his wife prevented him from indulging too freely; but away from home, and surrounded by gay companions, he went as full lengths as any.

Such indulgences could not continue long without showing their effects. George saw these, and remonstrated with him; but Josephine could not or did not observe them. If he did not arrive home at the customary hour, she ever had an excuse for his delay.

The arrival of another cargo of wines, etc., for Messrs. Laneville & Co., was duly acknowledged by another carousal in the cabins of the vessel, which ended in results far more destructive to the reputation of James, and to the happiness of himself and friends, than the former.

At a late hour Josephine sat waiting and watching, when the ring of the door-bell, the movement of the servant, the mingling of several suppressed voices, and the shuffle of footsteps on the entry-floor, aroused her from that listless inaction which fatigue had brought upon her. She sprang to the door of her room, and, opening it, was about to descend, when her brother met her and requested her not to do so.

"Why?" she inquired.

He gave no definite answer to her inquiry, but requested

her to retire for the night, saying that James would probably be home in the morning, bright and early as the dawn.

"And not before?" she inquired, in a tone of voice that startled her attentive brother. Then, as a stray thought of the former ship's party and its unfortunate results came into her mind, she exclaimed, "I *must* see him *now!* Let me know the worst. Nothing can keep me from him. James, my James!" and, bursting from her brother's embrace, she ran down stairs, and, notwithstanding the remonstrance of her friends, opened the door where half a dozen men and her husband had gathered.

James lay upon a sofa, nearly unconscious of what was transpiring around him. Josephine caught the hand that hung loosely at his side, threw herself on the floor beside him, smoothed back his dishevelled hair, and kissed his flushed cheek.

"James, James!" exclaimed she. He opened his eyes, gazed for a moment listlessly upon her, then closed them again. "O, James! don't you know me? James! say,—wake thee, dearest!"

She pressed his hand in her own, and, as the tears fell freely from her eyes, so unused to weep, she continued her calls upon him who lay insensate before her. She whispered in his ear the breathings of her heart, or in louder tones gave vent to the grief that wounded it.

Vainly did friends beseech her to retire; vainly did they tell her she could not hasten his restoration to reason. She declared her determination to remain with him till morning.

Day dawned. There, at the side of her husband, sat the faithful wife, as neglective of her own wants as she was attentive to his. James began to realize his condition, but not fully. He had vague ideas of being in his own house, but his mind was at times wandering, and his words betrayed its condition.

"Here I am," said he; "in a paradise, with an angel at my side, and beauty and rich fragrance all around me. See you how that diamond sparkles at the bottom of this brook flowing at my feet! Watch that dove as it comes down from the sky! See, it nestles in my angel's bosom. See how it folds its wings! See how she smooths down its ruffled plumage, and, hark ye, listen to its plaintive cooing! My angel, my sweet one, come near me, let me whisper in thine ear. Go, bring me that bunch of luscious grapes which is suspended on that sapphire cloud, and make me wine of them that gods might envy! Ah, see, she goes,— she wings her flight,— she grasps the rich fruit,— she comes! She presses the grapes, and here is wine,— from where? From paradise! Droop not, droop not, droop not, spirit of light! Do not weep! What are you weeping for? Here, let me wipe those tears away. Ah, they are pearls, they are not tears! I thought they were tears.— Going so soon?— Gone?"

He sank into a quiet sleep. Josephine had wept as she caught his words partly uttered in a whisper so low as to be scarcely distinguishable. Now, as he slept, she watched his breathings, and hoped that when he awoke he would be of a sane mind, and that a realization of what had occurred might influence his future career for the better.

CHAPTER VII.

"News!" exclaimed Capt. Thorndyke, as he shook the hand of his friend Basyl. "Have you not heard it? Why, it 's common talk. Young Clifton imbibes rather too freely. You know him,— Laneville & Co.'s clerk,— best judge of liquors in the states; strange that *he* will imbibe."

"Strange indeed, very strange, if he is really a judge and knows what they 're made of," said Basyl; "and stranger yet that he will sell. For my part, I consider a man that will sell liquor, in these days of light and knowledge, as bad as a highwayman, and no better than a pirate."

"Rather plain spoken."

"I know it, but, look ye, there's Follet, a fine man, a first-rate man, once worth half a million, but now not worth a guinea-pig. The man that sold him good wine in his better days sells him poor whiskey now; and the confounded dealer in fancy poisons has taken the houses of Mr. Follet, brick by brick, and piled them up in his own yard, so to speak. Why, no longer ago than yesternight, he took a fine black coat of Dick Pherson, and gave him in return a coarse, brown one and a glass of sin — gin, I mean. Fudge! talk about consistency! That rumseller is nominated for an alderman, and he'll be elected. He's rich; and all your say-so temperance men will vote for him, and when elected he'll go hand-in-hand with some lone star, who deems it advisable that men should be licensed to corrupt the morals of the community, in order to make it wise and virtuous!"

The captain acknowledged that his friend had a right view of the matter, and, as he bade him good-day, promised to take care of his vote at the coming election.

We doubt whether any man ever felt more deeply sensible of the wrong committed than did James, as he, the next morning, awaking from his long sleep, beheld his wife standing at his side, now weeping over him, now joyous and smiling at his returned consciousness, and closely attentive to his every want. He felt himself unworthy of such kindness, and for the first time in his life saw the evil of the doctrine he had all his lifetime advocated, namely, that a man can drink enough and not too much; in other words, that he can guide his evil passions as he will, and command them to stop in their course, nor trespass on forbidden ground.

But James even yet was opposed to the pledge, and, though George presented it with strong arguments, he refused to sign it, and laughed at the idea of his ever getting the worse for liquor again.

The employer of James Clifton had his name on the same ticket with that of the rumseller before mentioned, as a candidate for mayor. Election-day came. The two political parties had their tickets in the hands of scores of distributors. There was a third party, with its ticket, the caption of which —"Temperance Men and Temperance Measures"—was bandied about with gibes and sneers by the prominent men of both other parties.

Among the vote-distributors was a young man of exceedingly prepossessing appearance, and who, by means of the winning manner he possessed, disposed of a large number of tickets, even to men of the opposing party. "Vote for Laneville! vote for Laneville!" was his constant cry, save when he, in well-chosen words, proclaimed the ability and worthiness of his candidate. Some said he was urged on by selfish motives; that, as he was a clerk of Laneville's, the election of that candidate would be much to his pecuniary benefit. But James Clifton cared for none of these insinuations.

"Well, deacon, my dear, dear deacon, who do you vote for?" inquired a stanch teetotaller, as an old gentleman approached. The person addressed, after a little hesitation, during which a few nervous twinges of the mouth betrayed his nervousness of conscience, and the debate going on in his heart between consistency and principles on the one side, and party names and measures on the other, replied, "Well, well,"—then a pause,—"well, I don't know; go for the best man, I s'pose."

"Here's the ticket, sir! the best man, sir, is Laneville! vote for Laneville!" shouted James, as he thrust his ticket into the hands of the old gentleman, and, laying hold of his arm, led him into the room, and saw him deposit the vote of a temperance advocate for a rumseller! James laughed well over his victory, while the distributors of the temperance tickets felt somewhat ill at ease in seeing him whom they thought their truest friend desert them in the hour of need, and give his vote and influence for the other party.

The day ended; the votes were counted, and Laneville was proclaimed elected by a majority of *one!*

The night was one of carousal. The betting on both sides had been considerable, and the payment of these debts caused the small change to circulate pretty freely among the dispensers of eatables and drinkables.

This night James yielded more easily than ever before to the cravings of an appetite that began to master him.

Poor fellow! Deluded man! A fond, a devoted, a trusting wife waiting at home, watching the hands of the clock as they neared the mark of twelve, and listening for thy footfall! Thou, trusting in thine own strength, but to learn thy weakness, lying senseless among thy drinking mates in the hall of dissolute festivity!

Tom Moore may sing in praise of "wine and its sparkling tide;" but the sighing of wronged women and their tears shall toll the requiem of its praise.

CHAPTER VIII.

Notwithstanding the entreaties of George, added to those of Josephine, James continued in the way he had begun to walk, and which was leading him to ruin. The arguments of the one, and the tears of the other, were equally unavailing.

So far had he proceeded in a downward course that his employers remonstrated; and the same arguments they had used upon their former clerks were urged upon his consideration. Fearing the loss of situation, he repented, but it was only to fall again before the power of that appetite with which he had tampered as with a torpid viper, which now felt the warmth of his embrace, and became a living, craving creature within his bosom.

His old companions perceived the change he was undergoing, and, like butterflies that hovered about his path in sunshine, left him as clouds overshadowed his way. But he had friends who would not leave him. He had a wife who clung to him with all the affection of woman's love, and a brother whose hand was ever extended to aid him.

James saw the evil that threatened to overwhelm him; yet, strangely infatuated, he would not come to a fixed determination to reform so far as to sign the pledge.

The sun never shone with a brighter effulgence than it did on the morning of the 24th of July, 1849. The streets of Boston were filled with busy crowds, and banners and flags streamed from balconies and windows. Delegates of men from the suburbs poured into the city, and the sound of music filled the air. Men, women, and children, the rich and the poor, the merchant and the mechanic, the American and the foreigner, joined in the movement; and a stranger could not long remain ignorant of the fact that some great event was to transpire that day in the capital of the Old Bay State. Crowds gathered at the corners, and lined the principal thoroughfares.

"He has blist his own country, an' now he will bliss ours," said a well-dressed Irishman.

"An' that he will," was the response; "an' God bliss Father Mathew!"

"Amen," said half a dozen voices.

"He 's coming!" exclaimed another. The sound of distant music was heard, and far up the street was seen approaching a dense mass of people. White banners mingled with the stars and stripes. Nearer they approached, and more distinct became, to the Irishman and his friends, the peals of music and the hurras of the multitude.

THEOBALD MATHEW, the friend of Ireland, was making his entry into Boston! Never man was more gladly welcome. Never was man more enthusiastically received. It seemed as though all men strove to do him homage, for they looked upon one who was the instrument, under God, of saving five millions of human beings from the greatest curse sin brought into the world; lifting them, and bidding them stand up as their Maker intended they should.

The "apostle" was seated in an open barouche, with his head uncovered, bowing to the crowds of stout men and fair women that filled the windows on either side, often shaking hands with those who pressed near him to do so.

A young man stood upon the side-walk watching its approach; and when the carriage in which he was seated came near where he stood, he took off his hat, pressed through the assemblage, and, urging his way towards it, grasped the hand that was extended to him. The carriage stopped. Father Mathew arose, and, as his hand lay upon the head of the young man, he repeated the words of a pledge, which the latter, in a distinct tone, repeated after him. At its close, the words "*I do!*" were heard far and near, and James Clifton had taken the pledge!

This was done from no sudden impulse. During the previous week he had indulged rather freely, and when its effects were over he began for the first time to give serious thought upon the question whether it was not required of him to become a pledged man. He was becoming convinced that he was unsafe. He knew how often he had fallen, how liable he was to fall again, and that it might be never to rise. He found his companions did not look upon him with as much respect as formerly; and he determined to break down the pride of opinion, rather than have it break him down.

As he thought of his situation at Messrs. Laneville & Co.'s, he for a moment drew back, yet it was but for a moment. He resolved to leave it, and beg rather than continue to disgrace himself and bring ruin upon his relatives and friends. He was cheered by the thought that he had those around him who would furnish him with employment suited to his mind, and in the steady pursuit of which he might live well. This resolution was made a few days previous to the twenty-fourth, but he communicated it to no one.

James hurried from the crowd that gathered around him, and hastened to his home. The glad news preceded him, and his wife, meeting him at the door, caressed, blessed and welcomed him. George grasped his hand, and James, with tears in his eyes, asked pardon for the past, and promised much for the future.

"Once," said he, "I refused to sign. I trusted to my own self, and thought because I was young and strong I could resist temptation. I said I would not make myself a slave to a pledge, and clung to my promise till I found myself a slave to an appetite. I ask your pardon, George, for the manner in which I treated your request."

"I grant it."

"Then *I* am happy, *we* are happy, and the future shall redeem the past."

The door opened, and a bright-eyed boy, bounding into the room, sprang upon his father, and, with a smile, said, "Father, I'm a Cadet of Temperance! We formed a little society this morning, 'cause Father Mathew has come to Boston. We've got six names, and we are to have more."

James kissed his child, and encouraged him to go on in the cause he had so early espoused.

Messrs. Laneville & Co. engaged a new clerk,— a young man of seventeen, hopeful, promising. He had heard of the fate of his predecessors, of the narrow escape of him whose place he was being trained to fill; but, like them and him, he thought himself stronger than the tempter at his side. That firm is in the home-desolating business to-day, though James has used much endeavor to induce them to relinquish it. The young man is there to-day, open to temptations which have conquered many strong men, have destroyed many mighty. The *pledge* is with us to-day, open for those who have fallen, for those who yet stand,—an instrument of God, in human hands, to rescue the one and to preserve the other.

ANGELINA.

BLUE-EYED child, with flaxen ringlets,
'Neath my window played, one day ;
And its tiny song of gladness,
Sounded like an angel's lay.
Roses bright in beauty blossomed
Round the path the cherub trod
Yet it seemed that child was fairest,
Freshest from the hand of God.

Watched I her till hour of sunset
Told me of the coming night,
And the sun o'er rock and mountain
Shed its flood of golden light.
Yet she gambolled, though the dew-drops
Fell upon her thick and fast ;
Fearing ill, I went and told her, —
" Dearest child, the day hath past :

" Haste thee to thy home, — there waiting
Is thy parent, thee to bless."
Then she hasted from the play-ground,
To her mother's fond caress.
Stars shone forth in all their splendor,
And the moon with silver light
Rose in beauty, and presided
Queen o'er all the hosts of night.

Days had passed ; I had not seen her,
Had not heard her merry laugh,
Nor those joyous tones that told me
Of the joy her spirit quaffed.

Vain I asked whence Angelina
  Had departed, — none could tell;
Feared I then that sorrow gathered
  O'er the child I loved so well.

Funeral train passed by my window, —
  Banished were all thoughts of mirth;
And I asked of one who lingered,
  "Who hath passed to heaven from earth?"
In his eye a tear-drop glistened,
  As he, turning, to me said,
"Heaven now holds another angel, —
  Little Angelina 's dead!"

I could scarce believe the tidings,
  Till I stood above her grave,
And beheld those flaxen ringlets,
  That so late did buoyant wave,
Lie beside a face whose features
  Still in death did sweetly smile
And methought angelic beauty
  Lingered on her cheeks the while.

At the pensive hour of twilight,
  Oft do angel-footsteps tread
Near her grave, and flowers in beauty
  Blossom o'er the early dead;
And a simple marble tablet
  Thence doth unassuming rise,
And these simple words are on it, —
  "Here our Angelina lies."

Oft at night, when others slumber,
  One bends o'er that holy spot;
And the tear-drops fall unnumbered
  O'er her sad yet happy lot.
Friends, though oft they mourn her absence,
  Do in meek submission bow;
For a voice from heaven is whispering,
  "Angelina 's happy now."

FAREWELL, MY NATIVE LAND.

Written for KAH-GE-GA-GAH-BOWH, a representative from the North-west Tribes of American Indians to the Peace Convention in Frankfort-on-the-Maine, Germany; and recited by him on board the British steamship Niagara, at the hour of sailing from Boston, July 10th, 1850.

THE day is brightening which we long have sought;
I see its early light and hail its dawn;
The gentle voice of Peace my ear hath caught,
And from my forest-home I greet the morn.
Here, now, I meet you with a brother's hand—
Bid you farewell — then speed me on my way
To join the white men in a foreign land,
And from the dawn bring on the bright noon-day.
Noon-day of Peace! O, glorious jubilee,
When all mankind are one, from sea to sea.

Farewell, my native land, rock, hill, and plain!
River and lake, and forest-home, adieu!
Months shall depart ere I shall tread again
Amid your scenes, and be once more with you.
I leave thee now; but wheresoe'er I go,
Whatever scenes of grandeur meet my eyes,
My heart can but *one* native country know,
And that the fairest land beneath the skies.
America! farewell, thou art that gem,
Brightest and fairest in earth's diadem.

Land where my fathers chased the fleeting deer;
Land whence the smoke of council-fires arose;
Land whose own warriors never knew a fear;
Land where the mighty Mississippi flows;
Land whose broad surface spreads from sea to sea;
Land where Niagara thunders forth God's praise; —
May Peace and Plenty henceforth dwell with thee,
And o'er thee War no more its banner raise!
Adieu, my native land, — hill, stream, and dell!
The hour hath come to part us, — fare thee well.

UNLEARNED TO LOVE.

He hath unlearned to love; for once he loved
A being whom his soul almost adored,
And she proved faithless; turned in scorn upon
His heart's affections; to another gave
The love she once did pledge as all his own.
And now he doth not love. Within his heart
Hate dwells in sullen silence. His soul broods
Over its wrongs, over deluded hopes.
Fancy no more builds airy castles.
Amid the crowd he passes on alone.
The branches wave no more to please his eye,
And the wind singeth no sweet songs to him.
The murmuring brook but murmurs discontent,
And all his life is death since Love hath fled.

O, who shall count his sorrows? who shall make
An estimate of his deep, burning woes,
And place them all in order, rank on rank?
Language is weak to tell the heart's deep wrongs.
We think, and muse, and in our endless thought
We strive to grasp, with all the mind's vast strength,
The undefinable extent of spirit grief,
And fail to accomplish the herculean task.

WHAT WAS IT?

It was a low, black, miserable place;
Its roof was rotting; and above it hung
A cloud of murky vapor, sending down
Intolerable stench on all around.
The place was silent, save the creaking noise,
The steady motion of a dozen pumps,
That labored all the day, nor ceased at night.

Methought in it I heard a hundred groans;
Dropping of widows' tears, and cries of orphans;
Shrieks of some victim to the fiendish lust
Of men for gold; woe echoing woe,
And sighs, deep, long-drawn sighs of dark despair.
Around the place a dozen hovels stood,
Black with the smoke and steam that bathed them all;
Their windows had no glass, but rags and boards,
Torn hats and such-like, filled the paneless sash.
Beings, once men and women, in and out
Passed and repassed from darkness forth to light;
And children, ragged, dirty, and despised,
Clung to them. Children! heaven's early flowers,
In their spring-time of life, blighted and lost!
Children! those jewels of a parent's crown,
Crushed to the ground and crumbled to the dust.
Children! Heaven's representatives to man,
Made menial slaves to watch at Evil's gate,
And errand-boys to run at Sin's command.

I asked why thus it was; and one old man
Pushed up the visor of his cap, and said:
"That low, black building is the cause of all."
And would you know what 't was that wrought such ill,
And what the name of that low building was?
Go to thy neighbor, read to him these lines,
And if he does not tell thee right, at first,
Then come to me and you shall know its name.

LETTERS AND LETTER-WRITING.

THERE is nothing from which more real enjoyment can be derived than the art of letter-writing. All praise to the inventive genius that gave to man a written language, and with it the implements with which to talk across the world! Did you ever think, reader, what a world this would be without pen, ink, and paper? Then, the absence of friends were painful, and, as we grasped the friendly hand, bade our acquaintances "good-by," and saw the last, far-distant wave of the parting signal, we might turn aside to weep, as we thought we should never hear from them till we met face to face — perhaps never. But, as it is, when friends leave, we expect a message from their hearts soon, to solace our own. How we watch, and how we hope! What a welcome rap is the postman's! With what eagerness we loosen the seal; with what pleasure we read, from date to signature, every word!

It may not be uninteresting, nor wholly uninstructive, to examine the various modes of letter-writing, and to spend a brief half-hour with those who have by their letters made grave or gay impressions on the public mind.

Some write letters with great ease; others, with great difficulty. Miss Seward was an inveterate letter-writer. There have been published six large volumes of letters written by her; besides these, she left twelve quarto volumes of letters to a publisher of London, and these, it is said, are but a twelfth part of her correspondence. It seems as though she must have written nothing but letters, so many and various were they; but her fame as an authoress will convince any one that her industry overcame what might seem an impossibility, and that her genius in this particular resembled that of the steam-writing machine, Dumas, of the present time.

Lord Peterborough had such a faculty for this kind of composition, that, when ambassador to Turin, according to Pope, who says he was a witness of the performance, he employed nine *amanuenses*, who were seated in a room, around whom Lord Peterborough walked and dictated to each what he should write. These nine wrote to as many different persons, upon, perhaps, nine times as many subjects; yet the ambassador retained in his mind the connection of each letter so completely as to close each in a highly-finished and appropriate manner.

These facts show the ease and rapidity of some writers. In contradistinction to these are the letters of many eminent Latin writers, who actually bestowed several months of close attention upon a single letter. Mr. Owen says: "Such is the defect of education among the modern Roman ladies, that they are not troubled to keep up any correspondence, because they cannot write. A princess of great beauty, at Naples, caused an English lady to be informed that she was learning to write; and hoped, in the course of time, to acquire the art of correspondence."

There are many persons with whom it is the most difficult task of their existence to write a letter. They follow the old Latin writers, and make a labor of what with others is a recreation. They begin with the stereotyped words, "I take my pen in hand," as though a letter could be written without doing so. Then follows, "to inform you that I am well, and hope this will find you the same." There is a period — a full stop; and there are instances of persons going no further, but closing with, "This from your friend, JOHN SHORT."

This "difficulty" arises not from an inability, but from an excessive nicety — a desire to write a prize essay, instead of a good, sociable, familiar letter. To make a letter interesting, the writer must transfer his thoughts from his mind to his paper, as truly as the rays of the sun place the likeness of an object in front of the lens through which it acts upon the silvered plate. Seneca says, "I would have my letters be like my discourses when we sit or walk together, unstudied and easy."

Willis' letters are of a kind always "free and easy." His "Letters from Under a Bridge" are admirable specimens of letters as they should be; and his "Pencillings by the Way" owe much of their popularity to their easy, familiar, talkative style. The letters of Cicero and Pliny, of ancient, and Swift, Pope, Arbuthnot, Madame de Sévigné, and Lady Mary Wortley Montague, of modern times, are generally received as some of the best specimens extant of epistolary composition. The letters of Charles Lamb are a series of brilliances, though of kaleidoscope variety; they have wit without buffoonery, and seriousness without melancholy. He closes one of them by subscribing himself his friend's "afflicted, headachey, sorethroaty, humble servant, CHARLES LAMB."

Some men, and women too, of eminence, have written curiosities in the form of correspondence. The letter of the mother of Foote is a good example of this kind of correspondence. Mrs. Foote became embarrassed, and, being unable to meet a demand, was placed in prison; whereupon she wrote to Mr. Foote as follows:

"DEAR SAM: I am in prison for debt; come, and assist your loving mother, E. FOOTE."

It appears that "Sam" was equally entangled in the meshes of the law, for he answered as follows:

"DEAR MOTHER: — So am I; which prevents his duty being paid to his loving mother by her affectionate son,

"SAM FOOTE.

"P. S. — I have sent my attorney to assist you; in the mean time, let us hope for better days."

These laconic epistles are well matched by that of a French lady, who wrote to her husband this missive of intelligence, affection, &c., &c.:

"I write to you because I have nothing to do; I end my letter because I have nothing to say."

But these are left far in the rear by the correspondence of two Quakers, the one living in Edinburgh, the other in London. The former, wishing to know whether there was anything new in London, wrote in the corner of a letter-sheet a small interrogation note, and sent it to his friend. In due time he received an answer. He opened the sheet and found, simply, 0, signifying that there was none.

In the *London Times* of January 3d, 1820, is the following, purporting to be a copy of a letter sent to a medical gentleman:

"CER: Yole oblige me uf yole kum un ce me. I hev a Bad kowld, am Hill in my Bow Hills, and hev lost my Happy Tight."

William Cowper, the poet, being on very familiar terms with the Rev. Mr. Newton, amused himself and his friend with a letter, of which the following is a copy:

"MY VERY DEAR FRIEND: I am going to send, what, when you have read, you may scratch your head, and say, I suppose, there 's nobody knows, whether what I have got be verse or not; by the tune and the time, it ought to be rhyme; but if it be, did you ever see, of late or of yore, such a ditty before?

"I have writ Charity, not for popularity, but as well as I could, in hopes to do good; and if the reviewers should say, 'To be sure the gentleman's muse wears methodist shoes, you may know by her pace, and talk about grace, that she and her bard have little regard for the taste and fashions, and ruling passions, and hoydening play, of the modern day; and though she assume a borrowed plume, and now and then wear a tittering air, 't is only her plan to catch, if she can, the giddy and gay, as they go that way, by a production on a new construction; she has baited her trap, in hopes to snap all that may come, with a sugar-plum.' His opinion in this will not be amiss; 't is what I intend my principal end; and if I succeed, and folks should read, till a few are brought to a serious thought, I shall think I am paid for all I have said, and all I have done, though I have run, many a time, after rhyme, as far as from hence, to the end of my sense, and, by hook or crook, write another book, if I live and am here, another year.

"I heard before of a room, with a floor laid upon springs, and such like things, with so much art, in every part, that when you went in, you was forced to begin a minuet pace, with an air and a grace, swimming about, now in and now out, with a deal of state, in a figure of eight, without pipe or string, or any such thing; and now I have writ, in a rhyming fit, what will make you dance, and, as you advance, will keep you still, though against your will, dancing away, alert and gay, till you come to an end of what I have penned; which that you may do ere madam and you are quite worn out with jigging about, I take my leave; and here you receive a bow profound, down to the ground, from your humble me,

"W. C."

At one of those famous coteries, so fashionable in the time of George Selwyn, Selwyn declared that a lady never closed a letter without a postscript. One of his fair auditors defended her sex by saying that her next letter should prove he was wrong. Soon after, Selwyn received a letter from the lady, in which, after the name, was "P. S. Who is right now, you or I?"

"We have met the enemy, and they are ours" is an example for naval letters. Commodore Walton's letter, by which he gave information of his capture of a number of Spanish vessels of war, was as follows:

"We have taken or destroyed all the enemy's ships or vessels on the coast, as per margin."

General Taylor's letters are of the same class,— brief and to the point.

As a specimen of *ultra*-familiarity, see the Duke of Buckingham's letter to King James the First, which he commences as follows: "DEAR DAD AND GOSSIP," and concludes thus:— "Your Majesty's most humble slave and dog,

"STINIE."

Some letters have been distinguished for a play upon words. The following is supposed to have been written by one Zebel Rock, a stone-cutter, to a young lady for whom he cherished a love somewhat more than Platonic:

"DIVINE FLINT: Were you not harder than Porphyry or Agate, the Chisel of my love, drove by the Mallet of my fidelity, would have made some impression on thee. I, that have shaped as I pleased the most untoward of substances, hoped by the Compass of reason, the Plummet of discretion, the Saw of constancy, the soft File of kindness, and the Polish of good words, to have modelled you into one of the prettiest Statues in the world; but, alas! I find you are a Flint, that strikes fire, and sets my soul in a blaze, though your heart is as cold as marble. Pity my case, pray, madam, for I know not what I say or do. If I go to make a Dragon, I strike out a Cupid; instead of an Apothecary's Mortar, I make a

Church Font for Baptism; and, dear Pillar of my hopes, Pedestal of my comfort, and Cornice of my joy, take compassion upon me, for upon your pity I build all my hope, and will, if fortunate, erect Statues, Obelisks and Pyramids, to your generosity."

As a specimen of alliteration the following may be considered a fair off-hand epistle of love:

"ADORED AND ANGELIC AMELIA: Accept An Ardent And Artless Amorist's Affections; Alleviate An Anguished Admirer's Alarms, And Answer An Amorous Applicant's Avowed Ardor. Ah, Amelia! All Appears An Awful Aspect; Ambition, Avarice, And Arrogance, Alas, Are Attractive Allurements, And Abuse An Ardent Attachment. Appease An Aching And Affectionate Adorer's Alarms, And Anon Acknowledge Affianced Albert's Alliance As Agreeable And Acceptable. Anxiously Awaiting An Affectionate And Affirmative Answer, Accept An Ardent Admirer's Aching Adieu. ALBERT."

The custom of *espionage* among some nations, which led the government officials to open all letters supposed to contain matters at variance with the plans and purposes of their masters, induced the inventive to contrive various means of correspondence.

One of the most singular of these was that adopted by Histaus, the Milesian, as related by Herodotus. Histaus was "kept by Darius at Susa, under an honorable pretence, and, despairing of his return home, unless he could find out some way that he might be sent to sea, he purposed to send to Aristagoras, who was his substitute at Miletum, to persuade his revolt from Darius; but, knowing that all passages were stopped and studiously watched, he took this course: he got a trusty servant of his, the hair of whose head he caused to be shaved off, and then, upon his bald head, he wrote his mind to Aristagoras; kept him privately about him, till his hair was somewhat grown, and then bid him haste to Aristagoras, and bid him cause him to be shaved again, and then upon his head he should find what his lord had written to him."

A volume might be written of the Curiosities of Letter-writing, and it would be by no means an uninteresting production. Years ago, when New England missionaries first taught the wild men of the South Sea Islands, it so happened that one of the teachers wished to communicate with a friend, and having no pen, ink and paper at hand, he picked up a chip and wrote with a pencil his message. A native conveyed it, and, receiving some article in return, he thought the chip endowed with some miraculous power, and could he have obtained it would doubtless have treasured it as a god, and worshipped it. And so would seem to us this invaluable art of letter-writing, were we in like ignorance. We forget to justly appreciate a blessing while we have it in constant use; but let us be for a short time deprived of it, and then we lament its loss and realize its worth. Deprive mankind of pen, ink and paper, obliterate from the human mind all knowledge of letter-writing, — then estimate, if you can, the loss that would accrue.

The good resulting from a general intercommunication of thought among the people has brought about a great reduction in the rates of postage. We look forward to the time when the tens of millions now expended in war, and invested in the ammunition of death, shall be directed into other channels, and postage shall be free. What better defence for our nation than education? It is better than forts and vessels of war; better than murderous guns, powder and ball. Hail to the day when there shall be no direct tax on the means of education!

A VISION OF REALITY.

I HAD a dream: Methought one came
  And bade me with him go;
I followed, 'till, above the world,
  I wondering gazed below.
One moment, horror filled my breast;
  Then, shrinking from the sight,
I turned aside, and sought for rest,
  Half dying with affright.

My guide with zeal still urged me on;
"See, see!" said he, "what sin hath done;
How mad ambition fills each breast,
And mortals spurn their needed rest,
And all their lives and fortunes spend
To gain some darling, wished-for end;
And scarce they see the long-sought prize,
When each to grasp it fails and dies."

Once more I looked: in a lonely room,
  On a pallet of straw, were lying
A mother and child; no friends were near,
  Yet that mother and child were dying.

A sigh arose; she looked above,
  And she breathed forth, "I forgive;"
She kissed her child, threw back her head,
  And the mother ceased to live.

The child's blue eyes were raised to watch
  Its mother's smile of love;

She was not there, — her child she saw
  From her spirit-home above.

An hour passed by: that child had gone
  From earth and all its harms;
Yet, as in sleep, it nestling lay
  In its dead mother's arms.

I asked my guide, "What doth this mean?"
He spake not a word, but changed the scene.
  I stood where the busy throng
Was hurrying by; all seemed intent,
As on some weighty mission sent;
And, as I asked what all this meant,
  A drunkard passéd by.

He spake, — I listened; thus spake he:
"*Rum*, thou hast been a curse to me;
My wife is dead, — my darling child,
Who, when 't was born, so sweetly smiled,
And seemed to ask, in speechless prayer,
A father's love, a father's care,—
  He, he, too, now is gone!
How can I any longer live?
What joy to me can earth now give?
I 've drank full deep from sorrow's cup, —
When shall I drink its last dregs up?
When will the last, last pang be felt?
When the last blow on me be dealt?
  Would I had ne'er been born!"

As thus he spake, a gilded coach
  In splendor passéd by;
And from within a man looked forth, —
  The drunkard caught his eye.
Then, with a wild and frenzied look,
  He, trembling, to it ran;
He stayed the rich man's carriage there,
  And said, "*Thou* art the man!

"Yes, *thou* the man! *You* bade me come,
You took my gold, *you* gave me *rum;*
You bade me in the gutter lie,
My wife and child *you* caused to die;
You took their bread, — 't was justly theirs;
You, cunning, laid round me your snares,
Till I fell in them; then *you* crushed,
And robbed me, as my cries you hushed;
You 've bound me close in misery's thrall;
Now, take a drunkard's *curse* and fall!"

A moment passed, and all was o'er, —
He who 'd sold rum would sell no more
And *Justice* seemed on earth to dwell,
When by his victim's hand he fell.
Yet, when the trial came, she fled,
And *Law* would have the avenger dead.
The gilded coach may rattle by,
Men too may drink, and drunkards die,
And widows' tears may daily fall,
And orphans' voices daily call, —
Yet these are all in vain;
The dealer sells, and glass by glass
He tempts the man to ruin pass,
And piles on high his slain.

His fellows fall by scores, — what then?
He, being *rich* (though rich by fraud),
Is honored by his fellow-men,
Who bend the knee and call him "lord."

Again I turned;
Enough I 'd learned
Of all the misery sin hath brought;
I strove to leave the fearful spot,
And wished the scene might be forgot,
'T was so with terror fraught.

I wished to go,
No more to know.

I turned me, but no guide stood there;
Alone, I shrieked in wild dismay,
When, lo! the vision passed away,—
I found me seated in my chair.

The morning sun was shining bright,
Fair children gambolled in my sight;
A rose-bush in my window stood,
And shed its fragrance all around;
My eye saw naught but fair and good,
My ear heard naught but joyous sound.

I asked me, can it be on earth
Such scenes of horror have their birth,
As those that in my vision past,
And on my mind their shadows cast?

Can it be true, that men do pour
Foul poison forth for sake of gold?
And men lie weltering in their gore,
Led on by that their brethren sold?

Doth man so bend the supple knee
To Mammon's shrine, he never hears
The voice of conscience, nor doth see
His *ruin* in the wealth he rears?

Such questions it were vain to ask,
For Reason whispers, "It is so;"
While some in fortune's sunshine bask,
Others lie crushed beneath their woe.
And men do sell, and men do pour,
And for their gold return men death;
Though wives and children them implore,
With tearful eyes and trembling breath,
And hearts with direst anguish riven,
No more to sell,—'t is all in vain;
They, urged to death, by avarice driven,
But laugh and turn to sell again.

JEWELS OF THE HEART.

THERE are jewels brighter far
Than the sparkling diamonds are;
Jewels never wrought by art, —
Nature forms them in the heart!

Would ye know the names they hold?
Ah! they never can be told
In the language mortals speak!
Human words are far too weak

Yet, if you would really know
What these jewels are, then go
To some low, secluded cot,
Where the poor man bears his lot!
Or, to where the sick and dying
'Neath the ills of life are sighing.

And if there some one ye see
Striving long and patiently
To alleviate the pain,
Bring the light of hope again!
One whose feet do lightly tread,
One whose hands do raise the head,

One who watches there alone,
Every motion, every tone;
Unaware an eye doth see
All these acts of charity.

Know that in that lonely cot,
Where the wealth of earth is not,
These bright jewels will be found,
Shedding love and light around!

Say, shall gems and rubies rare
With these heart-shrined gems compare?

Constancy, that will not perish,
But the thing it loveth cherish,
Clinging to it fondly ever,
Fainting, faltering, wavering, never!

Trust, that will not harbor doubt;
Putting fear and shame to rout,
Making known how, free from harm,
Love may rest upon its arm.

Hope, that makes the future bright,
Though there come a darksome night;
And, though dark despair seems nigh,
Bears the soul up manfully!

These are gems that brighter shine
Than they of Golconda's mine.
Born amid love's fond caresses,
Cradled in the heart's recesses,
They will live when earth is old,
Marble crumble, perish gold!

Live when ages shall have past,
While eternity shall last;
Be these gems the wealth you share,
Friends of mind, where'er you are!

LIGHT FROM A BETTER LAND.

Here at thy grave I stand,
  But not in tears;
Light from a better land
  Banishes fears.

Thou art beside me now,
  Whispering peace;
Telling how happy thou
  Found thy release!

Thou art not buried here ;
  Why should I mourn ?
All that I cherished dear
  Heavenward hath gone !

Oft from that world above
  Come ye to this;
Breathing in strains of love
  Unto me bliss !

POOR AND WEARY!

In a low and cheerless cot
Sat one mourning his sad lot ;
All day long he 'd sought for labor ;
All day long his nearest neighbor
Lived in affluence and squandered
Wealth, while he an outcast wandered,
And the night with shadowy wing
Heard him this low moaning sing :
  " Sad and weary, poor and weary,
  Life to me is ever dreary ! "

Morning came ; there was no sound
Heard within. Men gathered round,
Peering through the window-pane :
They saw a form as if 't were lain
Out for burial. Stiff and gaunt
Lay the man who died in want.
And methought I heard that day
Angel voices whispering say,
  " No more sad, poor and weary,
  Life to me no more is dreary ! "

THE BANDBOX MOVEMENT.

"THERE! Mr. McKenzie, I declare! You are the most oncommon, oncivil man I ever sot eyes on!"

"Peace, my lady! I'll explain."

"Then do so."

"You must know, then, that I have a perfect hatred of bandboxes,— so great, in fact, that if I see one on the walk, I involuntarily raise my foot and kick it."

"So it appears," chimed in Mrs. McKenzie, with a significant *hunch* of the right shoulder.

"Therefore, ——"

"Well, go on! what you waitin' for?"

"Therefore, when I saw Arabella's bandbox in the entry, as I came down, sitting, as it did, directly at the foot of the stairs, I jumped on it, thinking I would come over it *that* time ——"

"An' crushed a new spring bonnet, that cost—let me see!"

"No matter!" said Mr. McKenzie; "that will be in the bill."

Mr. McKenzie, having said thus much, placed his hat on his head and rushed from the house, fearful of another onslaught of "oncommon oncivilities."

A little shop at the North End,— seven men seated round said shop,— a small dog growling at a large cat, a large cat making a noise resembling that produced by root-beer confined in a stone bottle by a cork bound down with a piece of twine. Reader, imagine you see and hear all this!

[Enter Mr. McKenzie.] "Gentlemen, something must be done to demolish the idea held by the 'rest of mankind' that they, the women, cannot exist without owning as personal property an indefinite number of bandboxes. I therefore propose that we at once organize for the purpose; that a committee be appointed to draft resolutions, and report a name for the confederacy."

Voted unanimously; whereupon, a committee being appointed, after a short session, reported the following "whereas, etc."

"Whereas, WE, in our perambulations up and down the earth, are frequently, oftentimes, and most always, beset with annoyances of various kinds; and, as the greatest, most perplexing, most troublesome and iniquitous of these, generally assumes the shape of a *bandbox*, in a bag or out of one; and, whereas, our wives, our daughters, our sisters, and our female acquaintances generally and particularly, manifest a determination to put said boxes in our way, at all times, and under all circumstances, therefore

"***Resolved***, That — we — wont — stand — it — any — longer!!!

"***Resolved***, That we form ourselves into a society for the purpose of annihilating this grievous evil, and all bandboxes, of every size and nature.

"***Resolved***, That this society be known by the name of 'The Bandbox Extermination Association.'"

The chairman of the committee made a few remarks, in which he stated that, in the performance of the duties which would devolve upon the members, they would, doubtless, meet with some opposition. "But, never mind," said he; "it is a glorious cause, and if we get the tongs at one time, and the hearth-brush another time, let 'em come!" He defined the duties of members to be, — first and foremost, to pay six and a quarter cents to defray expenses; to demolish a bandbox wherever and whenever there should be one; (for instance, if a fat woman was racing for the cars, with a bandbox in her arms, that box should be forcibly taken and burned on the spot, or whittled into such minute particles that it could no more be seen; if, in an omnibus warranted to seat twelve, fifteen men are congregated, and an individual attempts to enter with a bandbox, the box shall have notice to quit.)

"The manner of demolition," he said, further, "might be variously defined. If the owner was a nervous lady, to kick the box would wound her feelings, and it were best to apparently unintentionally seat yourself on it; then beg a thousand pardons, and, as you, in your efforts to make it better, only make it worse, give it up in despair, and console the owner by a reference to spilt milk and the uselessness of crying. As to the contents of the boxes, they must look out for themselves. If they get injured, hint that they should keep out of bad company."

The chairman sat down, and, the question being put, it was more than unanimously voted (inasmuch as one man voted with both hands *) to adopt the resolutions, the name, and all the remarks that had been made in connection with them. Members paid their assessments, and with a hearty good will.

Thus we see how "oaks from acorns grow." Mrs. McKenzie's fretfulness on account of her husband's patriotism led to the formation of a society that will make rapid strides towards the front rank of the army now at work for the amelioration of the condition of mankind.

* That was McKenzie.

NEW ENGLAND HOMES.

I 'VE been through all the nations, have travelled o'er the earth,
O'er mountain-top and valley, far from my land of birth;
But whereso'er I wandered, wherever I did roam,
I saw no spot so pleasant as my own New England home.

I 've seen Italia's daughters, beneath Italian skies;
Seen beauty in their happy smiles, and love within their eyes;
But give to me the fairer ones that grace New England's shore,
In preference to the dwellers in the valley of Lanore.

I 've watched the sun's departure behind the "Eternal Hills,"
When with floods of golden light the vaulted heaven it fills;
But Italy can never boast, with its poetic power,
More varied beauties than those of New England's sunset hour.

I love my own New England; I love its rocks and hills;
I love its trees, its mossy banks, its fountains and its rills;
I love its homes, its cottages, its people round the hearth;
I love, O, how I love to hear New England shouts of mirth!

Tell me of the sunny South, its orange-groves and streams,
That they surpass in splendor man's most enraptured dreams;
But never can they be as fair, though blown by spicy gales,
As those sweet homes, those cottages, within New England vales.

O, when life's cares are ending, and time upon my brow
Shall leave a deeper impress than gathers on it now;
When age shall claim its sacrifice, and I no more shall roam,
Then let me pass my latter days in my New England home!

LOVE THAT WANES NOT.

O, WHEN should Love's true beacons glow the brightest,
If not when darkness shrouds the path we tread?
When should its tokens, though they be the slightest,
Be given, if not when clouds are overhead?

When light is 'round us, and when joys are glowing,
Some hand may press our own, and vow to cherish
A love for us which ne'er shall cease its flowing,—
And yet *that* love, when darkness comes, may perish.

But there is love which will outlive all sorrow,
And in the darkest hour be nigh to bless,—
Which need not human art or language borrow,
Its deep affection fondly to express.

The mother o'er the child she loveth bending
Need not in words tell others of her love;
For, on the wings of earnest prayer ascending,
It rises, and is registered above.

O, such *is* love—all other is fictitious;
All other 's vanquished by disease and pain;
But this, which lives when fate is unpropitious,
Shall rise to heaven, and there an entrance gain.

ONWARD COURAGEOUSLY.

BEND thee to action—nerve thee to duty!
Whate'er it may be, never despair!
God reigns on high,—pray to him truly,
He will an answer give to thy prayer.

Shrinketh thyself from crosses before thee?
Art thou so made as to tremble and fear?
Confide in thy God; he will watch o'er thee;
Humbly and trustingly, brother, draw near!

Clouds may be gathering, light may depart,
  Earth that thou treadest seem crumbling away;
New foes, new dangers, around thee may start,
  And spectres of evil tempt thee astray.

Onward courageously! nerved for the task,
  Do all thy duty, and strength shall be thine;
Whate'er you want in humility ask,
  Aid shall be given from a source that 's divine.

Do all thy duty faithful and truly;
  Trust in thy Maker, — he 's willing to save
Thee from all evil, and keep thee securely,
  And make thee triumphant o'er death and the grave.

A FOREST PIC-NIC SONG.

WITHIN these woods, beneath these trees,
  We meet to-day a happy band;
All joy is ours, — we feel the breeze
  Blow gently o'er our native land.
How brightly blooms each forest flower!
  What cheerful notes the wild bird sings!
How nature charms our festive hour,
  What beauty round our pathway springs!

The aged bear no weight of years;
  The good old man, the matron too,
Forget their ills, forget their fears,
  And range the dim old forests through
With youth and maiden on whose cheek
  The ruddy bloom of health doth glow,
And in whose eyes the heart doth speak
  Oft more than they would have us know.

How pleasant thus it is to dwell
  Within the shadow of this wood,
Where rock and tree and flower do tell
  To all that nature's God is good!

Here nature's temple open stands,—
  There 's none so nobly grand as hers,—
The sky its roof; its floor, all lands,
  While rocks and trees are worshippers.

There 's not a leaf that rustles now,
  A bird that chants its simple lays,
A breeze that passing fans our brow,
  That speaks not of its Maker's praise.
O, then, let us who gather here
  Praise Him who gave us this glad day,
And when the twilight shades appear
  Pass with his blessing hence away!

THE WARRIOR'S BRIDE.

CHAPTER I.

Rome was enjoying the blessings of peace; and so little employment attended the soldier's every-day life, that the words "as idle as a soldier" became a proverb indicative of the most listless inactivity.

The people gave themselves up to joy and gladness. The sound of music was heard from all parts of the city, and perfumed breezes went up as an incense from the halls of beauty and mirth.

It was, indeed, a blessed time for the city of the seven hills; and its people rejoiced as they had not for many a long, long year — ay, for a century.

"Peace, sweet peace, a thousand blessings attend thy glad reign. See you how quietly the peasant's flocks graze on our eternal hills? The tinkling bell is a sweeter sound than the trumpet's blast; and the curling smoke, arising from the hearth-stones of contented villagers, is a truer index of a nation's power than the sulphurous cloud from the field of battle. What say you, Alett,— is it not?"

Thus spake a youth of noble mien, as he stood with one arm encircling the waist of a lady, of whose beauty it were useless to attempt a description. There are some phases of beauty which pen cannot describe, nor pencil portray,— a beauty which seems to hover around the form, words, and motions of those whose special recipients it is; a sort of ethereal loveliness, concentrating the tints of the rainbow, the sun's golden rays, and so acting upon the mind's eye of the observer as almost to convince him that a visitant from a sphere of perfection is in his presence.

Such was that of Alett. She was the only daughter of a distinguished general, whose name was the terror of all the foes, and the confidence of all the friends, of Italy — his eldest daughter; and with love approaching idolatry he cherished her. She was his confidant. In the privacy of her faithful heart he treasured all his plans and purposes. Of late, the peaceful security in which the nation dwelt gave him the opportunity of remaining at home, where, in the companionship of a wife he fondly loved, children he almost idolized, and friends whose friendship was not fictitious, he found that joy and comfort which the camp could never impart.

Alett was ever in the presence of her father, or the young man whose apostrophe to peace we have just given.

Rubineau was not the descendant of a noble family, in the worldly acceptation of the term. It was noble, indeed, but not in deeds of war or martial prowess. Its nobleness consisted in the steady perseverance in well-doing, and a strict attachment to what conscience dictated as right opinions. The general loved him for the inheritance he possessed in such traits of character, and the love which existed between his daughter and the son of a plebeian was countenanced under such considerations, with one proviso; which was, that, being presented with a commission, he should accept it, and hold himself in readiness to leave home and friends when duty should call him to the field of battle.

We have introduced the two standing on a beautiful eminence, in the rear of the general's sumptuous mansion.

The sun was about going down, and its long, golden rays

streamed over hill and dale, palace and cot, clothing all in a voluptuous flow of rich light.

They had stood for several moments in silence, gazing at the quiet and beautiful scene before them, when the musical voice of Rubineau broke forth in exclamations of delight at the blessings of peace.

Alett was not long in answering. It was a theme on which she delighted to dwell. Turning the gaze of her large, full eyes up towards those of Rubineau, she said,

"Even so it is. Holy Peace! It is strange that men will love the trumpet's blast, and the smoke and the heat of the conflict, better than its gentle scenes. Peace, peace! blessings on thee, as thou givest blessings!"

Rubineau listened to the words of his Alett with a soul of admiration. He gazed upon her with feelings he had never before felt, and which it was bliss for him to experience.

She, the daughter of an officer, brought up amid all the glare and glitter, show and blazonry, of military life,— she, who had seen but one side of the great panorama of martial life,— to speak thus in praise of peace, and disparagingly of the profession of her friends — it somewhat surprised the first speaker.

"It is true," he replied; "but how uncertain is the continuance of the blessings we now enjoy! To-morrow may sound the alarm which shall call me from your side to the strife and tumult of war. Instead of your gentle words, I may hear the shouts of the infuriated soldiery, the cry of the wounded, and the sighs of the dying."

"Speak not so," exclaimed Alett; "it must not be."

"Do you not love your country?" inquired the youth.

"I do, but I love Rubineau more. There are warriors enough ready for the battle. It need not be that you go. But why this alarm? We were talking of peace, and, behold, now we have the battle-field before us — war and all its panoply ! "

" Pardon me, my dearest Alett, for borrowing trouble; but at times, when I am with you, and thinking of our present joy, the thought will arise that it may be taken from us." No more words were needed to bring to the mind of Alett all that filled that of Rubineau. They embraced each the other more affectionately than ever, and silently repaired to the house of the general.

CHAPTER II.

" To remain will be dishonor; to go may be death! When a Roman falls, the foe has one more arrow aimed at his heart; an arrow barbed with revenge, and sent with unerring precision. Hark ! that shout is music to every soldier's ear. Hear you that tramp of horsemen ? that rumbling of chariot-wheels ? "

Twelve months had passed since the time of the last chapter, and, after repeated threatenings, war had actually begun.

Instead of idle hours, the soldiers had busy moments, and every preparation was made to meet the opposing array in a determined manner, and with a steadiness of purpose that should insure success.

The general watched for some time the fluctuating appearance of public affairs, and it was not until war was not only certain, but actually in progress, that he called upon Rubineau to go forth.

A week hence Rubineau and Alett were to be united in marriage; and invitations had been extended far and near, in anticipation of the event. It had been postponed from week to week, with the hope that the various rumors that were circulated respecting impending danger to the country might prove untrue, or at least to have a foundation on some weak pretence, which reasonable argument might overthrow.

Day by day these rumors increased, and the gathering together of the soldiery betokened the certainty of an event which would fall as a burning meteor in the midst of the betrothed and their friends.

The call for Rubineau to depart was urgent, and its answer admitted of no delay.

"To remain," said the general, "will be dishonor; to go may be death: which will you choose?"

It was a hard question for the young man to answer. But it must be met. The general loved him, and with equal unwillingness the question was presented and received.

"I go. If Rubineau falls ——"

"If he returns," exclaimed the general, interrupting him, "honor, and wealth, and a bride who loves and is loved, shall be his — all his."

It was a night of unusual loveliness. The warm and sultry atmosphere of the day had given place to cool and gentle breezes. The stars were all out, shining as beacons at the gates of a paradise above; and the moon began and ended her course without the attendance of one cloud to veil her beauties from the observation of the dwellers on earth.

Rubineau and Alett were seated beneath a bower, cultivated by the fair hand of the latter.

The next morning Rubineau was to depart. All the happy scenes of the coming week were to be delayed, and the thought that they might be delayed long — ay, forever — came like a shadow of evil to brood in melancholy above the place and the hour.

We need not describe the meeting, the parting.

"Whatever befalls me, I shall not forget you, Alett. Let us hope for the best. Yet a strange presentiment I have that I shall not return."

"O that I could go with you!" said Alett. "Think you father would object?"

"That were impossible. Nothing but love, true and enduring, could make such a proposal. It would be incurring a two-fold danger."

"Death would be glorious with you, — life insupportable without you!"

In such conversation the night passed, and when the early light of morning came slowly up the eastern sky, the sound of a trumpet called him away.

The waving of a white flag was the last signal, and the general, all unused to tears as he was, mingled his with those of his family as the parting kiss was given, and Rubineau started on a warfare the result of which was known only to Him who governs the destinies of nations and of individuals.

And now, in the heat of the conflict, the war raged furiously. Rubineau threw himself in the front rank, and none was more brave than he. It seemed to his fellow-officers that he was urged on by some unseen agency, and guarded from injury by some spirit of good.

To himself but one thought was in his mind; and, regardless of danger, he pressed forward for a glorious victory, and honor to himself and friends.

Those whose leader he was were inspirited by his courageous action, and followed like true men where he led the way.

They had achieved several victories, and were making an onset upon numbers four-fold as large as their own, when their leader received a severe wound, and, falling from his noble horse, would have been trampled to death by his followers, had not those who had seen him fall formed a circle around as a protection for him.

This serious disaster did not dampen the ardor of the soldiers; they pressed on, carried the point, and saw the foe make a rapid retreat.

The shouts of victory that reached the ears of Rubineau came with a blessing. He raised himself, and shouted, "On, brave men!" But the effort was too much for him to sustain for any length of time, and he fell back completely exhausted.

He was removed to a tent, and had every attention bestowed upon him. As night approached, and the cool air of evening fanned his brow, he began to revive, but not in any great degree.

The surgeon looked sad. There was evidently reason to fear the worst; and, accustomed as he was to such scenes, he was now but poorly prepared to meet it.

"Rubineau is expiring," whispered a lad, as he proceeded quietly among the ranks of soldiers surrounding the tent of the wounded.

And it was so. His friends had gathered around his couch, and, conscious of the approach of his dissolution, he bade them all farewell, and kissed them.

"Tell her I love, I die an honorable death; tell her that her Rubineau fell where the arms of the warriors clashed the closest, and that victory hovered above him as his arm grew powerless; and, O, tell her that it was all for her sake,—love for her nerved his arm, and love for her is borne upward on his last, his dying prayer. Tell her to love as I ——"

"He is gone, sir," said the surgeon.

"Gone!" exclaimed a dozen voices.

"A brave man has fallen," remarked another, as he raised his arm, and wiped the flowing tears from his cheek.

CHAPTER III.

At the mansion of the old general every arrival of news from the war sent a thrill of joy through the hearts of its inmates. Hitherto, every despatch told of victory and honor; but now a sad chapter was to be added to the history of the conflict.

Alett trembled as she beheld the slow approach of the messenger, who, at all previous times, had come with a quick step. In her soul she felt the keen edge of the arrow that was just entering it, and longed to know all, dreadful though it might be.

Need we describe the scene of fearful disclosure? If the reader has followed the mind of Alett, as from the first it has presumed, conjectured, and fancied,— followed all its hopes of future bliss, and seen it revel in the sunshine of honor and earthly fame,— he can form some idea, very faint though it must be, of the effect which followed the recital of all the facts in regard to the fallen.

In her wild frenzy of grief, she gave utterance to the deep feelings of her soul with words that told how deep was her sorrow, and how unavailing every endeavor which friends exerted to allay its pangs.

She would not believe him dead. She would imagine him at her side, and would talk to him of peace, "sweet peace," and laugh in clear and joyous tones as she pictured its blessings, and herself enjoying with him its comforts.

Thus, with enthroned reason, she would give vent to grief; and, with her reason dethroned, be glad and rejoice.

And so passed her lifetime.

Often, all day long, attired in bridal raiment, the same in which she had hoped to be united indissolubly to Rubineau, she remained seated in a large oaken chair, while at her side stood the helmet and spear he had carried forth on the morning when they parted. At such times, she was as calm as an infant's slumberings, saying that she was waiting for the sound of the marriage-bells; asked why they did not ring, and sat for hours in all the beauty of loveliness — the Warrior's Bride.

THE ADVENT OF HOPE.

ONCE on a time, from scenes of light
An angel winged his airy flight;
Down to this earth in haste he came,
And wrote, in lines of living flame,
These words on everything he met, —
"Cheer up, be not discouraged yet!'

Then back to heaven with speed he flew,
Attuned his golden harp anew;
Whilst the angelic throng came round
To catch the soul-inspiring sound;
And heaven was filled with new delight,
For HOPE had been to earth that night.

CHILD AND SIRE.

"KNOW you what intemperance is?"
I asked a little child,
Who seemed too young to sorrow know,
So beautiful and mild.
It raised its tiny, blue-veined hand,
And to a church-yard near
It pointed, whilst from glistening eye
Came forth the silent tear.

PAGE 164.

"Yes, for yonder, in that grave,
Is my father lying;
And these words he spake to me
While he yet was dying:

"'Mary, when the sod lies o'er me
And an orphan child thou art, —
When companions ask thy story,
Say intemperance aimed the dart.
When the gay the wine-cup circle,
Praise the nectar that doth shine,
When they 'd taste, then tell *thy* story,
And to earth they 'll dash the wine.'

"And there my dear-loved mother lies, —
What bitter tears I 've shed
Over her grave! — I cannot think
That she is really dead.
And when the spring in beauty blooms,
At morning's earliest hour
I hasten there, and o'er her grave
I plant the little flower.

"And patiently I watch to see
It rise from out the earth,
To see it from its little grave
Spring to a fairer birth.
For mother said that thus would she,
And father, too, and I,
Arise from out our graves to meet
In mansions in the sky.

"O, what intemperance is, there 's none
On earth can better tell.
Intemperance me an orphan made,
In this wide world to dwell;
Intemperance broke my mother's heart,
It took my father's life,
And makes the days of man below
With countless sorrows rife."

"Know you what intemperance is?"
I asked a trembling sire,
Whose lamp of life burned dim, and seemed
As though 't would soon expire.
He raised his bowéd head, and then
Methought a tear did start,
As though the question I had put
Had reached his very heart.

He raised his head, but 't was to bow
It down again and sigh;
Methought that old man's hour had come
In which he was to die.
Not so; he raised it up again,
And boldly said, "I can!
Intemperance is the foulest curse
That ever fell on man.

"I had a son, as fair, as bright
As ever mortal blest;
And day passed day, and year passed year,
Whilst I that son carest.
For all my hopes were bound in him;
I thought, from day to day,
That when old age should visit me
That son would be my stay.

"I knew temptations gathered near,
And bade him warning take, —
Consent not, if enticed to sin,
E'en for his father's sake.
But in a fearful hour he drank
From out the poisonous bowl,
And then a pang of sorrow lodged
Within my inmost soul.

"A year had passed, and he whom I
Had strove in vain to save
Fell, crushed beneath intemperance,
Into a drunkard's grave.

O, brother, I *can* tell to thee
  What vile intemperance is,
When one in whom I fondly hoped
  Met such an end as his!

"This was not all; a daughter I
  Was blest with, and she passed
Before me like an angel-form
  Upon my pathway cast.
She loved one with a tender love,
  She left her father's side,
And stood forth, in her robes of white,
  A young mechanic's bride.

"She lived and loved, and loved and lived,
  For many a happy year;
No sorrow clouded o'er her path,
  But joy was ever near.
Ay, those were pleasant hours we spent,
  Were joyful ones we passed;
Alas! too free from care were they
  On earth to always last.

"Then he was tempted, tasted, drank,
  And then to earth he fell;
And ever after misery
  Within that home did dwell.
And soon he died, as drunkards die,
  With scarce an earthly friend,
Yet *one* bent o'er him tenderly
  Till life itself did end.

"And when life's chord was broken, when
  His spirit went forth free,
In all her anguish then she came
  To bless and comfort me.
Yet she, too, died, ere scarce twelve months
  Had passéd o'er her head,
And in yon much-loved church-yard now
  She resteth with the dead.

"That little child you spoke to is
  The child she left behind;
I love her for her mother's sake,
  And she is good and kind.
And every morning, early, to
  Yon flowery grave she 'll go;
And I thank my God she 's with me
  To bless me here below.

"I had a brother, but he died
  The drunkard's fearful death;
He bade me raise a warning voice
  Till Time should stay my breath.
And thousands whom in youth I loved
  Have fallen 'neath the blast
Of ruin which intemperance
  Hath o'er the wide world cast."

He spoke no more, — the gushing tears
  His furrowed cheeks did leap;
The little child came quick to know
  What made the old man weep.
He, trembling, grasped my hand and said
  (The little child grasped his),
"May you ne'er know, as I have known,
  What sad intemperance is!"

And since that hour, whene'er I look
  Around me o'er the earth,
And see the wine-cup passing free
  'Mid scenes of festive mirth,
I think how oft it kindleth up
  Within its raging fire,
And fain would tell to all the truths
  I heard from "Child and Sire."

A BROTHER'S WELCOME.

Welcome, brother, welcome home!
Here 's a father's hand to press thee;
Here 's a mother's heart to bless thee;
Here 's a brother's will to twine
Joys fraternal close with thine;
Here 's a sister's earnest love,
Equalled but by that above;
Here are friends who once did meet thee,
Gathered once again to greet thee.

Welcome, brother, welcome home!
Thou hast wandered far away;
Many a night and many a day
We have thought where thou might'st be,
On the land or on the sea;
Whether health was on thy cheek,
Or that word we dare not speak
Hung its shadowy wing above thee,
Far away from those who love thee.

Welcome, brother, welcome home!
Here, where youthful days were spent
Ere life had its labor lent,
Where the hours went dancing by,
'Neath a clear, unclouded sky.
And our thanks for blessings rendered
Unto God were daily tendered,
Here as ever pleasures reign,
Welcome to these scenes again!

THE IMMENSITY OF CREATION.

It is well for man to consider the heavens, the work of God's hands; the moon and the stars, which He has created. To look forth upon the universe, of which we form a part, fills us with high and ennobling thoughts, and inspires us with an earnest desire to press onward in the endless path, at every step of which new wonders and new joys spring up to greet our vision, and to gladden our souls.

Whichever way we look, above or below us, to the right or the left, we find a boundless expanse teeming with life and its enjoyments. This earth, large as it may appear to us, is less than a grain of sand in size, when compared with the vastness around it.

Take your soul away from earth, and send it on a mission of research among other worlds. Let it soar far away to where the dog-star, Sirius, holds its course; and then, though *nineteen billion two hundred million miles from earth*, a distance so great, that light, travelling, as it does, at the rate of six million six hundred and twenty thousand miles a minute, would require three years to pass it, — even then, when the journeying spirit had reached such a point, it might pass on and on, — new worlds meeting its gaze at every advance, and new wonders being seen as far beyond the point it had attained as the inconceivable length of the path it had already travelled multiplied a myriad of times.

We can scarcely comprehend the vast distance of Sirius; yet, great as this distance is, it is the *nearest* star to our system, and stars have been seen whose distance from the earth is estimated to be a thousand times as great!

Can human mind mark *that* range? A thousand times nineteen billion two hundred million! And were we to stand on the last of these discovered stars, we might look yet far beyond, and see "infinity, boundless infinity, stretching on, unfathomed, forever."

To have an idea of the vastness of creation, we must possess the mind of the Creator. What are we? We live and move and have our being on a grain of creation, that is being whirled through boundless space with inconceivable rapidity. And we affect to be proud of our estate! We build houses, and we destroy them; we wage war, kill, brutify, enslave, ruin each other; or, we restore, beautify, and bless. We are vain, sometimes. We think the world was made for *us*; the stars shine for *us*, and all the hosts that gem the drapery of night created for *our* special benefit. Astonishing presumption! — born of ignorance and cradled in credulity!

The mind grows dizzy as it attempts to conceive of constellation beyond constellation, on and on, through endless space.

Commencing with this earth, the mind given up to serious reflection muses upon its broad extent of territory, its continents and its oceans, and it appears very large indeed. Forgetting, for a moment, its knowledge of other planets, it believes that this world is the whole universe of God; that the sun, moon and stars, are but lights in the firmament of heaven to give light upon the earth. But truth steps in and changes the mind's view. It shows that, large and important as this earth may appear, the sun, which is spoken of as inferior, is three hundred and fifty-four thousand nine hundred and thirty-six times larger; and the stars, that seem like diamond points above us, are, many of them, larger than the sun, one being one billion eight hundred million miles in diameter. Yet, such a bulk, when compared to the universe, is less than a monad.

A "monad" is an indivisible atom. It is as incomprehensible as the mysteries of creation, or the duration of eternity.

Tripoli, or rotten-stone, an article used in every family, and tons of which are daily employed in manufactories, is composed entirely of animalculæ. In each cubic inch there are forty-one billion, that is, forty-one million-million of these living, breathing creatures, each of whom has organs of sight, hearing and digestion. Think, if you can, of the internal organization of beings a million of whom could rest on the point of a cambric needle!

But there are more minute forms of creation than even those. Deposit a grain, the four hundred and eightieth part of an ounce of musk, in any place, and, for twenty years, it will throw off exhalations of fragrance, without causing any perceptible decrease of weight. The fragrance that for so many years goes forth from that minute portion of matter is composed of particles of musk. How small must each of those particles be, that follow each other in ceaseless succession for twenty years, without lessening, to any perceptible degree, the weight of the deposit! And yet we have not reached the monad. A celebrated author * made a computation which led to the conclusion that six billion as many atoms of light flow from a candle in *one second* as there are grains of sand in the whole earth, supposing each cubic inch to contain one million!

Here we *must* stop. Further advances are impossible, yet our end is not attained; we have not yet reached the monad, for the animalculæ and the less sentient particles of matter, light, are not, for they are divisible.

The insect can be divided, because it has limbs with which

* Niewentyt.

to move; and an intelligence higher than man can doubtless see emanations from those particles of light. But a monad is indivisible! Think of each cubic inch of this great earth containing a million grains of sand, and those countless grains multiplied by one billion, or a million-million, and that the product only shows the number of particles of light that flow from a candle in one second of time! — and not a monad yet! Minds higher than ours can separate each of these particles, and yet perhaps they find not the indivisible, but assign over to other minds the endless task.

With such thoughts let us return to our first point, and remark that the star tens of billions of miles distant, one billion eight hundred million miles in diameter, is but a monad when compared with the creations of the vast universe of God!

Here the mind sinks within itself, and gladly relinquishes the herculean task of endeavoring to comprehend, for a single moment, a fractional part of the stupendous whole.

Deep below us, high above us, far as the eye of the mind can see around us, are the works of our Creator, marshalled in countless hosts. All animated by his presence, all breathed upon by his life, inspired by his divinity, fostered by his love, supported by his power.

And in all things there is beauty — sunbeams and rainbows; fragrant flowers whose color no art can equal. In every leaf, every branch, every fibre, every stone, there is a perfect symmetry, perfect adaptation to the conditions that surround it. And thus it is, from the minutest insect undiscernible by human eye, to the planet whose size no figures can represent. Each and all the works of God order governs, symmetry moulds, and beauty adorns.

There are all grades of beings, from the monad to the highest intelligences, and man occupies his position in the endless chain. Could you hear and see, as seraphs listen and behold, you would hear one continuous song of glad praise go up from all creation; you would see all things radiant with smiles, reflecting the joys of heaven. And why? Because they follow nature's leading, and, in doing so, live and move in harmony.

Who can scale the heights above us, or fathom the depths below us? Who can comprehend the magnitude of countless worlds that roll in space — the distance that separates the nearest orb from our earth, the worlds of being in a drop of water, the mighty array of angel forms that fill immensity?

Well may we exclaim, "Great and marvellous are thy works, O Lord of Hosts, and that my soul knoweth right well!"

A VISION OF HEAVEN.

Night had shed its darkness round me;
Wearied with the cares of day,
Rested I. Sleep's soft folds bound me,
And my spirit fled away.

As on eagle pinions soaring,
On I sped from star to star,
Till heaven's high and glistening portals
Met my vision from afar.

Myriad miles I hasted over;
Myriad stars I passéd by:
On and on my tireless spirit
Urged its ceaseless flight on high.

Planets burned with glorious radiance,
Lighting up my trackless way;
On I sped, till music coming
From the realms of endless day

Fell upon my ear, — as music
Chanted by celestial choirs
Only can, — and then my spirit
Longed to grasp their golden lyres

Stood I near that portal wondering
Whether I could enter there:
I, of earth and sin the subject,
Child of sorrow and of care!

There I stood like one uncalled for,
Willing thus to hope and wait,
Till a voice said, "Why not enter?
Why thus linger at the gate?

"Know me not? Say whence thou comest
  Here to join *our* angel band.
Know me not? Here, take *thy* welcome —
  Take thine angel-sister's hand."

Then I gazed, and, gazing, wondered;
  For 't was she who long since died, —
She who in her youth departed,
  Falling early at my side.

"Up," said she, "mid glorious temples!
  Up, where all thy loved ones rest!
They with joy will sing thy welcome
  To the mansions of the blest.

"Mansions where no sin can enter,
  Home where all do rest in peace;
Where the tried and faithful spirit
  From its trials finds release;

"Golden courts, where watchful cherubs
  Tune their harps to holy praise;
Temples in which countless myriads
  Anthems of thanksgiving raise."

I those shining portals entered,
  Guided by that white-robed one,
When a glorious light shone round me,
  Brighter than the noonday sun!

Friends I met whom death had severed
  From companionship below;
All were there — and in each feature
  Immortality did glow.

I would touch their golden lyres,
  When upon my ear there broke
Louder music ——— at that moment
  I from my glad vision woke.

All was silent; scarce a zephyr
  Moved the balmy air of night;

And the moon, in meekness shining,
Shed around its hallowed light.

THERE 'S HOPE FOR THEE YET.

WHAT though from life's bounties thou mayest have fallen?
What though thy sun in dark clouds may have set?
There is a bright star that illumes the horizon,
Telling thee truly, "There 's hope for thee yet."

This earth may look dull, old friends may forsake thee;
Sorrows that never before thou hast met
May roll o'er thy head; yet that bright star before thee
Shines to remind thee "there 's hope for thee yet."

'T is but folly to mourn, though fortune disdain thee,
Though never so darkly thy sun may have set;
'T is wisdom to gaze at the bright star before thee,
And shout, as you gaze, "There 's hope for me yet."

SOLILOQUY OVER THE GRAVE OF A WIFE.

IT cannot be that thou art dead; that now
I watch beside thy grave, and with my tears
Nourish the flowers that blossom over *thee;*
I cannot think that thou art dead and gone;
That naught remains to me of what thou wert,
Save that which lieth here, — dust unto dust.

When the bright sun arises, and its rays
Pass noiseless through my chamber, then methinks

That thou art with me still; that I can see
Thy flowing hair; and thy bright glancing eye
Beams on me with a look none other can.
And when at noon life's busy tumult makes
My senses reel, and I almost despair,
Thou comest to me and I 'm cheered again;
Thine own bright smile illuminates my way,
And one by one the gathered clouds depart,
Till not a shadow lies upon my path.

Night, with its long and sombre shadows, treads
Upon the steps that morn and noon have trod;
And, as our children gather round my knee,
And lisp those evening prayers *thy* lips have taught,
I cannot but believe that thou art near.
But when they speak of "mother," when they say
"'T is a long time since she hath left our side,"
And when they ask, in their soft infant tones,
When they again shall meet thee, — then I feel
A sudden sadness o'er my spirit come:
And when sleep holds them in its silken bands
I wander here, to this fair spot they call
Thy grave (as though this feeble earth could hold
Thee in its cold embrace), and weep and sigh;
Yet, trusting, look above to yon bright sphere,
And feel thou art *not* dead, but *living* there.

It is not *thou* that fills this spot of earth,
It is not *thou* o'er whom these branches wave,
These blooming roses only mark the spot
Where but remaineth that thou couldst not wear
Amid immortal scenes.
Thou livest yet!
Thy feet do tread the golden courts of heaven;
Thy hands have touched the harps that angels use;
Thy eyes have seen the glory of our Lord;
Thy ears have listened to that song of praise
Which angels utter, and which God accepts.

THE FUGITIVES.

THEY had escaped the galling chain and fetters,
Had gained the freedom which they long had sought,
And lived like men — in righteous deeds abettors,
Loving the truth which God to them had taught
Some at the plough had labored late and early;
And some ascended Learning's glorious mount;
And some in Art had brought forth treasures pearly,
Which future history might with joy recount
As gems wrought out by hands which God made free,
But man had sworn should chained and fettered be.

They lived in peace, in quietness, and aided
In deeds of charity — in acts of love;
Nor cared though evil men their works upbraided,
While conscience whispered of rewards above.
And they had wives to love, children who waited
At eve to hear the father's homeward tread,
And clasped the hand, — or else, with joy elated,
Sounding his coming, to their mother sped.
Thus days and years passed by, and hope was bright,
Nor dreamed they of a dark and gloomy night.

Men came empowered, with handcuffs and with warrants,
And, entering homes, tore from their warm embrace
Husbands and fathers, and in copious torrents
Poured forth invective on our northern race,
And done all "lawfully," because 't was voted
By certain men, who, when they had the might,
Fosteréd plans on which their passions doted,
Despite of reason and God's law of right;
And, bartering liberties, the truth dissembled,
While Freedom's votaries yielded as they trembled.

* * * * * *

Shall we look on and bear the insult given?
O, worse than "insult" is it to be chained,
To have the fetters on thy free limbs riven,
When *once* the prize of Freedom has been gained.

No! by the granite pointing high above us,
By Concord, Lexington, and Faneuil Hall,
By all these sacred spots, by those who love us,
We pledge to-day our hate of Slavery's thrall;
And give to man, whoever he may be,
The power we have to make and keep him free.

THE UNIVERSAL JUBILEE.

What shouts shall rise when earth shall hold
Its universal jubilee!
When man no more is bought and sold,
And one and all henceforth are free!
Then songs they 'll sing,
That loud shall ring
From rock to rock, from shore to shore.
"Hurra!" they 'll shout, "we 're free, we 're free,
From land to land, from sea to sea,
And chains and fetters bind no more!"

Let every freeman strive to bring
The universal jubilee;
All hail the day when earth shall ring
With shouts of joy, and men are free!
Then each glad voice
Shall loud rejoice,
And chains shall fall from every hand,
Whilst myriad tongues shall loudly tell
The grateful joy of hearts that swell,
Where Freedom reigns o'er sea and land.

THE WIDOW'S STORY.

TAPVILLE was situated on the borders of one of the most beaütiful rivers that grace and refresh the soil of New England. It was once a quiet place, once as perfect in its character as any of its sisterhood. A moral atmosphere pervaded it, and the glorious and divine principle of doing unto others as they would have others do unto them governed its inhabitants; and, therefore, it was not strange that its farmers and storekeepers kept good the proverbial honesty and hospitality of their progenitors. Tradition said (but written history was silent) that a few of those who landed at Plymouth Rock separated from the main body, and took up their abode further in the interior; and that, from these "few," a flourishing company arose, and the place they inhabited was "Springvale." But time and circumstances, having much to do with the concerns of earth's inhabitants, changed the character as well as the name of this ancient town, and "Springvale" became "Tapville."

One evening, in the year one thousand eight hundred and I don't remember what, after a somewhat fatiguing ride on horseback all day, my heart was cheered on coming in view of the town. I had never visited Tapville, but, from accounts I had heard, judged it to be a sort of Pandemonium — a juvenile Bedlam. As I entered, troops of children greeted me with shouts, and my horse with stones. Despite of my treatment, I could not but compare their appearance, to say nothing of their conduct, with those I had last seen in another town, thirty miles distant. These were attired in rags, those in good clothing; these with unwashed faces, uncombed hair, and bearing every mark of neglect,— those bright and smiling, happy themselves, and making all around them so.

I did not much fancy my reception, I assure you. My horse seemed wondering at the cause of it, for he suddenly halted, then turned slowly about, and began to canter away with a speed that I thought quite impossible for a beast after a long day's work. I reined him in, turned about, and entered the town by a small and not much frequented pathway.

There was a large building at my left, with a huge sign over its principal door, from which I learned that "Good Entertainment for Man and Beast" might be had within. Appearances, however, indicated that a beast must be a very *bad* beast who would accept its "entertainment."

A fat man, wearing a green jacket on his back, an old torn and tattered straw hat on his head, and both hands in his pockets, stood lazily at the door; before which half a score of dirty children were playing with marbles, and a short distance from which a couple of children were fighting, upon whose pugilistic exercises a woman, with a child in her arms and a pipe in her mouth, was gazing with intense interest.

The general appearance of the town was far from pleasing. At nearly every window, hats, or shingles, or bundles of rags, took the place of glass, and the doors, instead of being hung on hinges, were "*set up*," liable to be *set down* by the first gust of wind.

Near one miserable shantee, poor, *very* poor apology for a dwelling-house, one man was endeavoring to get another into the house; at least, so I thought; but both were so much intoxicated that I could not tell, for my life, which the latter was. At one moment, the man with the blue coat with the tails cut off seemed to be helping the man without a coat; the next moment, I thought the coatless man was trying to help the other. The fact was, both needed help, which neither could give; so they remained "in a fix."

Now and then, a bare-footed little child would run across my path, and hurry out of sight, as if fearful of being seen where so much that was neither of heaven nor of earth was discernible.

In striking contrast with the want and desolation around, stood a beautiful mansion. Around it was a garden of choice flowers, and the vine, with its rich clusters of luscious grapes, shaded the path to the entrance of the house.

I continued on. Far up a shaded avenue I perceived a small, yet neat cottage, so different in general appearance from those around it, that I turned my way thither, in hopes of resting in quiet, and, if possible, of learning something relative to the town. I alighted, knocked, and soon an old lady requested me to enter, saying that Tommy would see that my horse was cared for. It was a small room that I entered; everything was as neat and clean as a New Year's gift, and there was so much of New England about it, that I felt at home. Near an open window, in an easy-chair, sat a young lady of decidedly prepossessing appearance, but evidently wasting beneath that scourge of eastern towns and cities — consumption. There was a hue upon her cheek that was in beautiful contrast with the pure white of her high forehead, and the dark, penetrating eye that flashed with the deep thoughts of her soul.

The old lady was one of those good-natured, motherly women, whom you will find at the firesides of New England homes, generous to a fault; and whom you cannot but love, for the interest she takes in you, and the solicitude she manifests for your welfare.

A repast was soon at hand, and when it was over the lady said,

You are from Boston, then?"

"Yes," I replied; "and, having heard considerable respecting this place, have come hither to satisfy myself whether or not any good would be likely to result from a temperance lecture here."

"Temperance lecture!" she exclaimed, as she grasped my hand. "Do, sir, for Heaven's sake, do something, do anything you possibly can, to stay the ravages of the rum fiend in this place!"

She would have said more, but she could not. The fountains of her heart seemed breaking, and a flood of tears flowed from her eyes. The daughter buried her face in her hands, and the sighs that arose from both mother and child told me that something had been said that deeply affected them.

Tommy at this moment came in, happy and joyous; but, as soon as he saw his mother and sister weeping, his whole appearance changed. He approached his mother, and, looking up in her face, said, "Don't cry, mother. Jenny will be better soon, and Tommy will work and make you and her happy. Don't cry, mother!"

The child's simple entreaty brought more copiously the tears to the mourner's eyes, and some time elapsed before they became in the least degree comforted.

"You will excuse me, sir," said she, "I know you will, for my grief; but, O, if temperance had been here ten years ago, we should have been so happy!"

"Yes," said the boy; "then father would not have died a drunkard!"

The surmises I had entertained as to the cause of this sorrow were now confirmed; and, at my request, she told me her story, with a hope that it might prove a warning to others.

"You must know, sir, that when we came here to live

we were just married. Alfred, my husband, was a good mechanic, industrious, frugal and kind-hearted. He had by his labor and economy accumulated a small amount, enough to purchase an estate consisting of a house, shop and farm. He had many and good customers, and our prospects were very fair. We attended church regularly, for we thought that, after enjoying the bounties of a beneficent Ruler all of six days, it was our duty, as well as privilege, to devote the seventh to His praise.

"Years passed by, when one morning Jenny, who was then about seven years old, came running in, and told me that a new store had been opened; that the man had nothing but two or three little kegs, and a few bottles and tumblers. I went out, and found it as she had stated. There was the man; there was his store; there were his kegs, bottles and tumblers.

"The next day some changes were made; a few signs were seen, and the quiet villagers gazed in wonder, if not admiration, at the inscriptions, 'Rum,' 'Gin,' 'Brandies,' 'Wines and Cigars.' Old men shook their heads, and looked wise. Old women peered from beneath their specs, and gave vent to many predictions. Children asked what the words meant.

"That night I talked with my husband about it. He thought that there was no danger; that social enjoyment would harm no one; and seemed astonished, to use his own words, 'that such a sensible woman as I was should express any anxiety about the matter.' That night, to me, was a long and sad one. I feared the result of the too much dependence on self which he seemed to cherish.

"The rumseller soon gathered a number of townsmen about him. His establishment became a place of frequent resort by many, and soon we had quarrelling neighbors, and disturbances at night. Boys became dishonest, and thus the fruits of the iniquitous traffic became visible.

"I noticed that Alfred was not as punctual in his return

as formerly; and my fears that he visited this pest-house of the town were soon confirmed. I hinted to him my suspicions. He was frank, and freely admitted that he visited the bar-room; said he had become acquainted with a few choice spirits, true friends, who had sworn eternal friendship. 'Danger,' said he, 'there is none! If I thought I endangered *your* happiness, I would not visit it again.' I recollect the moment. He looked me steadily in the face, and, as he did so, a tear escaped my eye. He, smiling, wiped it away, promised that when he saw evil he would avoid it, and left me alone to my reflections.

"But I will be brief. I need not tell you how, step by step, he descended that ladder whose end rested in the grave. I need not tell you how I warned him of danger; how I entreated him to avoid it; how I watched him in sickness, and bathed his fevered brow; how my heart was gladdened when I saw his health returning, and heard his solemn promise to reform.

"Nor need I tell you how he was again led astray, and his hand encircled that cup which he had once dashed aside. O, sir, he was a good man; and, in his sober moments, he would weep like a child, as he thought of his situation! He would come to me and pour out his soul in gratitude for my kindness; and would beg my forgiveness in the tenderest manner, till his heart became too full for utterance, and his repentance found vent in his tears.

"What could I do but forgive him, as I did a hundred times!

"Disheartened, I became sick. I was not expected to survive; and Jenny, poor child, watched by my side, and contracted an illness, from which, I fear, she will not be freed till the God she loves calls her home to himself.

"When I recovered, Alfred remained for some time sober and happy. But he fell! Yes, sir; but God knows he tried to stand, and would have done so had not the owner of that groggery, by foul stratagem, hurled him to the ground. I went, my daughter went, friends went, to ask the destroyer of our happiness to desist; but he turned us away with an oath and a laugh, saying, 'he would sell to all who wanted.'

"Frequent exposure brought disease; disease brought death, and my husband died.

"All our property was sold to meet the demands of merciless creditors, the principal one of whom was this very rum-seller who turned me from his doors. A friend furnished us with the cottage in which we have since lived. Many kind-hearted friends have gathered around us, and we have been happy, save when the recollections of the past rise before us. Others, beside myself, have had cause to mourn; and our town, once inhabited by happy, quiet and contented families, has become noted as a seat of iniquity.

"He who has caused this change is now the wealthiest man in town. You might have seen his stately palace as you rode up, environed with fruits and flowers. He lives there; but, within the shade of that mansion, are the wretched hovels of those upon whose ruin he sits enthroned. He has roses and fruits at his door, but they have been watered by widows' tears; and the winds that reach his home amid rich vines and laden trees may bear to his ears the orphan's cry, from whose mouth he has taken the daily bread."

When the old lady had finished her narrative, she could restrain her tears no longer, and they burst forth as freely as at first.

I inquired whether there were any beside herself who would become interested in a temperance movement. She replied that there were many, but they wished some one to start it.

I had left a gentleman at the town I last came from, who

was an eloquent advocate; and my first act, after listening to the widow's narrative, was to write a note, and send it in all possible haste to him.

The next day he came; and, if you could have seen the joy of that family as I told them that we had announced a meeting, you would have some faint idea of the happiness which the temperance reform has produced.

From what I had learned, I expected that we should meet with some opposition from the wealthy individual before alluded to, or from his agents, who were so blinded to their own interests that they could not be easily induced to move for their own good.

The evening came, and the room we had engaged was well filled. My friend arose, when a stone, hurled at him from without, missed its aim, and struck a lamp at his side, dashing it into a hundred fragments. Little disconcerted at this, he began his address; and, in a short time, gained the attention of the audience in so perfect a manner, that they heeded not the attempts of a noisy crowd without to disturb them.

He continued on. Men leaned forward to catch his words, and some arose and stood as motionless as statues, with eyes fixed intently on the speaker. Women wept; some in sorrow for the past, others in joy for the future. A deep feeling pervaded all. The disturbance without ceased, and one by one the disturbers came to the door; one by one they entered, and began to feel the truths which the speakers uttered.

The only interruption was made by an aged man, who bowed his silvery head, and, in trembling accents, moaned out, "My son, my son!" These words, uttered at the expiration of every few minutes, increased the solemnity of the occasion, and added power to the lecturer's remarks, for all knew the story of his son, and all knew that he was carried home dead from the groggery.

When, at the end of the lecture, it was asked who would sign the pledge, the whole assembly started to respond to the call, and each one that night became pledged to total abstinence.

The next day a great excitement existed relative to the groggeries in town; a meeting was called, and a committee appointed to act in a manner they thought best calculated to promote the interests of the people at large.

This committee determined to present the facts to the keepers of the places in question, and request them to renounce the traffic.

The facts were presented. They saw that *their customers had all left them*, and why should they continue? It would be a losing business.

The effect of the moral suasion had been powerful; it labored with the very soul of the traffic, with those who put the pence in the dealers' coffers. It was more powerful than all laws that could have been enacted. Forbidding them to sell while customers crowded their doors would have had no effect, unless to create riot; inducing their customers to leave them soon induced them to leave the business, for where there are none to buy there will be none to sell.

In view of all this, the rumsellers of *Tapville* gave up; and, strange to say, joined with the people that night in their rejoicing, and made a bonfire of their stock in trade.

By the light of that fire my friend and I left the town; and when far away we could see its glare, and hear the shouts of a disenthralled people.

After a few months' travel in the south and west, I revisited *Tapville*, or rather the place where it once stood; but no Tapville was there. The town had regained its former sobriety and quiet, and became "Springvale."

I called at the widow's cottage; Tommy ran out to meet me, and I received a welcome I shall never forget. But Jenny was no more; with her last breath she had blessed the temperance cause, and then her pure spirit winged its way to that home where sorrows never come, and where the troubles of earth are forgotten amid the joys of heaven.

THE BATTLE OF THE RED MEN.

'T WAS cold, bleak winter, on a rock-bound coast,
  When bands of exiles trod its frozen shore.
Who then stood forth to greet the coming host
  And shelter freely give when storms did pour?
    Old Samoset — peace to his memory still! —
    He bade them welcome, welcome, with good will.

Then was the red man's nation broad and strong —
  O'er field and forest he held firm control;
Then power was his to stay the coming throng,
  And back the wave of usurpation roll.
    He might have crushed them on old Plymouth's rock,
    And freedom to this day have felt the shock.

Not so he willed it; he would have them sit
  In peace and amity around his door;
The pipe of peace in friendship would have lit,
  And, as its white cloud up towards heaven did soar,
    Learned that like it the spirits pure and white
    Ascend, to live in never-ceasing light.

But what return did they profusely give
  Who were dependent on the red man's corn?
Not even to them the privilege to live,
  But war and fire, torture, hate and scorn!
    Hunted like wild beasts through the forests' track;
    For food and welcome such they gave him back.

Then roused to madness was the Indian's soul,
Then grasped with firmness every one his bow;
No mortal power his purpose could control,
Till he had seen the traitors lying low.
Revenge! revenge! was sounded far and wide,
O'er every field and every river's tide.

The little child that scarce could lisp a word
Was taught to hate the white man; maidens fair
Were roused to fearful vengeance, as they heard
Their brothers' wrongs, and madly tore their hair;
Old men urged on the young, and young men fled
Swift to increase the armies of the dead.

And thus the war began, — the fearful war
That swept o'er happy homesteads like a flood;
The white and red man knew no other law
Than that which wrote its every act in blood.
Daylight beheld the ball and arrow's flight,
And blazing homes made terrible the night.

The rifle's sharp report, the arrow's whiz,
The shout, the yell, the fearful shriek of death;
Despair in him who saw the last of his,
And heard "good-by" from children's dying breath;
The last sad look of prisoners borne away,
And groan of torture, marked the night and day.

With arms more skilful — not with hearts more true,
Or souls more brave to battle for the right —
The white the unjust warfare did pursue,
Till, inch by inch, the red man took his flight
From homes he loved, from altars he revered,
And left, forever, scenes to him endeared.

O, what an hour for those brave people that!
Old men, whose homes were loved as homes can be;
Young men and maidens who had often sat
In love and peace beneath the forest tree;
Parents who 'd planted flowers, and with warm tears
Watered the graves of dearest-gone for years!

From every tree a voice did seem to start,
  And every shrub that could a shadow cast
Seemed to lament the fate that bade them part,
  So closely twined was each one with the past.
    O, was it strange they fought with furious zeal?
    Say, men who think, and have warm hearts to feel.

And thus they went, — a concourse of wronged men, —
  Not with a speedy flight; each inch they gave,
Each blade of grass that passed beyond their ken,
  Was sold for blood, and for a patriot's grave;
    And white men paid the price — and now they hold
    This broad, broad land for cost more dear than gold.

And yet 't is not enough; the cry for more
  Hath vexed the Indian, till the Atlantic's wave
Now blends with it the thunder of its roar,
  And soon shall sound the requiem o'er the grave
    Of the last Indian, — last of that brave band
    Who once held sway o'er all this fertile land.

Methinks to-day I see him stand alone,
  Drawing his blanket close around his form;
He hath braved all, hath heard the dying moan
  Rise from the fields of strife; and now the storm
    That hath swept all before it, age on age,
    On him, the last, seeks to pour forth its rage.

Raising his hand appealing to the sun,
  He swears, by all he hath or now could crave,
That when his life is closed, his life-race run,
  A white man ne'er shall stand above his grave.
    Shall he, the last of a once noble race,
    Consign himself to such a dire disgrace?

Never! let rock to rock the word resound;
  Never! bear witness all ye gods to-day;
Never! ye streams and rivers, as ye bound,
  Write "Never" on your waves, and bear away;
    Tell to the world that, hunted, wronged, abused,
    With such reproach he ne'er shall be accused,

The red man's brethren, tell him where are they;
The red man's homes and altars, what their fate?
Shall he who stands the last, the last to-day,
Forget with his last breath to whisper hate?
Hate, deep and fathomless, and boundless too,
Such as to fiendish cruelty is due.

He cannot bear the white man's presence now,
Or bear to hear his name or see his works;
He thinks that wrong is stamped upon his brow,
That in his good deeds selfish purpose lurks.
Has he a cause for this? — review the past,
And see those acts which prompt hate to the last.

Sons of the Pilgrims, who to-day do boast
Of Freedom's favors, ye whose wealth doth lie
From the Atlantic to the Pacific coast!
Let not the race you have supplanted die;
Perish like forest-leaves from off their lands,
Without a just requital at your hands.

O, give them homes which they can call their own,
Let Knowledge light its torch and lead the way;
And meek Religion, from the eternal throne,
Be there to usher in a better day;
Then shall the past be blotted from life's scroll,
And all the good ye may do crown the whole.

SUNLIGHT ON THE SOUL.

O, THAT some spirit form would come,
From the fair realms of heaven above,
And take my outstretched hand in hers,
To bathe me in angelic love!
O that these longing, peering eyes,
Might pierce the shadowy curtain's fold,

And see in radiant robes arrayed,
  The friends whose memory I do hold
Close, close within my soul's deep cell!
O, that were well! O, that were well!

I 've often thought, at midnight's hour,
  That round my couch I could discern
A shadowy being, from whose eye
  I could not, ah! I would not turn.
It seemed so sisterly to me,
  So radiant with looks of love,
That ever since I 've strove to be
  More like the angel hosts above.
The hopes, the joys were like a spell,
And it was well! Yes, it was well!

And every hour of day and night
  I feel an influence o'er me steal,
So soothing, pure, so holy, bright,
  I would each human heart could feel
A fraction of the mighty tide
  Of living joy it sends along.
Then why should I complain, and ask
  Why none of heaven's angelic throng
Come to this earth with me to dwell,
For all is well, — all, all is well!

A SONG FROM THE ABSENT.

TO THE LOVED ONE AT HOME.

Away from home, how slow the hours
  Pass wearily along!
I feel alone, though many forms
  Around my pathway throng.

There 's none that look on me in love,
  Wherever I do roam;
I 'm longing for thy gentle smile,
  My dearest one, at home.

I walk around; strange things I see,
  Much that is fair to view;
Man's art and Nature's handiwork,
  And all to me is new.
But, ah! I feel my joy were more,
  If, while 'mid these I roam,
It could be shared with thee I love,
  My dearest one, at home.

Blow, blow ye winds, and bear me on
  My long and arduous way!
Move on, slow hours, more swiftly move,
  And bring to life the day
When, journey done, and absence o'er,
  No more I distant roam;
When I again shall be with thee,
  My dearest one, at home.

TWILIGHT FOREST HYMN.

THE HOUR OF PARTING.

Friends who here have met to-day,
Let us sing our parting lay,
Ere we hence do pass away,
  Ere the sun doth set.
As we 've trod this grassy earth,
Friendships new have had their birth,
And this day of festive mirth
  We shall ne'er forget.

Rock, and hill, and shading tree,
Streamlet dancing to the sea,
Gladly though we 'd stay with thee,
  We must leave you all ;
On the tree and on the flower
Comes the evening's twilight hour,
And upon each forest bower
  Evening's shadows fall.

Part we now, but through our life,
Hush of peace or jar of strife,
Memory will still be rife
  With glad thoughts of thee ;
Wheresoe'er our feet may stray,
Memory will retain this day ;
Fare thee well — we haste away,
  Farewell rock and tree !

THE SUMMER SHOWER.

Up from the lake a mist ascends,
  And forms a sea of cloud above,
  That hangs o'er earth as if in love
With its green vales ; then quick it sends
  Its blessings down in cooling rain,
  On hill and valley, rock and plain.
Nature, delighted with the shower,
Sends up the fragrance of each flower ;
  Birds carol forth their cheeriest lays,
  The green leaves rustle forth their praise.
Soon, one by one, the clouds depart,
  And a bright rainbow spans the sky,
That seems but the reflective part
  Of all below, fixed there on high.

AUTOBIOGRAPHY OF AN AUTOMATON.

EARLY one bright summer morning, as I was perambulating beneath those noble trees that stand the body-guard of one of the most beautiful places of which city life can boast, — Boston Common, — I encountered a man who attracted my special attention by his apparent carelessness of action, and humble bearing. He looked dejected likewise, and I seated myself on the stone seat beside him.

He took me by the sleeve of my coat, and whispered in my ear, " I 'm an Automaton, sir." A few more words passed between us, after which, at my request, he gave me a sketch of his life, which I propose to give you in language as nearly his own as possible.

" I was born. I came into this world without any consent of my own, sir, and as soon as I breathed the atmosphere of this mundane state I was bandaged and pinned, and felt very much as a mummy might be supposed to feel. I was then tossed from Matilda to Jerusha, and from Jerusha to Jane, and from Jane to others and others. I tried to laugh, but found I could n't; so I tried to cry, and succeeded most admirably in my effort.

" 'He 's sick,' said my aunt; and my aunt called a doctor, who, wise man, called for a slip of paper and an errand-boy.

" The next I knew, my head was being held by my aunt, and the doctor was pouring down my throat, which he distended with the handle of a spoon, a bitter potion; pouring it down without any consent of my own, sir.

"Whether I got better or worse I don't know; but I slept for a time, and had a strange dream, of a strange existence, upon which I seemed to have suddenly entered.

"The subsequent year was one in which I figured not largely, but considerably. I made a noise in the world, and was flattered so much by my mother's acquaintances that my nose has been what is vulgarly called 'a pug,' ever since. I did n't have my own way at all, except when I screamed. In that I was not an Automaton. I was myself in that particular; and the more restraint they put upon me, the more freedom I had. I cried independently of all my aunts and cousins. They could n't dictate me in that.

"Years passed on, and I grew older, as a matter of course. I grew without any consent of my own, sir, and found myself in jacket and trousers ditto. I was sent to school, and was told to study Greek and Latin, and Algebra, and Pneumatics, and Hydrostatics, and a dozen or twenty other things, the very names of which I have forgotten, but which I well remember bothered me considerably in those days. I had much rather have studied the laws of my own being; much rather have examined and become acquainted with the architecture of my own bodily frame; much rather have studied something more intimately connected with the realities of my own existence; but they made me study what was repulsive to my own mind, and speak big words which I did n't understand, and which my teacher could n't explain without the aid of a dictionary.

"My parents labored under the strange delusion that I was a wonderful child. I don't know why, unless it was because I did n't know anything of life, and I could repeat a little Latin, stumble through a sentence of Greek, and, after having solved a problem seventy-six thousand times to show my wonderful precociousness, could do it again when called upon. Perhaps I 'm extravagant. It was n't more than half that number of times. At any rate, sir, I was thought a prodigy — a most astonishing intellectual — I don't know what,— call it mushroom,— because what I had done so many times I could do again.

"I recollect there was a little youngster of my acquaintance,— a charming, flaxen-haired, blue-eyed boy,— who told me, one day, that he did n't care for the *dead* languages, he had rather know the live ones. I thought so too, and we talked a long time, down behind old Turner's barn, about what should be and what should n't. But I had to go home. I had to be pulled about, this arm with this wire, and that foot with that wire. I had to do this and that, to study this and study that, because — why, because I was an Automaton, sir. I was born such. 'T was in my bones to be an Automaton.

"My school-days passed, and the minister told my father that if he was him he 'd send me to college. He — my father — did n't sleep any, that night. He and my mother kept awake till daylight prognosticating my career, and fixing upon a day when I should go to Cambridge.

"That day came. I remember it was a cloudy day. There was a dull shadow over everything. Yes, even over my heart. I did n't want to go to college. I knew I had n't been allowed to learn anything I wanted to learn out of it; and I knew I should n't do any better shut up within its old dingy, musty, brick walls. I knew I should n't learn anything there. I had rather be out in the world. I had rather be studying in Nature's great college. I had rather graduate with a diploma from God, written on my heart, than to waste years of life away from the great school of human life; to be told by another how *I* should go, what *I* should believe, and how *I* should act, in the great drama of life. But I had to go, sir,— go to college; for I was an Automaton.

"As I before said, the day was cloudy. Mother dressed

me up. For a week preparations had been making for my exit, and finally I went. I was put in a stage where three men were smoking. I objected, and intimated that it would be much better if those who smoked rode on the outside; but my father said, 'hush,' and told me that smoking was common at college, and I must get used to it. When the stage stopped to change horses, the men got out, and swore, and drank brandy; and I asked whether such things were common at college, and whether I had got to get used to them too. But I could n't get any answer.

"The wind blew cold, but my coat was made so small that I could n't button it together. *I* would have had it loose and easy, and warm and comfortable; but 't was n't fashionable to have it so. Father followed fashion, and I suffered from the cold. I had a nice, soft cap, that I used to wear to church at home; but father thought that, as I was going to the city, I must have a hat; so he had bought me one, and the hard, stiff, ungainly thing was stuck on my head. I had as lieves have had a piece of stove-pipe there. It made my head ache awfully.

"If I had n't been what I was, I should have worn a nice, easy pair of shoes; but I *was* an Automaton. I was n't anybody; so I was made to wear a pair of thin boots, that clung to my feet a great deal closer than my skin did,— a great deal, sir.

"Well, we reached Cambridge. It 's a pretty place, you know; and I rather liked it until I arrived at the college buildings. Then I did n't like the looks of anything, except the green trees, and the grass, and the shady walks. And I wondered where I could learn the most useful knowledge, within or without the college.

"I was ushered in, and my college life began. To narrate to you all that made up that life, would be irksome to me and tedious to you. I was taught much that I did n't believe then, and don't believe now, and don't think I ever shall. I was made to subscribe to certain forms, and with my lips to adopt certain views, which my heart all the time rebelled against, and reason told me were false. But I said I believed, and I did believe after the fashion of the times; for I believe it 's fashionable to believe what you don't know anything about, and the more of this belief you have the better you are. So I believed what my teachers told me, because — why, because I was an Automaton.

"When I returned home, I found myself, quite unexpectedly, a lion. All the neighbors flocked in to see the young man who 'd been to college, and in the evening a dozen young ladies — marriageable young ladies — called on me. I tried to have a pleasant time; and should have had, if I had n't been pulled and pushed, and made a puppet-show of; made to go through all my college exercises, to please the pride of my immediate relatives, and minister to the wonder-loving souls of their friends. But, though I did n't want to do all this, though I had much preferred to have sat down and had a quiet talk with one or two,— talked over all that had taken place during my absence, our lives and loves,— yet I was obliged to, sir. I was an Automaton.

"One day,—it was but a week after I had returned,— my father took me into his room, and said he had something to say to me. I knew very well, before he said so, that something out of the usual course was to take place; for, all the morning, he had been as serious and reserved as a deacon at a funeral, and I had caught him holding sly talks with my mother in out-of-the-way places.— I knew something was to happen.

"I sat down, and he did. And then he went on to say that I had probably had some thoughts of marriage. I merely responded, 'Some.'

"He then remarked that every young man should calculate

to get a wife and settle down; and that 'old folks' had had experience, and knew a vast deal more about such things than young folks did; and that the latter, when they followed the advice of the former, always were well-to-do in the world, always were respected.

"I began to see what he was driving at. I looked very serious at him, and he a great deal more so at me.

"He talked to me half an hour; it was the longest half-hour I had known since I first measured time. He expatiated on the wisdom of old people; told me I was inexperienced. *I*, who had been to college! *I*, who had lived a city life! *I* was inexperienced! But I let him go on — I could n't help it — you know what I was.

"He then drew his chair closer mine, lowered the tone of his voice, and said,

"'I 've picked out a wife for you. It 's Squire Parsons' daughter, Susan Jane Maria. She 'll be an excellent wife to you, and mother to your children.'

"If I had been anything else than what I was, I should have sprang up and declared my own ability to choose a wife for me and 'a mother for my children;' but I did n't do any such thing. I nodded a calm assent to all he said; for you know, sir, I was an Automaton.

"I was to go with my father, that night, and see Susan,— she that was to be *my* Susan,— O, no, not so; *I* was to be her Jacob. So, when tea was over, and I had been 'fixed up,'— I *was* fixed, I tell you,— father led the way over Higginses' rough pasture. *I* should have gone round, in the road, where it was decent walking, if I had been anybody; but I was n't any one; I was a — well, you know what. I got one of my boots full of water, and father fell down and bruised his nose; but I took off my boot and poured the water out, and he put a piece of court-plaster on his nose,—

a great black piece,—and we did n't look as bad as we might, so he said; and so I said, 'of course.'

"Susan was at home, seated in the middle of a great room, as if on exhibition; and perhaps she was,—I thought so. I had seen Susan before, and always disliked her. There was nothing in her personal appearance, or her mind, that pleased me. I never met her without marking her future life as that of an old maid. But she was to be *my* wife; father said so, mother shouted amen; and I was to love her, and so I said I did, 'of course.'

"It seemed to me that she knew all about what I came for; for she put out her little slim hand, that never made a loaf of bread nor held a needle, but had only fingered the leaves of Greek and Latin Lexicons, and volumes of Zoology and Ornithology, and thrummed piano-keys,—all very well in their place (don't think I depreciate them), but very bad when their place is so large that there 's no room for anything else,—very bad, sir.

"As she took my hand she attempted to kiss me; but, being rather shy, I dodged when I saw her lips a-coming, and they went plump on to father's nose, and exploded on his piece of court-plaster.

"It was all fixed that night, and I was to be married one week from the ensuing Sunday.

"We went home. I received a smile from those who were so considerate as to hunt me up a wife.

"If you 'd seen the *Greentown Gazette* a fortnight after, and had looked at the list of marriages, you might have read, '*Married:* In this town, by Rev. Ebenezer Pilgrade, Mr. Jacob Jenkins, Jr. (recently from college), to Susan Jane Maria Parsons, estimable daughter of Nehemiah Q. Parsons; all of this place.'

"We lived at home. My wife soon found out what I was, found out that I was an Automaton, and she pulled the wires and put me in motion, in any way she wished. I opened an office, put out a sign, and for a time practised law and physic, and when the minister was sick took his place and preached. I preached just what they wanted me to. I felt more like an Automaton than ever, stuck up in a high box, talking just what had been talked a thousand times from the same place. It would n't do, I was told, to have any ideas of my own; and, if had them, I must n't speak them. So my parish and me got along pretty well.

"Of course I had joined the church. I was told that I must, and so I did; but I won't tell you what my thoughts were in regard to what I was told to believe, for that 's delicate ground. I don't know what your religion is, sir, and I might offend you, and I would n't do so for the world. You see I am an Automaton yet. I 'll do just as you want me to. I hate to be so; but, somehow or other, I can't be otherwise. It 's my nature.

"You think I 'm prosy. I won't say much more, for I see you take out your watch as though you wished I 'd stop, that you might go; so I 'll close with 'finally,' as I do in preaching.

"Well, then, finally, father died, mother died, Susan run off, and I 've become almost discouraged. I have three children to take care of, but they are good children. They do just precisely as I tell them, and won't do anything without asking me whether it 's right; and I ask somebody else. They have n't got any minds of their own, any more than I have. They 'll do just as I tell them. I 've nobody in particular now to tell *me* what I shall do; so I take everybody's advice, and try to do as everybody wants me to do. I 've come to Boston on a visit, and shall go back to-night, if you think best.

"Now I 've given you my autobiography. You can do just what you want to with it,—print it, if you like. People, perhaps, will laugh at me when they read it; but perhaps there are other Automatons besides me."

He came to a full stop here; and, as it was getting late, I arose, wished him well, bade him good-by, and left. I had proceeded but a few steps, when I felt a touch on my shoulder, and, turning, found it was the Automaton, who had come to ask me whether I thought he had better go home that night.

TO THE UNKNOWN DONOR OF A BOUQUET.

Richest flowers of every hue,
Lightly fringed with evening dew;
Sparkling as from Eden's bowers,
Brightly tinted — beauteous flowers!
Thee I 've found, and thee I 'll own,
Though from one to me unknown;
Knowing *this*, that one who 'll send
Such a treasure is my friend.

Who hath sent thee? — Flora knows,
For with care she reared the rose.
Lo! here 's a name! — it is the key
That will unlock the mystery;
This will tell from whom and why
Thou didst to my presence hie.
Wait — the hand 's disguised! — it will
Remain to me a mystery still.

But I 'm a "Yankee," and can "guess"
Who wove this flowery, fairy tress.
Yea, more than this, I *almost know*
Who tied this pretty silken bow,
Whose hand arranged them, and whose taste
Each in such graceful order placed.
Yet, if unknown thou 'dst rather be,
Let me wish this wish for thee:

May'st thou live in joy forever,
Naught from thee true pleasure sever;
From thy heart arise no sigh;
May no tear bedew thine eye.

Joys be many, cares be few,
Smooth the path thou shalt pursue;
And heaven's richest blessings shine
Ever on both thee and thine.

Round thy path may fairest flowers,
As in amaranthine bowers,
Bloom and blossom bright and fair,
Load with sweets the ambient air!
Be thy path with roses strewn,
All thy hours to care unknown;
Sorrow cloud thy pathway never,
Happiness be thine forever.

TO A SISTER IN HEAVEN.

Sister, in thy spirit home,
  Knowest thou my path below?
Knowest thou the steps I roam,
  And the devious road I go?
Many years have past since I
  Bade thee here a sad farewell;
Many past since thou didst die,
  Since I heard thy funeral knell.

Thou didst go when thou wast young;
  Scarcely hadst thou oped thine eyes
To the world, and it had flung
  Its bright sunshine from the skies,
Ere thy Maker called for thee,
  Thou obeyed his high behest;
Then I mourned, yet knew thou 'dst be
  Throned on high among the blest.

Gently thou didst fold thy wing,
  Gently thou didst sink in sleep;
Birds their evening songs did sing,
  And the evening shades did creep

Through the casement, one by one,
  Telling of departing day;
Then, thou and the glorious sun
  Didst together pass away.

Yet that sun hath rose since then,
  And hath brought a joy to me;
Emblem 't is time will be when
  Once again I shall see thee, —
See thee in immortal bloom,
  Numbered with the ransomed throng,
Where no sorrow sheds its gloom
  O'er the heart, or chills the song.

Spirit sister, throned on high,
  Now methinks I hear thee speak
From thy home within the sky,
  In its accents low and meek.
Thou art saying, "Banish sadness;
  God is love, — O, trust him ever!
Heaven is filled with joy and gladness —
  It shall be thy home forever."

This thou sayest, and thy voice,
  Like to none of earth I 've heard,
Bids my fainting soul rejoice;
  Follow God's revealéd word,
Follow that, 't is faithful true;
  'Mid the trackless maze of this,
It will guide the pilgrim through
  To a world of endless bliss.

Sister, in thy spirit home,
  Thou dost know my path below,
Thou dost know the steps I roam,
  And the road I fain would go.
If my steps would err from right,
  If I 'd listen to the wrong,
If I 'd close my eyes to light,
  Mingle with earth's careless throng:

Then wilt thou with power be nigh;
  Power which angel spirits wield,
That temptation may pass by,
  Be thou near my soul to shield!
As I close this simple lay,
  As I over it do bow,
Sister, thou art round my way,
  Thou art standing near me now.

I DREAMED OF THEE, LAST NIGHT, LOVE!

I DREAMED of thee last night, love,
  And I thought that one came down
From scenes of azure light, love,
  The most beautiful to crown.

He wandered forth where diamonds
  And jewels rich and rare
Shone brightly 'mid the glittering throng,
  Yet crownéd no one there.

He passéd by all others,
  Till he came to where thou stood;
And chose *thee* as the beautiful,
  Because thou wast so good.

And said, as there he crowned thee,
  That Goodness did excel
The jewels all around thee
  In which beauty seemed to dwell.

For Goodness is that beauty
  Which will forever last;
Then, crowning thee most beautiful,
  From earth to heaven he passed.

THEY TELL OF HAPPY BOWERS.

They tell of happy bowers,
Where rainbow-tinted flowers
Bloom bright with sweetest fragrance, and never, never die;
Where friends are joined forever,
Where parting hours come never,
And that that happier land is far beyond the sky; —

That when this life is ended
The spirit there ascended
Shall meet in happy unison the spirits gone before;
And all that here hath vexed us,
With seeming ill perplexed us,
We shall see was for the best, and God of all adore.

Then, brother, hope and cheer thee,
For glorious hours are near thee,
If thou but livest holy, and hope, and trust, and wait;
Soon, trials all departed,
Thou, heavenward, homeward started,
Shalt find a glorious entrance at heaven's golden gate.

MAN CANNOT LIVE AND LOVE NOT.

Man cannot live and love not;
Around, beneath, above,
There is that 's bright and beautiful,
And worthy of his love;
There is in every object
That works out nature's plan,
Howe'er so low and humble,
That 's worth the love of man.

Each blade of grass that springeth
From earth to beauty fair;
Each tiny bird that wingeth
Its course through trackless air;

Each worm that crawls beneath thee,
  Each creature, great and small,
Is worthy of thy loving;
  For God hath made them all.

Should earthly friends forsake thee,
  And earth to thee look drear;
Should morning's dark forebodings
  But fill thy soul with fear,
Look up! and cheer thy spirit—
  Up to thy God above;
He 'll be thy friend forever—
  Forever!—"God is Love!"

BETTER THAN GOLD.

"Find we Lorenzo wiser for his wealth?
What if thy rental I inform, and draw
An inventory new to set thee right?
Where is thy treasure? Gold says, 'Not in me!'
And not in me, the diamond. Gold is poor,
Indies insolvent——. Seek it in thyself,
Seek in thy naked self, and find it there."

GOLD is, in itself, harmless — brilliant, beautiful to look upon; but, when man entertains an ungovernable, all-absorbing love of it, gold is his curse and a mill-stone around his neck, drawing him down to earth. How much sorrow that love has caused! O, there is love that is angelic! But high and holy as love is when bestowed upon a worthy object, in like proportion is it base and ignoble when fixed upon that which is unworthy.

It may well be questioned whether, taking a broad view of the matter, gold has not produced more evil than good. Point out, if you can, one crime, be it the most heinous and inhuman of which you can possibly conceive, that has not been perpetrated for the sake of gold, or has not its equal in the history of the battle for wealth. We can conceive of no worse a thing than a human soul idolizing a mass of shining metal, and counting out, with lean and tremulous hands, the coined dollars. Late and early the devotee bows at the shrine. No motive can induce him to remove his fixed gaze from the god he worships. No act too base for him to execute if gold holds out its glittering purse. No tears of widows, no orphan's cry, no brother's famishing look, no parent's imploring gaze, no wife's loving appeal, doth he heed; but on, and on, day by day, night by night, he rakes together the scattered fragments, rears his altar, and lays his soul upon it, a burnt sacrifice to *his* God.

It was the first day of the trial, and the excitement was intense. The court-house was filled at an early hour to its utmost capacity, whilst the lanes leading to it were completely blocked up with crowds of inquisitive inquirers. The professor left his study, the trader his accounts, and the mechanic dismissed for a while the toil of his avocation.

The judges had arrived; the counsel of both parties were at their respective desks; all were eager to get a full sight — if not this, a passing glance — at the prisoner's face. They were looking for his arrival, and if a close carriage drew near, they believed he was within, until the carriage passing by withered all their hopes, and blasted their fond expectations. Such was the state of feeling when a rumor began to pass round that he, the prisoner, had been privately conveyed into court. Some believed, and some disbelieved; some went away, whilst others remained, not giving up all hope of having their desire gratified. — But why all this ?

Pedro Castello, a young man, an Italian by birth, had been indicted, and was soon to be tried, charged with two heinous crimes — murder and robbery. The murdered was an aged person, one of a very quiet and sedate character, whose every movement seemed to be by stealth, and who seemed to care for none but himself, but who took particular interest in what he did care for. This individual had, for quite a number of years, been a resident in the town where the incidents we now propose to relate transpired.

Lorenzo Pedan had the reputation of being wealthy. Whether he was so or not, no one could positively determine; at least, many thought so, and here a farmer, there a mechanic, offered to bet all that he was worth that "Renzo," as he was called, could show his fifty thousand. It was well known that he was once in prosperous business; that then, as the saying is, he moved on "swimmingly." But, two or three years previous to the time we now speak of, he suddenly gave up business, closed his store, hired a small and retired house, and lived in as secluded a state as living in the world and not in a forest would admit of. He was his own master, his own servant, cook and all else. Visitors seldom if ever darkened his door; and, when necessity obliged him to leave his house, it was with the utmost precaution he made fast his door before starting. Proceeding a short distance, he became possessed with the idea that all was not right, and would return to his dwelling closely to scrutinize every part. This and many other characteristics of Pedan induced a belief in the minds of his townsmen that he had by degrees become possessed of an avaricious disposition, and that his miserly views of the "whole duty of man" had induced him to secrete huge boxes of silver, and bags of gold in crevices of his cellar, vacancies in his chimney, and musty and dusty corners of his garret.

Various were the tricks played upon Lorenzo by the boys of the town. At times they would place logs of wood against his door, and arrange them in such a position that when the door was opened they would inevitably fall in; yet he did not care for this,— we mean he found no fault with this trick, for he usually claimed the fuel for damages occasioned by its coming in too close proximity with his aged self.

Sometimes these "villanous boys," as widow Todd, a notorious disseminator of town scandal, called them, would fasten his door; then, having hid behind some bushes, laugh heartily as they beheld Mr. Pedan exhibit himself at the window, at which place he got out. We will not attempt to relate one half or one quarter of these tricks; we will say nothing of sundry cats, kittens, etc., that were crowded into boxes and marked "Pedro — this side up with infinite care;" nor about certain black, white, and yellow dogs, that were tied to all his door-handles, and made night hideous in the exercise of their vocal powers. We will not weary our readers with such details. Suffice it to say that they were all perpetrated, and that he, the aforesaid Lorenzo Pedan, received the indignities heaped upon him with a degree of patience and fortitude rivalled only by that of the martyrs of the dark ages. He was, in fact, a martyr to his love of gold; and a recompense for all his outward troubles was the satisfaction of knowing that he might be rich some time, if he was prudent.

Lorenzo was undoubtedly rich, yet he derived no enjoyment from his abundance; on the contrary, it caused him much trouble, care, and watchfulness; and not possessing any benevolent feelings, prompting him to spend his gold and silver for his own good or the good of his fellow-men, the poorest man, with all his poverty, — he who only by his daily toil earned his daily bread,— was far more wealthy than he.

He passed on in this way for some time, when, on a certain morning, he not having made his appearance for some days previous, his door was burst open, and the expectations of not a few realized upon finding him murdered. All the furniture and even the wainscotings of the house were thrown about in dread disorder; scarcely an article seemed to be in its right place. The robber or robbers were undoubtedly on the alert for money, and they left no spot untouched where possibly they might find it. They pulled up parts of the floor, tore away the ceiling, and left marks of their visit from cellar to garret.

Immediate efforts were made and measures taken to ferret out the perpetrator of this daring crime. These were, for a considerable length of time, fruitless, and, the excitement that at first arose being somewhat quelled, some thought the search that had been instituted was given, or about to be given, up, when a man by the name of Smith came forward, and stated that, about nine days previous to the discovery, as he was passing the house of the deceased, he heard a faint cry, as of one in distress, and, turning round, noticed a young man running in great haste. He, at the time, thought little of this incident, as he supposed the boys were engaged in some of their tricks. It had entirely passed his recollection, until, hearing of the murder, he instantly recollected the circumstance, and now he did not entertain a doubt that the young man whom he saw was the murderer.

It appeared strange to some that this man had not made all this known before; and that now, at so late a period, he should come forward and with such apparent eagerness make the disclosures. Being asked why he had not come forward before, he promptly replied that he did not wish to suspect any person, for fear he might be mistaken.

Efforts were now made, and excitement had again risen, to find out a young man answering the description given by Smith, whom he alleged to be one short in stature, and wearing a fur cap. Pedro Castello, by birth an Italian, by trade a jeweller, who had resided in the town a few years, was of this description. He was not very tall, neither very short; but the fur cap he wore made up all deficiencies in stature. Smith swore to his identity, and, at his instigation, he was arrested, and with great coolness and self-possession passed through a short examination, which resulted in his being placed in custody to await his trial at the next session of a higher court. The only evidence against him was that of Smith and his son; that of the former was in substance what has already been stated, and that of the latter only served to support and partially confirm the evidence of the former. A host of townsmen appeared to attest to the good character of the accused; and, with such evidence for and against, he was committed.

Never was man led to prison who behaved with a greater degree of composure. Conscious of his innocence, he acted not the part of a guilty man, but, relying upon justice for an impartial trial, he walked with a firm step, and unflinchingly entered a felon's cell.

In two months his trial was to commence, and that short period soon elapsed. The morning of the trial came; all was excitement, as we have before said. A trial for murder! Such an event forms an era in the history of a town, from which many date. That one so long esteemed as an excellent neighbor, and of whose untarnished character there could be no doubt, should be suddenly arrested, charged with the committal of a crime at the thought of which human nature revolts, was a fact the belief of which was hardly credible. He himself remained not unmoved by the vast concourse of spectators; he thought he could read in the pitying glance of each an acquittal. An acquittal at the bar of public opinion always has and always will be esteemed of more value than one handed in by a jury of twelve; yet by that jury of twelve men he was to be tried,—he must look to them for his release, if he was to obtain it. Their decision would condemn him to an ignoble death, or bid him go forth once more a free man. He had obtained the best of counsel, by whose advice he selected, from twenty-five jurors, twelve, whose verdict was to seal his fate.

The trial commenced. A deep silence prevailed, broken only by the voice of the government officer, who briefly stated an outline of the facts, to wit: "That murder and robbery had been committed; that a young man was seen hastily leaving the spot upon which the crime was committed; that the appearance of the defendant was precisely that of the person thus seen; said he should not enter into an examination of the previous character of the prisoner, giving as a reason that a man may live long as a person of unquestionable character, and after all yield to some strong temptation and fall from the standard of excellence he had hitherto attained; he should present all the facts that had come to his knowledge, tending to substantiate the charge, and would leave it to the prisoner and his counsel to undermine the evidence he presented, and to prove the accused innocent, if possible; all that he should do would be to attempt to prove him guilty; if he failed to do so a verdict must be rendered accordingly." Having said this, he called upon his witnesses. Those who first discovered the outrage were called and testified to what they saw. John Smith was next called, and gave in as evidence what has before been stated; at the close of a strict cross-examination he returned to his seat. His son Levi was next called, and stated that his father was out the night he himself stated he was; he went out about half-past six or seven; did not say where he was going, or how long he should be out; he came home about eleven.

Prisoner's counsel here inquired whether it was usual, upon his father's going out, to state where he was going or when he should return. He answered in the affirmative. This was all the knowledge Levi Smith had of the affair, and with this the evidence for the government closed.

The counsel for the defendant stated, in the opening, that all he should attempt to prove would be the bad character of the principal witness, John Smith, and the unexceptionable character of the prisoner. He would prove that the reputation of Smith for truth and veracity was bad, and that therefore no reliance could be placed upon his statements. He should present the facts as they were, and leave it to them to say whether his client was innocent or guilty.

A person by the name of Renza was first called, who

stated that for about two years he had resided in the house with the prisoner; that he esteemed him as a friend; that the prisoner had treated him as a brother,—had never seen anything amiss in his conduct,—at night he came directly home from his place of business, was generally in at nine, seldom out later than ten,—remembered the night in question,—thought he was in about ten, but was not certain on that point,—had been acquainted with John Smith for a number of years,—had not said much to him during that time,—had often seen him walking about the streets,—had known him to be quarrelsome and avaricious, easily provoked, and rather lacking in good principle. After a few cross-questions the witness took his seat.

Seven others were called, whose testimony was similar to the above, placing the evidence of the principal government witness in rather a disagreeable light. The evidence being in on both sides, the prisoner's counsel stood forth to vindicate the innocence of Castello. For three hours he faithfully advocated the cause, dwelt long upon the reputation of Smith, and asked whether a man should be convicted upon such rotten evidence. He brought to light the character of Smith, and that of Castello; placed them in contrast, and bade them judge for themselves. He wished to inquire why Smith, when he heard the terrible scream, when he saw a person running from the place whence the sound proceeded, why, when he heard and beheld all this, he did not make an alarm; why did Smith keep it a secret, and not till nine days had elapsed make this known? "Perhaps he would reply," argued the counsel, "that he did not wish to suspect any person, fearing the person suspected might be the wrong one; if so, why did he not inform of the person he saw running? If he was not the doer of the deed, perhaps he might relate something that would lead to the detection of him who was. Beside, if he had doubts whether it was right to inform *then*, why does he do so now with so much eagerness? It would be natural for one, after hearing such fearful noises,— after seeing what he testifies to having seen,—to have related it to some one; but no—Smith keeps all this important information treasured up, and not till two weeks had nearly passed does he disclose it. But, gentlemen, I have my doubts as to the truth of John's evidence. It is my firm belief that he never saw a person running from that house; he might have heard the noise—I will not dispute that. I believe his story has been cut and dried for the occasion, and surely nine days and nights have afforded him ample time to do so. The brains of an ox could concoct such ideas in nine days. Now comes the inquiry, why should he invent such a story? Of what benefit can it be to him to appear in a crowded court-room? Gentlemen, I confess myself unable to give you his reasons; to him and to his God they are only known. The veil which, in my opinion, now shrouds this affair, will some day be withdrawn, and we shall *know* the truth, even as it is."

The defence here closed. The officer for the prosecution now arose, and with equal faithfulness and ability argued his side of the question. He thought the reasons why Smith had not before informed were full and explicit; and, as to the testimony of the eight as to the past good character of the prisoner, he saw no reason why a man should be always good because for two or more years he had been so. A great temptation was presented; he was young—perhaps at the moment regardless of the result, the penalty of the crime; he did not resist, but yielded; and as to the argument of the learned counsel, that Mr. S. did not see what he testifies to have seen, it is useless to refute such an unfounded allegation. Can you suppose Smith to be benefited by this prosecution further than to see justice have its dues? Settle it then in your minds that Mr. Smith did actually see all he says he did. We come next to the description given by Smith of the man seen. He said he was short in stature, and wearing a fur cap. Look at the prisoner,— is he not short? — and the testimony of two of the previous witnesses distinctly affirm that for the past six weeks he has worn a fur cap. What more evidence do you want to prove his guilt?

The prosecuting officer here closed. We have given but a faint outline of his remarks; they were forcible and to the point.

It was near the dusk of the second day's trial that the judge arose to charge the jury. He commented rather severely upon the attempt to impeach the character of Smith. His address was not lengthy, and in about thirty minutes the jury retired, while a crowded audience anxiously waited their return. It was not till the rays of the morning sun began to be seen that it was rumored that they had arrived at a decision and would soon enter. All was silent as the tomb. The prisoner, although aware that his life was at stake, sat in great composure, frequently holding converse with his friends who gathered around. How anxiously all eyes were turned towards the door by which they were to enter, wishing, yet dreading, to hear the final secret! The interest of all watched their movements and seemed to read acquittal upon each juror's face. The prisoner arose, the foreman and he looking each other in the face. The clerk put the question, "Guilty, or not guilty?" The ticking of the clock was distinctly heard. "Guilty!" responded the foreman. A verdict so unexpected by all could not be received in silence, and, as with one voice, the multitude shouted "False! *false!* FALSE!" With great difficulty were they silenced and restrained from rescuing the prisoner, who, though greatly disappointed, heard the verdict without much agitation. Innocent, he was convinced that justice would finally triumph, though injustice for a moment might seem to have the ascendency.

One week had passed. Sentence had been pronounced upon the young Italian, and, notwithstanding the strenuous efforts his friends made for his pardon, he was committed to prison to await the arrival of that day when innocence should suffer in the place of guilt, and he should by the rough hands of the law be unjustly dragged to the gallows, and meet his death at so wretched a place; yet far better was it for him, and of this was he aware, to be led to that place free from the blood of all men, than to proceed there a guilty criminal, his hands dyed in the warm blood of a fellow-creature, pointed out as a murderer, and looked upon but with an eye of condemnation. He was certain that in the breasts of hundreds a spark, yea, a burning flame, of pity shone for him,— that he met not his death uncared for,— that many a tear would flow in pity for him, and that he would wend his way to the scaffold comforted by the consciousness of his innocence, and consoled by many dear friends.

* * * * * *

The day had arrived for the execution, and crowds of people flocked to the spot to gratify their love of sight-seeing — to allay their curiosity — even though that sight were nothing less than the death of a fellow-being. Crowds had assembled. A murder had been committed, and now another was to follow. To be sure it was to be executed "according to law," but that law was inspired with the spirit of revenge. Its motto was "blood for blood." It forgot the precepts of Christ, "forgive your enemies;" and that that which is a wrong when committed by one in secret, is no less a wrong when committed by many, or by their sanction, in public. The condemned stood upon the death-plank, yet he hoped justice would be done. "Hope!" what a cheering word! 't will nerve man for every trial. Yes, Castello hoped, and relied upon that kind arm that had hitherto supported him, and had enabled him to bear up under an accumulated mass of affliction. He had a full consciousness of innocence, and to the oft-repeated inquiry as to his state of mind he replied, "I am innocent, and that truth is to me better than gold."

It lacks but five minutes of the appointed time — now but three — but two. But yonder the crowd seem excited. What is the cause of the sudden movement? But a few moments since and all were silently gazing at the centre of attraction, the scaffold. Lo, a messenger, breathless with haste, shouting "INNOCENT! INNOCENT! INNOCENT!" and a passage is made for him to approach, whilst thousands inquire the news. He answers not, save by that shrill shout, "INNOCENT!" and pressing forward touches the gallows just as Castello is about to be launched forth. The stranger ascends the steps and begs that the execution may be deferred, at least until he can relate some recent disclosures. His wish is granted, and he speaks nearly as follows:

"The testimony of the principal witness was doubted. Last night I remained at the house of Smith. Owing to the great excitement I did not retire to rest, and sat in a room adjoining that in which Smith lodged. About midnight I heard a voice in that room. I went to the door, and, fearing he was sick and desired aid, I entered. He was asleep, and did not awake upon my entering, but continued talking. I thought it strange, and thinking I might be amused, and having nothing else to do, I sat and listened. He spoke in somewhat this manner, and you may judge of my surprise while I listened:

"'I'm rich; too bad Pedro should die; but I'm rich; no matter, I'm rich. Kings kill their millions for a little money. I only kill one man; in six months 't will be forgotten; then I'll go to the bank of earth back of the red mill and get the gold; I placed it there safe, and safe it is.

Ha, ha! I made that story in nine days — so I did, and might have made it in less; let him die. But supposing I should be detected; then it may be that I shall find that Pedro is right when he says there is something better than gold. But I am in no danger. The secret is in my own heart, locked up, and no one has the key but myself; so cheer thee, my soul, I'm safe! — and yet I don't feel right. I shall feel, when Pedro dies, that I kill him; but why should I care? I, who have killed one, may kill another!'

"After waiting some time, and hearing no more, I hastened to the spot he had alluded to, for the purpose of satisfying myself whether what he had ramblingly spoken of was truth or fancy. After searching the hill for over an hour, I found a stone, or rather stumbled against it; I threw it aside, so that others might not stumble over it as I had, when to my astonishment I found it to be a large flat one, beneath which I found a collection of bags and boxes, which upon opening I found filled with gold and silver coin, and in each box a small paper,— one of which I hold in my hand; all are alike, and written upon each are these words:

"'This gold and silver is the property of Pedan, who enjoyed it but little himself; he leaves it to posterity, and hopes that they may find more pleasure and more satisfaction in its use than he ever did.'

"Not content with this, I pushed my researches still further, and, having taken out all the bags and boxes, I found this knife, all bloody as you see it, and this hatchet in nearly the same condition. Now I ask if it is not the course of justice to delay the execution of this young man until more examinations can be made?"

The executioner obeyed the mandate of the sheriff, and stayed his avenging hand.

"Better than gold!" shouted the prisoner, and sank helpless upon the platform.

That day John Smith was arrested, and, being bluntly charged with the murder, confessed all. Castello was immediately released, and went forth a free man.

In four weeks Smith was no more of earth; he had paid the penalty of his crimes, and died not only a murderer but a perjured man.

The next Sabbath the pastor of the church discoursed upon the subject, and an indescribable thrill pervaded the hearts of some of the people as they repeated the words, "Forgive us *our* trespasses as *we* forgive those who trespass against us."

GONE AWAY.

HERE, where now are mighty cities,
  Once the Indians' wigwam stood;
Once their council-fires illumined,
  Far and near, the tangled wood.
Here, on many a grass-grown border,
  Then they met, a happy throng;
Rock and hill and valley sounded
  With the music of their song.
Now they are not, — they have vanished,
  And a voice doth seem to say,
Unto him who waits and listens,
  "Gone away, — gone away."

Yonder in those valleys gathered
  Many a sage in days gone by;
Thence the wigwam's smoke ascended,
  Slowly, peacefully, on high.
Indian mothers thus their children
  Taught around the birchen fire, —
"Look ye up to the great Spirit!
  To his hunting-grounds aspire."
Now those fires are all extinguished;
  Fire and wigwam, where are they?
Hear ye not those voices whispering,
  "Gone away, — gone away!"

Here the Indian girl her tresses
  Braided with a maiden's pride;
Here the lover wooed and won her,
  On Tri-mountain's grassy side.
Here they roamed from rock to river,
  Mountain peak and hidden cave;

Here the light canoe they paddled
  O'er the undulating wave.
All have vanished ; — lovers, maidens,
  Meet not on these hills to-day,
But unnumbered voices whisper,
  " Gone away, — gone away ! "

" Gone away ! " Yes, where the waters
  Of the Mississippi roll,
And Niagara's ceaseless thunders
  With their might subdue the soul,
Now the noble Indian standeth
  Gazing at the eagle's flight,
Conscious that the great good Spirit
  Will accomplish all things right.
Though like forest-leaves they 're passing,
  They who once held boundless sway,
And of them 't will soon be written,
  " Gone away, — gone away ! "

As they stand upon the mountain,
  And behold the white man press
Onward, onward, never ceasing,
  Mighty in his earnestness ;
As they view his temples rising,
  And his white sails dot the seas,
And his myriad thousands gathering,
  Hewing down the forest trees ;
Thus they muse : " Let them press onward,
  Not far distant is the day
When of *them* a voice shall whisper,
  ' Gone away, — gone away ! ' "

LINES TO MY WIFE.

Thou art ever standing near me,
  In wakeful hours and dreams ;
Like an angel-one, attendant
  On life and all its themes ;

And though I wander from thee,
In lands afar away,
I dream of thee at night, and wake
To think of thee by day.

In the morning, when the twilight,
Like a spirit kind and true,
Comes with its gentle influence,
It whispereth of you.
For I know that thou art present,
With love that seems to be
A band to bind me willingly
To heaven and to thee.

At noon-day, when the tumult and
The din of life is heard,
When in life's battle each heart is
With various passions stirred,
I turn me from the blazonry,
The fickleness of life,
And think of thee in earnest thought,
My dearest one — my wife!

When the daylight hath departed,
And shadows of the night
Bring forth the stars, as beacons fair
For angels in their flight,
I think of thee as ever mine,
Of thee as ever best,
And turn my heart unto thine own,
To seek its wonted rest.

Thus ever thou art round my path,
And doubly dear thou art
When, with my lips pressed to thine own,
I feel thy beating heart.
And through the many joys and griefs,
The lights and shades of life,
It will be joy to call thee by
The holy name of "wife!"

20

I love thee for thy gentleness,
  I love thee for thy truth;
I love thee for thy joyousness,
  Thy buoyancy of youth
I love thee for thy soul that soars
  Above earth's sordid pelf;
And last, not least, above these all,
  I love thee for thyself.

Now come to me, my dearest,
  Place thy hand in mine own;
Look in mine eyes, and see how deep
  My love for thee hath grown;
And I will press thee to my heart,
  Will call thee "my dear wife,"
And own that thou art all my joy
  And happiness of life.

CHEER UP.

Cheer up, cheer up, my own fair one!
  Let gladness take the place of sorrow;
Clouds shall not longer hide the sun, —
  There is, there *is* a brighter morrow!

'T is coming fast. I see its dawn.
  See! look you, how it gilds the mountain!
We soon shall mark its happy morn,
  Sending its light o'er stream and fountain.

My bird sings with a clearer note;
  He seems to know *our* hopes are brighter,
And almost tires his little throat
  To let us know *his* heart beats lighter.

I wonder if he knows how dark
  The clouds were when they gathered o'er us!

No matter,— gayly as a lark
He sings that bright paths are before us.

So cheer thee up, my brightest, best!
For clear 's the sky, and fair 's the weather.
Since hand in hand we 've past the test,
Hence heart in heart we 'll love together.

TRUST THOU IN GOD.

Trust thou in God! he 'll guide thee
When arms of flesh shall fail;
With every good provide thee,
And make his grace prevail.
Where danger most is found,
There he his power discloseth;
And 'neath his arm,
Free from all harm,
The trusting soul reposeth.

Trust thou in God, though sorrow
Thine earthly hopes destroy;
To him belongs the morrow,
And he will send thee joy.
When sorrows gather near,
Then he 'll delight to bless thee!
When all is joy,
Without alloy,
Thine earthly friends caress thee.

Trust thou in God! he reigneth
The Lord of lords on high;
His justice he maintaineth
In his unclouded sky.
To triumph Wrong may seem,

The day, yet justice winneth,
And from the earth
Shall songs of mirth
Rise, when its sway beginneth.

When friends grow faint and weary,
When thorns are on thy way,
When life to thee is dreary,
When clouded is thy day,
Then put thy trust in God,
Hope on, and hoping ever;
Give him thy heart,
Nor seek to part
The love which none can sever!

THE MINISTRATION OF SORROW.

There 's sorrow in thy heart to-day,
There 's sadness on thy brow;
For she, the loved, hath passed away,
And thou art mourning now.
The eye that once did sparkle bright,
The hand that pressed thine own,
No more shall gladden on thy sight, —
Thy cherished one hath flown.

And thou didst love her well, 't is true;
Now thou canst love her more,
Since she hath left this world, and you,
On angel wings to soar
Above the world, its ceaseless strife,
Its turmoil and its care,
To enter on eternal life,
And reign in glory there.

O, let this thought now cheer thy soul,
And bid thy tears depart;

A few more days their course shall roll,
  Thou 'lt meet, no more to part.
No more upon thine ear shall fall,
  The saddening word " farewell ·"
No more a parting hour, but all
  In perfect union dwell.

This world is not the home of man ;
  Death palsies with its gloom,
Marks out his life-course but a span,
  And points him to the tomb ;
But, thanks to Heaven, 't is but the gate
  By which we enter bliss ;
Since such a life our spirits wait,
  O, cheer thy soul in this,—

And let the sorrow that doth press
  Thy spirit down to-day
So minister that it may bless
  Thee on thy pilgrim way ;
And as thy friends shall, one by one,
  Leave earth above to dwell,
Say thou to God, " Thy will be done,
  Thou doest all things well."

GIVING PUBLICITY TO BUSINESS.

From the earliest ages of society some means have been resorted to whereby to give publicity to business which would otherwise remain in comparative privacy. The earliest of modes adopted was the crying of names in the streets; and before the invention of printing men were employed to traverse the most frequented thoroughfares, to stand in the market-places and other spots of resort, and, with loud voices, proclaim their message to the people. This mode is not altogether out of use at the present time; yet it is not generally considered a desirable one, inasmuch as it does not accomplish its purpose so readily or completely as any one of the numerous other methods resorted to.

Since the invention of printing, handbills, posters, and newspapers, have been the principal channels of communication between the inside of the dealer's shop and the eye of the purchaser, and from that to the inside of his purse. So advantageous have these modes been found, that it is a rare thing to find a single individual who does not, either on a large or small scale, rein the press into the path he travels, and make its labor conducive to the profits of his own.

England and France have taken the lead in this mode of giving publicity to business; but the United States, with its unwillingness to be beat in any way, on any terms, has made such rapid strides of late in this enterprise, that the English lion will be left in the rear, and the French eagle far in the background.

In London many curious devices have been used or proposed. Of these was that of a man who wished to prepare a sort of bomb-shell, to be filled with cards or bills, which, on reaching a certain elevation above the city, would explode, and thus scatter these carrier doves of information in all conceivable directions. In that city, butchers, bakers, and fishmongers, receive quite an income from persons who wish their cards attached to the various commodities in which they deal. Thus, a person receiving a fish, a loaf, or a piece of meat, finds the advertisement of a dealer in silks and satins attached to the tail of the fish; that of an auction sale of domestic flannels wrapped around the loaf; and perhaps flattering notices of a compound for the extermination of rats around the meat.

In the evening, transparencies are carried about the streets, suspended across the public ways, or hung upon the walls.

In this country, no person has taken the lead of a famous doctor in the way of advertising. Nearly every paper in the Union was one-fourth filled with ably-written articles in praise of his compound. In fact, he published papers of his own, the articles in which were characterized by the "one idea principle," and that one idea was contained in a bottle of Dr. ——'s save all and cure all, "none true but the genuine," "warranted not to burst the bottles or become sour." In addition to these, he issued an almanac — millions of them — bearing glad tidings to the sick and credulous, and sad tidings to the "regulars" in the medical fraternity. These almanacs were distributed everywhere. They came down on the American people like rain-drops. The result was, as we all know, the doctor flourished in a fortune equal to his fame, and disposed of his interest in the business, a few years since, for one hundred thousand dollars.

The amount of capital invested in advertising is very great, some firms expending thousands of dollars monthly in this mode of making known their business. It has been truly said that a card in a newspaper, that costs but a few dollars, is of far more value than costly signs over one's door. The former thousands behold, and are directed to your place of business; the latter very few notice who do not know the fact it makes known before they see it.

Attracted by the good fortune of those who have advertised, nearly every one has adopted the means that led to it, and the advertising system has become universal.

We have been seated in a car, waiting impatiently for the sound of the "last bell," when a person in a brown linen coat entered with an armful of books, and gave to each passenger a copy, without a hint about pay. Thanking him for the gift, and astonished at his generosity, we proceeded to open it, when "Wonderful cures," "Consumption," "Scrofula," "Indigestion," and "Fits," greeted our eyes on every page. Illustrated, too! Here was represented a man apparently dying, and near by a figure that would appear to be a woman were it not for two monstrous wings on its back, throwing obstacles in the way of death in the shape of a two-quart bottle of sarsaparilla syrup. Presumptive man in a brown linen coat, to suppose that we, just on the eve of a pleasure excursion, are troubled with such complaints, and stand in need of such a remedy!

You buy a newspaper, go home, seat yourself, and, in the anticipation of a glorious intellectual feast, open its damp pages, when, lo and behold! a huge show-bill falls from its embrace, and you are informed of the consoling truth that you can have all your teeth drawn for a trifle, and a new set inserted at a low price, by a distinguished dentist from London. The bill is indignantly thrown aside, and you commence reading an article under the caption of "An interesting incident," which, when half finished, you find to refer to a young lady whose complexion was made beautiful by the free use of

"Chaulks Poudres," a box of which can be obtained at 96 Azure-street, for 25 cts. After reading another column, headed "An act of mercy," you find at its close a most pathetic appeal to your tender sensibilities in an affectionate request for you to call on Dr. Digg and have your corns extracted without pain. Despairing of finding the "intellectual treat," you lay the paper aside, and resolve upon taking a walk.

Before you are monstrous show-bills, emblazoned with large letters and innumerable exclamation-points. Above you, flaunting flags with flaming notices. Beneath you, marble slabs inscribed with the names of traders and their goods. Around you, boys with their arms full of printed notices, and men encased with boards on which are mammoth posters. Sick of seeing these, you close your eyes; but you don't escape so easily; — a dinner-bell is rung in your ears, and a voice, if not like mighty thunder, at least like an embryo earthquake, proclaims an auction sale, a child lost, or news for the afflicted.

And thus it is, the world is one great Babel. All is business, business, and we ask for "some vast wilderness" in which to lie down and get cool, and keep quiet.

In Paris, the people long since adopted a plan which has not yet come in vogue among us. A long story is written; in the course of this story, a dozen or more establishments receive the author's laudations, which are so ingeniously interwoven, that the reader is scarcely aware of the design. For instance, Marnetta is going to an evening party. In the morning she goes out, and is met by a sprig of gentility, a young man of fashion, who cannot allow her to omit entering the unrivalled store of Messrs. Veuns, where the most beautiful silks, etc., are to be seen and purchased. Leaving this, she next encounters a young lady acquaintance of prudent and economical habits, by whom "our heroine" is led into a store where beauty and elegance are combined with durability and a low price. She wishes perfumery; so she hastens to Viot & Sons; for none make so good as they, and the fragrance of their store has been wafted on the winds of all nations.

Thus is the story led on from one step to another, with its interest not in the least abated, to the end. This embraces "puffery," as it is called. And, while on this subject, we may as well bring up the following specimen of this species of advertising. It was written by Peter Seguin, on the occasion of the first appearance in Dublin of the celebrated Mrs. Siddons. It caused much merriment at the time among some, while in others, who could not relish a joke, it excited anger.

"The house was crowded with hundreds more than it could hold, with thousands of admiring spectators that went away without a sight. This extraordinary phenomenon of tragic excellence! this star of Melpomene! this comet of the stage! this sun of the firmament of the Muses! this moon of blank verse! this queen arch-princess of tears! this Donnellan of the poisoned bowl! this empress of the pistol and dagger! this child of Shakspeare! this world of weeping clouds! this Juno of commanding aspects! this Terpsichore of the curtains and scenes! this Proserpine of fire and earthquake! this Katterfelto of wonders! exceeded expectation, went beyond belief, and soared above all the natural powers of description! She was nature itself! she was the most exquisite work of art! She was the very daisy, primrose, tuberose, sweet-brier, furze-blossom, gilliflower, wallflower, cauliflower, aurica and rosemary! In short, she was the bouquet of Parnassus! Where expectation was raised so high, it was thought she would be injured by her appearance; but it was the audience who were injured; several fainted before the curtain drew up! but when she came to the scene of parting with her wedding-ring, ah! what a sight was there! The fiddlers in the orchestra, 'albeit unused to the melting mood!' blubbered like hungry children crying for their bread and butter; and when the bell rang for music between the acts, the tears ran from the bassoon player's eyes in such plentiful showers, that they choked the finger-stops, and, making a spout of the instrument, poured in such torrents on the first fiddler's book, that, not seeing the overture was in two sharps, the leader of the band actually played in one flat. But the sobs and sighs of the groaning audience, and the noise of corks drawn from the smelling-bottles, prevented the mistakes between the flats and sharps being discovered. One hundred and nine ladies fainted! forty-six went into fits! and ninety-five had strong hysterics! The world will hardly credit the truth, when they are told that fourteen children, five women, one hundred tailors, and six common-council men, were actually drowned in the inundation of tears that flowed from the galleries, the slips and the boxes, to increase the briny pond in the pit; the water was three feet deep, and the people that were obliged to stand upon the benches were in that position up to their ancles in tears."

There is nothing in the present style of criticism that can exceed the above. The author actually reached the climax, and all attempts to overtop him would be useless.

Of advertisements there have been many worthy of preservation: some on account of the ingenuity displayed in their composition; some in their wit; some for their domesticativeness,— matrimonial offers, for example,— and others for the conceitedness exposed in them, the ignorance of the writers, or the whimsicality of the matter advertised. In 1804 there was advertised in an English paper, as for sale, "*The walk of a deceased blind beggar* (*in a charitable neighborhood*), *with his dog and staff.*"

In the *St. James Chronicle* of 1772 was the following:

"Wanted, fifteen hundred or two thousand pounds, by a person not worth a groat; who, having neither houses, lands, annuities, or public funds, can offer no other security than that of a simple bond, bearing simple interest, and engaging the repayment of the sum borrowed in five, six, or seven years, as may be agreed on by the parties," &c.

We do not know whether the advertiser obtained his pounds or not, but such an advertisement, now-a-days, would draw forth a laugh much sooner than the money; or, if "pounds" came, they would, most probably, fall upon the recipient's shoulders, instead of into his pocket.

The Chinese are not behind the age in this business. The following is an instance in proof:

"ACHEU TEA CHINCOEU, sculptor, respectfully acquaints masters of ships trading from Canton to India that they may be furnished with figure-heads, any size, according to order, at one-fourth of the price charged in Europe. He also recommends, for private venture, the following idols, brass, gold and silver: The hawk of Vishnoo, which has reliefs of his incarnation in a fish, boar, lion and bull, as worshipped by the pious followers of Zoroaster; two silver marmosets, with gold ear-rings; an aprimanes for Persian worship; a ram, an alligator, a crab, a laughing hyena, with a variety of household idols, on a small scale, calculated for family worship. Eighteen months credit will be given, or a discount of fifteen per cent. for prompt payment, on the sum affixed to each article. Direct, Canton-street, Canton, under the marble Rhinoceros and gilt Hydra."

We subjoin another, in which self-exaltation is pretty well carried out.

"At the shop Tae-shing (prosperous in the extreme) —

very good ink; fine! fine! Ancient shop, great-grandfather, grandfather, father and self, make this ink; fine and hard, very hard; picked with care, selected with attention. I sell very good ink; prime cost is very great. This ink is heavy; so is gold. The eye of the dragon glitters and dazzles; so does this ink. No one makes like it. Others who make ink make it for the sake of accumulating base coin, cheat, while I make it only for a name. Plenty of A-kwan-tsaes (gentlemen) know my ink — my family never cheated — they have always borne a good name. I make ink for the 'Son of Heaven,' and all the mandarins in the empire. As the roar of the tiger extends to every place, so does the fame of the 'dragon's jewel' (the ink). Come, all A-kwan-tsaes, come to my shop and see the sign Tae-shing at the side of the door. It is Seou-shwuy-street (Small Water-street), outside the south gate."

THE MISSION OF KINDNESS.

* * * * *

Go to the sick man's chamber ; low and soft
Falls on the listening ear a sweet-toned voice ;
A hand as gentle as the summer breeze,
Ever inclined to offices of good,
Smooths o'er the sick man's pillow, and then turns
To trim the midnight lamp, moisten the lips,
And, passing over, soothe the fevered brow.
Thus charity finds place in woman's heart ;
And woman kind, and beautiful, and good,
Doth thus administer to every want,
Nor wearies in her task, but labors on,
And finds her joy in that which she imparts.

Go to the prisoner's cell ; to-morrow's light
Shall be the last on earth he e'er shall see.
He mutters hate 'gainst all, and threatens ill
To every semblance of the human form.
Deep in his soul remorse, despair and hate,
Dwell unillumined by one ray of light,
And sway his spirit as the waves are swayed
By wind and storm. He may have cause to hold
His fellow-men as foes ; for, at the first
Of his departure from an upright course,
They scorned and shunned and cursed him.
They sinnéd thus, and he, in spite for them,
Kept on his sullen way from wrong to wrong.
Which is the greatest sinner ? He shall say
Who of the hearts of men alone is judge.

Now, in his cell condemned, he waits the hour,
The last sad hour of mortal life to him.

His oaths and blasphemies he sudden stays!
He thinks he hears upon his prison door
A gentle tap. O, to his hardened heart
That gentle sound a sweet remembrance brings
Of better days — two-score of years gone by,
Days when his mother, rapping softly thus,
Called him to morning prayer. Again 't is heard.
Is it a dream? Asleep! He cannot sleep
With chains around and shameful death before him!
Is it the false allurement of some foe
Who would with such enticement draw him forth
To meet destruction ere the appointed time?

Softened and calmed, each angry passion lulled,
By a soft voice, "Come in," he trembling calls.
Slow on its hinges turns the ponderous door,
And "Friend," the word that falls from stranger lips.
As dew on flowers, as rain on parchéd ground,
So came the word unto the prisoner's ear.
He speaks not — moves not. O, his heart is full,
Too full for utterance; and, as floods of tears
Flow from his eyes so all unused to weep,
He bows down low, e'en at the stranger's feet.

He had not known what 't was to have a friend.
The word came to him like a voice from heaven,
A voice of love to one who 'd heard but hate.
"Friend!" Mysterious word to him who 'd known no friend.
O, what a power that simple word hath o'er him!
As now he holds the stranger's hand in his,
And bows his head upon it, he doth seem
Gentle and kind, and docile as a child.
Repentance comes with kindness, goodness rears
Its cross on Calvary's height, inspiring hope
Which triumphs over evil and its guilt.

O, how much changed! and all by simple words
Spoken in love and kindness from the heart.
O, love and kindness! matchless power have ye
To mould the human heart; where'er ye dwell
There is no sorrow, but a living joy.

There is no man whom God hath placed on earth
That hath not some humanity within,
And is not moved with kindness joined with love.
The wildest savage, from whose firelit eye
Flashes the lightning passions of his soul,
Who stands, and feeling that he hath been wronged,
That he hath trusted and been basely used,
And that to him revenge were doubly sweet,
Dares all the world to combat and to death,—
Even *he* hath dwelling in his inmost heart
A chord that quick will vibrate to kind words.
Go unto such with kindness, not with wrath;
Let your eye look love, and 't will disarm him
Of all the evil passions with which he
Hath mailed his soul in terrible array.

Think not to tame the wild by brutal force.
As well attempt to stay devouring flames
By heaping fagots on the blazing pile.
Go, do man good, and the deep-hidden spark
Of true divinity concealed within
Will brighten up, and thou shalt see its glow,
And feel its cheering warmth. O, we lose much
By calling passion's aid to vanquish wrong.
We should stand within love's holy temple,
And with persuasive kindness call men in,
Rather than, leaving it, use other means,
Unblest of God, and therefore weak and vain,
To force them on before us into bliss.

There is a luxury in doing good
Which none but by experience e'er can know.
He 's blest who doeth good. Sleep comes to him
On wings of sweetest peace; and angels meet
In joyous convoys ever round his couch;
They watch and guard, protect and pray for him.
All mothers bend the knee, and children too
Clasp their fair hands and raise their undimmed eyes,
As if to pierce the shadowy veil that hangs
Between themselves and God — then pray that he
Will bless with Heaven's best gifts the friend of man.

A PLEA FOR THE FALLEN.

Pity her, pity her! Once she was fair,
Once breathed she sweetly the innocent's prayer;
Parents stood by in pride o'er their daughter;
Sin had not tempted, Vice had not caught her;
Hoping and trusting, believing all true,
Nothing but happiness rose to her view.
She, as were spoken words lovers might tell,
Listened, confided, consented, and fell!
Now she 's forsaken; nursing in sorrow,
Hate for the night, despair for the morrow!

She 'd have the world think she 's happy and gay, —
A butterfly, roving wherever it may;
Sipping delight from each rose-bud and flower,
The charmed and the charmer of every hour.
She will not betray to the world all her grief;
She knows it is false, and will give no relief.
She knows that its friendship is heartless and cold;
That it loves but for gain, and pities for gold;
That when in their woe the fallen do cry,
It turns, it forsakes, and it leaves them to die!

But after the hour of the world's bright show,
When hence from her presence flatterers go;
When none are near to praise or caress her,
No one stands by with fondness to bless her;
Alone with her thoughts, in moments like this,
She thinks of her days of innocent bliss,
And she weeps! — yes, she weeps penitent tears
O'er the shame of a life and the sorrow of years:
She turns for a friend; yet, alas! none is there;
She sinks, once again, in the deepest despair!

Blame her not! O blame not; ye fathers who hold
Daughters you value more dearly than gold!
But pity, O, pity her! take by the hand
One who, though fallen, yet nobly may stand.

Turn not away from her plea and her cries;
Pity and help, and the fallen may rise!
Crush not to earth the reed that is broken,
Bind up her wounds — let soft words be spoken;
Though she be low, though worldlings reject her,
Let not Humanity ever neglect her.

JOY BEYOND.

Beyond the dark, deep grave, whose lowly portal
Must yet be passed by every living mortal,
There gleams a light;
'T is not of earth. It wavers not; it gloweth
With a clear radiance which no changing knoweth,
Constant and bright.

We love to gaze at it; we love to cherish
The cheering thought, that, when this earth shall perish,
And naught remain
Of all these temples, — things we now inherit,
Each unimprisoned, no more fettered spirit
Shall life retain.

And ever, through eternity unending,
It shall unto that changeless light be tending,
Till perfect day
Shall be its great reward; and all of mystery
That hath made up its earthly life, its history,
Be passed away!

O, joyous hour! O, day most good and glorious!
When from the earth the ransomed rise victorious,
Its conflict o'er;
When joy henceforth each grateful soul engages,
Joy unalloyed through never-ending ages,
Joy evermore!

THE SUMMER DAYS ARE COMING.

THE summer days are coming,
  The glorious summer hours,
When Nature decks her gorgeous robe
  With sunbeams and with flowers;
And gathers all her choristers
  In plumage bright and gay,
Till every vale is echoing with
  Their joyous roundelay.

No more shall frosty winter
  Hold in its cold embrace
The water; but the river
  Shall join again the race;
And down the mountain's valley,
  And o'er its rocky side,
The glistening streams shall rush and leap
  In all their bounding pride.

There 's pleasure in the winter,
  When o'er the frozen snow
With faithful friend and noble steed
  Right merrily we go!
But give to me the summer,
  The pleasant summer days,
When blooming flowers and sparkling streams
  Enliven all our ways.

THE MAN WHO KNOWS EVERYTHING.

Sansecrat is one of that class of persons who think they know everything. If anything occurs, and you seek to inform him, he will interrupt you by saying that he knows it all,— that he was on the spot when the occurrence happened, or that he had met a man who was an eye-witness.

Such a person, though he be the possessor of much assurance, is sadly deficient in manners; and no doubt the superabundancy of the former is caused by the great lack of the latter.

Such men as he *will* thrive; there is no mistake about it. This has been called an age of invention and of humbug. Nothing is so popular, or so much sought after, as that which cannot be explained, and around which a mysterious shroud is closely woven.

My friend *Arcanus* came sweating and puffing into my room. I had just finished my dinner, and was seated leisurely looking over a few pages of manuscript, when he entered.

"News!" said he; and before I could hand him a chair he had told me all about the last battle, and his tongue flew about with so much rapidity, that a conflagration might have been produced by such excessive friction, had not a rap at the door put a clog under the wheels of his talkative locomotive, and stayed its progress, which luckily gave me an opportunity to take his hat and request him to be seated.

The door was opened, and who but *Sansecrat* stood before me.

"Have you heard the news?" was the first interrogatory of my friend Arcanus, in reply to which Sansecrat said that he knew it all half an hour previous,— was at the railroad station when the express arrived, and was the first man to open the Southern papers.

In vain Arcanus told him that the information came by a private letter. He averred, point blank, that it was no such thing; that he had the papers in his pocket; and was about to exhibit them as proof of what he had said, when he suddenly recollected that he had sold them to an editor for one-and-sixpence.

Notwithstanding the proverb of "Man, know thyself," Sansecrat seems to know everything but himself. Thousands of times has it been said that man can see innumerable faults and foibles in his neighbors, but none in himself. Very true; and man can see his own character, just as he can see his own face in a mirror. His own associates mirror forth his own character; and the faults, be they great or small, that he sees in them, are but the true reflection of his own errors. Yet, blind to this, and fondly imagining that he is the very "pink of excellence," he flatters his own vain feeling with the cherished idea that, while others have faults, he has none, and so slumbers on in the sweet repose of ignorance.

Sansecrat imagines that he knows everything; that to teach him would be like "carrying coals to Newcastle," or sending ship-loads of ice to Greenland, or furnaces to the coast of Africa; yet he is as ignorant as the greatest dunce, who, parrot-like, repeats that he has heard, without having the least understanding of what he says.

Strange as it may seem, it is nevertheless true that Sansecrat will prosper in the world; for, though destitute of those qualifications which render their possessor worthy of success, he has an abundance of brazen-facedness, with which he will work himself into the good opinion of not a few, who look more closely upon exterior appearance than they do upon inward worth, and judge their fellow-men more by the good quality of their cloth than by the good quality of their hearts, and set more value on a shining hat and an unpatched boot than they do on a brilliant intellect and a noble soul.

PRIDE AND POVERTY.

I CANNOT brook the proud. I cannot love
The selfish man; he seems to have no heart;
And why he lives and moves upon this earth
Which God has made so fair, I cannot tell.
He has no soul but that within his purse,
And all his hopes are centred on its fate;
That lost, and all is lost.

I knew a man
Who had abundant riches. He was proud, —
Too oft the effect of riches when abused, —
His step was haughty, and his eye glanced at
The honest poor as base intruders on
The earth he trod and fondly called his own;
Unwelcome guests at Nature's banqueting.

Years passed away, — that youth became a man;
His beetled brow, his sullen countenance,
His eye that looked a fiery command,
Betrayed that his ambition was to rule.
He smiled not, save in scorn on humble men,
Whom he would have bow down and worship him.
Thus with his strength his pride did grow, until
He did become aristocrat indeed.
The humble beggar, whose loose rags scarce gave
Protection to him from the cold north wind,
He scarce would look upon, and vainly said,
As in his hand he held the ready coin,
"No mortal need be poor, — 'tis his own fault
If such he be; — if he court poverty,
Let all its miseries be his to bear."

'T is many years since he the proud spake thus,
And men and things have greatly changed since then.

No more in wealth he rolls, — men's fortunes change.

I met a lonely hearse, slowly it passed
Toward the church-yard. 'T was unattended
Save by one old man, and he the sexton.
With spade beneath his arm he trudged along,
Whistling a homely tune, and stopping not.
He seemed to be in haste, for now and then
He 'd urge to quicker pace his walking beast,
With the rough handle of his rusty spade.
Him I approached, and eagerly inquired
Whose body thus was borne so rudely to
Its final resting-place, the deep, dark grave.
"His name was Albro," was the prompt reply.
"Too proud to beg, we found him starved to death,
In a lone garret, which the rats and mice
Seemed greatly loth to have him occupy.
An' I, poor Billy Matterson, whom once
He deemed too poor and low to look upon,
Am come to bury him."
The sexton smiled, —
Then raised his rusty spade, cheered up his nag,
Whistled as he was wont, and jogged along.
Oft I have seen the poor man raise his hand
To wipe the eye when good men meet the grave, —
But Billy Matterson, he turned and smiled.

The truth flashed in an instant on my mind,
Though sad, yet deep, unchanging truth to me.
'T was he, thus borne, who, in his younger days,
Blest with abundance, used it not aright.
He, who blamed the poor because they were such ;
Behold his end ! — *too proud to beg, he died.*
A sad example, teaching all to shun
The rock on which he shipwrecked, — warning take,
That they too fall not as he rashly fell.

WORDS THAT TOUCH THE INNER HEART.

Words, words! O give me these,
Words befitting what I feel,
That I may on every breeze
Waft to those whose riven steel
Fetters souls and shackles hands
Born to be as free as air,
Yet crushed and cramped by Slavery's bands, —
Words that have an influence there.

Words, words! give me to write
Such as touch the inner heart;
Not mere flitting forms of light,
That please the ear and then depart;
But burning words, that reach the soul,
That bring the shreds of error out,
That with resistless power do roll,
And put the hosts of Wrong to rout.

Let others tune their lyres, and sing
Illusive dreams of fancied joy;
But, my own harp, — its every string
Shall find in Truth enough employ.
It shall not breathe of Freedom here,
While millions clank the galling chain;
Or e'en *one* slave doth bow in fear,
Within our country's broad domain.

Go where the slave-gang trembling stands,
Herded with every stable stock, —
Woman with fetters on her hands,
And infants on the auction-block!
See, as she bends, how flow her tears!
Hark! hear her broken, trembling sighs;
Then hear the oaths, the threats, the jeers,
Of men who lash her as she cries!

* * * *

O, men! who have the power to weave
  In poesy's web deep, searching thought,
Be truth thy aim; henceforward leave
  The lyre too much with fancy fraught!
Come up, and let the words you write
  Be those which every chain would break,
And every sentence you indite
  Be *pledged to Truth for Freedom's sake.*

OUR HOME.

  Our home shall be
A cot on the mountain side,
Where the bright waters glide,
  Sparkling and free;
Terrace and window o'er
Woodbine shall graceful soar;
Roses shall round the door
  Blossom for thee.

  There shall be joy
With no care to molest,—
Quiet, serene and blest;
  And our employ
Work each other's pleasure;
Boundless be the treasure;
Without weight or measure,
  Free from alloy.

  Our home shall be
Where the first ray of light
Over the mountain height,
  Stream, rock and tree,
Joy to our cot shall bring,
While brake and bower shall ring
With notes the birds shall sing,
  Loved one, for thee.

SPECULATION AND ITS CONSEQUENCE.

SPECULATION is business in a high fever. Its termination is generally very decided, whether favorable or otherwise, and the effect of that termination upon the individual most intimately connected with it in most cases unhealthy.

It was a truth long before the wise man wrote it, that making haste to be rich is an evil; and it always will be a truth that the natural, unforced course of human events is the only sure, the only rational one.

The desire to be rich, to be pointed out as wealthy, is a very foolish one, unless it be coupled with a desire to do good. This is somewhat paradoxical; for the gratification of the last most certainly repels that of the first, inasmuch as he who distributes his gains cannot accumulate to any great extent.

Wealth is looked at from the wrong stand-point. It is too often considered the end, instead of the means to an end; and there never was a greater delusion in the human mind than that of supposing that riches confer happiness. In ninety-nine cases out of every hundred the opposite is the result. Care often bears heavily on the rich man's brow, and the insatiate spirit asks again and again for more, and will not be silenced. And this feeling will predominate in the human mind until man becomes better acquainted with his own true nature, and inclines to minister to higher and more ennobling aspirations.

In one of the most populous cities of the Union there

resided, a few years since, a person in moderate circumstances, by the name of Robert Short. Bob, as he was usually called, was a shoemaker. With a steady run of custom, together with prudence and economy combined, he was enabled to support his family in an easy and by no means unenviable style. He did not covet the favors and caresses of the world. He looked upon all,— the rich, the poor, the prince, the beggar,— alike, as his brethren. He believed that all stood upon one platform, all were bound to the same haven, and that all should be equally interested in each other's welfare. With this belief, and with rules of a similar character, guided by which he pursued his course of life, it was not to be wondered at that he could boast of many friends, and not strange that many should seek his acquaintance. There is a desire planted in the hearts of honest men to associate with those who, ambitious enough to sustain a good character, are not so puffed up with pride, or so elevated in their own estimation, as to despise the company of what are termed "the common people." It was pleasant, of a winter's evening, to enter the humble domicile of Mr. Short, and while the howling storm raged fiercely without, and the elements seemed at war, to see the contentment and peace that prevailed within. Bob, seated at his bench, might be seen busily employed, and, as the storm increased, would seem to apply himself more diligently to his task. Six or perhaps eight of his neighbors might also be seen gathered around, seated upon that article most convenient,— whether a stool or a pile of leather, it mattered not,— relating some tale of the Revolution, or listening to some romantic story from the lips of the respected Mr. Short. 'T was upon such an evening, and at such a place, that our story commences. Squire Smith, Ned Green, and a jovial sort of a fellow by the name of Sandy, were seated around the red-hot cylinder. Squire Smith was what some would term a "man of consequence,"— at least, he thought so. Be it known that this squire was by no means a daily visitor at the work-shop of our hero. He came in occasionally, and endeavored to impress upon his mind that which he had settled in his own, namely, that he, Robert Short, *might* be a great man.

"I tell you what," said he, with an air of importance, "I tell you what, it is against all reason, it is contrary to common sense and everything else, that you remain any longer riveted down to this old bench. It will be your ruin; 'pend upon it, it will be your ruin."

"How so?" eagerly inquired Mr. Short.

"Why," replied the squire, "it's no use for me to go into particulars. But why do you not associate with more respectable and fashionable company?"

"Is not the present company respectable?" resumed Mr. Short; "and as for the fashion, I follow my own."

Squire Smith did not reply to this inquiry, but stood shaking his head, and appeared at a loss for words with which to answer.

"Perhaps your ideas of respectability," continued the squire, "are not in accordance with mine."

"Ay, ay; true, true," interrupted Sandy, with a shrug of the shoulder.

Mr. Smith continued his remarks, appearing not to notice the interruption. "Perhaps," said he, "one may be as honest as the days are long; but, sir, he is far from being respectable, in my humble opinion, if he is not genteel,—and certainly if he is not fashionably dressed he is not. He does not think *enough* of himself; *that's it*, my dear Mr. Short, he does not think enough of himself."

"But he is honest," replied Mr. Short. "Supposing he does *not* dress so fashionably as you would wish, would you condemn him for the cut of his coat, or the quality of his cloth? Perhaps his means are not very extensive, and will not admit of a very expensive outlay, merely for show. It is much better, my dear sir, to be clothed in rags and out of debt, than to be attired in the most costly apparel, and that not paid for. Sir, to hold up your head and say you owe no man, is to be free, free in the truest sense of the word."

"Ah, I must be on the move," interrupted the squire, at the same time looking at his "gold lever." And off he started.

Squire Smith had said enough for that night; to have said more would have injured his plan. Mr. Green and Sandy shook hands with their friend Robert, and, it being late, they bade him "good-by," and parted. Our hero was now left alone. Snuffing the candle, that had well-nigh burnt to the socket, he placed more fuel upon the fire, and, resting his hands upon his knees and his head upon his hands, he began to think over the sayings of his friend the squire.

Robert Short saw nothing of the squire for many days after the event just described transpired. One day, as he began his work, the door was suddenly thrown open, and the long absent but not forgotten squire rushed in, shouting "Speculation! speculation!" Mr. Short threw aside his *last*, and listened with feelings of astonishment to the eloquent words that fell from the lips of his unexpected visitor. "Gull, the broker," continued the squire, "has just offered me a great bargain. I have come to make a proposition, which is, that you and I accept his offer, and make our fortunes."

"Fortunes!" exclaimed the son of Crispin; "speculate in what?"

"In eastern land," was the reply.

Bob Short's countenance assumed a desponding appearance; he had heard of many losses caused by venturing in these speculations, and had some doubts as to his success, should he accept. Then, again, he had heard of those who had been fortunate, and he inquired the conditions of sale.

"Why," replied Mr. Smith, Esq., "old Varnum Gull has three thousand acres of good land, upon which are, as he *assures* me, some beautiful watering places. It is worth five dollars an acre; he offers it to me for one, and a grand chance it is; the terms are cash."

"Are you certain as to the quality of the land?" inquired Mr. Short.

"Perfectly certain," was the reply. "I would not advise you wrong for the world; but I now think it best to form a sort of co-partnership, and purchase the land. There is no doubt but that we can dispose of it at a great advantage. Will you not agree to my proposals, and accept?"

"I will," answered Mr. Short. "But how can I obtain fifteen hundred dollars? I have but a snug thousand."

"O, don't trouble yourself about that," replied the delighted squire. "I will loan you the balance at once. You can return it at some convenient time. What say you? will you accompany me to the broker's, and inform him of the agreement?"

Mr. Short, after a moment's delay, arose, and, laying aside his leather apron, took the squire by the arm, and both sallied forth in search of the office of Varnum Gull. After wending their way through short streets and long lanes, narrow avenues and wide alleys, they came to a small gate, upon which was fastened a small tin sign with the following inscription: "V. Gull, broker, up the yard, round the corner, up two pair of stairs." The squire and Mr. Short followed the directions laid down, and, having gone up the yard and turned round the corner, they found themselves at the foot of the stairs. They stood for a moment silent, and were about to ascend, when a voice from above attracted their attention.

"'Ollo, Squire, 'ere's the box; walk right up 'ere; only look out, there 's an 'ole in the stairs."

Our hero looked above, and perceived a man with green spectacles drawing his head in.

"We will go up," said the squire, "and look out for the hole; but, as the stairway is rather dark, we shall not see much; therefore we shall be obliged to feel our way."

They ascended, and escaped without injury. A little short man met them at the door, holding in his hand a paper bearing some resemblance to a map.

"Really, Mr. Smith, I feared you would lose that 'ere bargain I expatiated on. I 'ave received many good offers, but 'ave reserved it for you. Your friend, ha?" he continued, at the same time striking Mr. Short in no gentle manner upon the shoulder.

"Not friend *Hay*, but friend *Short*," replied the squire.

"Hall the same, only an error in the spelling," resumed the broker. "Good-morning, Mr. Short; s'pose you 'ave become 'quainted with the rare chance I 've offered, *an't ye?* and wish to accept it, *don't ye?* and can pay for it, *can't ye?* Such an opportunity is seldom met with, by which to make one's fortune."

"Well," replied Mr. Short, improving the time Mr. Gull stopped to breathe, "well, I had some idea of so doing."

"Hidea!" quickly responded the broker; "why will you 'esitate? read that!" and he handed a paper to Mr. Short, which paper he kept for reference, and pointed out to him an article which read as follows:

"It is astonishing what enormous profits are at present realized by traders in Eastern Land. One of our neighbors purchased a thousand acres, at one dollar and twenty-five cents per acre, of Gull, our enterprising broker, and sold it yesterday for the round sum of three thousand dollars, receiving thereby the enormous profit of nineteen hundred and seventy-five dollars. He was a poor man, but by this lucky movement has become rich."

As soon as our hero had read this cheering intelligence, he became elated with the prospect, and soon came to a final agreement with the squire to accept the offer. Papers were drawn up, signed by each, and a check given to the broker, for which was returned a deed for the land. They then left the office, Mr. Gull politely bidding them good-by, with a caution to look out for the "'ole." They did look out for the hole, but it might have been that the cunning broker referred to a hole of more consequence than that in the stairs. The squire on that day invited Mr. Short to his house to dine. This, however, he did not accept, but returned to his shop. One week had passed away, during which time the squire was often at the shop of Bob Short, but no customer had yet applied for the land. It was near dusk on the eighth day succeeding the purchase, as they were talking over the best way by which to dispose of it, when a short man entered, wrapped up in a large cloak, and a large bushy fur cap upon his head.

"I understand," said he, "you have a few acres of land you wish to dispose of."

"Exactly so," answered the squire.

"And how much do you charge per acre?" inquired the stranger.

"That depends upon the number you wish. Do you wish to purchase all?"

"That depends upon the price charged," was the reply.

"If you wish all," continued Mr. Smith, "we will sell for four dollars an acre. That is dog cheap, and a great sacrifice."

"Well," resumed the stranger, "I will take it on conditions; namely, I will pay you your price, and if the land answers my purpose I will keep it,— if not, you will return me the amount of money I pay."

"That is rather a hard bargain. I *know* it to be good land," answered the squire.

"Then," continued the stranger, "if you *know* it to be good, certainly there can be no danger in disposing of it on the conditions I have named."

After a few moments' conversation with Mr. Short, they agreed to sell to the stranger. Papers were immediately drawn up and signed by Messrs. Smith and Short, agreeing to return the money provided the land did not give satisfaction. The sum of twelve thousand dollars was paid in cash to the signers, and the papers given into the hands of the purchaser, who then left. Robert Short on that night did really feel rich. This was six thousand dollars apiece; after Mr. Short had paid the fifteen hundred borrowed, he had forty-five hundred left. Both were equally certain that the land would give entire satisfaction, and acted according to this belief. With a light heart he went home, and communicated the joyful intelligence to his wife, who had from the first been opposed to the trade. He did not, however, inform her of the terms on which he had sold. In a few days he had disposed of his shop and tools to one of his former workmen. Many were surprised when the sign of "Robert Short" was taken from its long resting-place over the door. Mr. Short now began to think the house in which he had for many years resided was not quite good enough, and therefore engaged a larger and more expensive one. He ordered new furniture, purchased a carriage and horses, and had his new house fitted out under the direction of his friend, the squire. He rented a large store; bought large quantities of shoes and leather, partly on credit. His business at first prospered, but in a short time became quite dull; his former customers left, and all business seemed at a stand-still. In the mean time, the broker had left town, having sold out his office to a young man. Matters stood thus, when, early in the morning on a pleasant day in June, as the squire and Mr. Short were seated in the counting-room of the latter, a man dressed in a light summer dress entered.

"Good-morning," said the visitor. "Business is quite lively, I suppose?"

"O, it's moderate, nothing extra," replied Mr. Short; "won't you be seated?"

The stranger seated himself.

"Mr. Robert Short is your name, is it not?" he inquired.

"It is, sir."

"Did I not make a bargain with you about some eastern land, a few months since?"

"Yes, some person did;" and Mr. Short immediately recognized him as the purchaser. The new comer then took from his pocket the paper of agreement, and presented it for the inspection of the two gentlemen.

"Are you not satisfied with your bargain?" inquired Mr. Smith.

"Not exactly," replied the stranger, laughing.

"Why, what fault is there in it?"

"Well," replied the stranger, "I suppose a report of my examination will be acceptable."

"Certainly, sir," replied Mr. Short.

"Then I can give it in a few words. It is a good *watering* place, being WHOLLY COVERED WITH WATER; and is of no value unless it could be drained, and that, I think, is impossible."

The squire was astonished; Mr. Short knew not what to

"What is the name of the water bought for land?" inquired Squire Smith.

"The location of it is in a large pond of water, twelve miles in length, and about six in width, and is known in those parts by the name of the 'Big Pond.' But," continued the stranger, "I must be gone; please return me my money, according to agreement."

After some talk, the stranger agreed to call the next day. The next day came, and with it came the stranger. Mr. Short had tried in vain to obtain the requisite sum, and was obliged to request him to call the next day. He came the next day, and the next, and the next, but received no money; and he was at length obliged to attach the property of the squire, as also that of Mr. Short. His other creditors also came in with their bills. All the stock of Mr. Short was sold at auction, and he was a poor man. He obtained a small house, that would not compare with the one he had lived in in former years. He had no money of his own, and was still deeply in debt. He was obliged to work at such jobs as came along, but at length obtained steady employment. The squire, who was the prime cause of all his trouble, sailed for a foreign port, leaving all his bills unpaid. In a short time Mr. Short obtained a sufficient sum to buy back his old shop, in which to this day he has steadily worked, with a vivid remembrance of the *consequence of speculation.*

RETROSPECTION.

He had drank deep and long from out
  The bacchanalian's bowl;
Had felt its poisonous arrows pierce
  The recess of his soul;
And now his footsteps turned to where
  His childhood's days were cast,
And sat him 'neath an old oak tree
  To muse upon the past.
Beneath its shade he oft had sat
  In days when he was young;
Ere sorrow, like that old oak tree,
  Its own deep shadows flung;
Beneath that tree his school-mates met,
  There joined in festive mirth,
And not a place seemed half so dear
  To him, upon the earth.

The sun had passed the horizon,
  Yet left a golden light
Along a cloudless sky to mark
  A pathway for the night;
The moon was rising silently
  To reign a queen on high,
To marshal all the starry host,
  In heaven's blue canopy.
In sight the schoolhouse stood, to which
  In youth he had been led
By one who now rests quietly
  Upon earth's silent bed.
And near it stood the church whose aisles
  His youthful feet had trod;

Where his young mind first treasured in
  The promises of God.

There troops of happy children ran
  With gayety along;
'T was agony for him to hear
  Their laughter and their song.
For thoughts of youthful days came up
  And crowded on his brain,
Till, crushed with woe unutterable,
  It sank beneath its pain.
Pain! not such as sickness brings,
  For that can be allayed,
But pain from which a mortal shrinks
  Heart-stricken and dismayed:
The *body* crushed beneath its woe
  May some deliverance find,
But who on earth hath power to heal
  The agony of mind?

O Memory! it long had slept;
  But now it woke to power,
And brought before him all the past,
  From childhood's earliest hour.
He saw himself in school-boy prime;
  Then youth, its pleasures, cares,
Came up before him, and he saw
  How cunningly the snares
Were set to catch him as he ran
  In thoughtless haste along,
To charm him with deceitful smiles,
  And with its siren song:
He saw a seeming friendly hand
  Hold out the glittering wine,
Without a thought that deep within
  A serpent's form did twine.

Then manhood came; then he did love,
  And with a worthy pride
He led a cherished being to
  The altar as his bride;

And mid the gay festivity
  Passed round the flowing wine,
And friends drank, in the sparkling cup,
  " A health to thee and thine."
A *health!* O, as the past came up,
  The wanderer's heart was stirred
And as a madman he poured forth
  Deep curses on that word.
For well he knew *that* " health " had been
  The poison of his life ;
Had made the portion of his soul
  With countless sorrows rife.

Six years passed by — a change had come,
  And what a change was that!
No more the comrades of his youth
  With him as comrades sat.
Duties neglected, friends despised,
  Himself with naught to do,
A mother dead with anguish, and
  A wife heart-broken too.
Another year — and she whom he
  Had promised to protect
Died in the midst of poverty,
  A victim of neglect.
But ere she died she bade him kneel
  Beside herself in prayer,
And prayed to God that he would look
  In pity on them there:

And bless her husband, whom she loved,
  And all the past forgive,
And cause him, ere she died, begin
  A better life to live.
She ceased to speak, — the husband rose,
  And, penitent, did say,
While tears of deep contrition flowed,
  " I 'll dash the bowl away ! "
A smile passed o'er the wife's pale face,
  She grasped his trembling hand,

Gave it one pressure, then her soul
  Passed to a better land.
He bent to kiss her pale cold lips,
  But they returned it not;
And then he felt the loneliness
  And sorrow of his lot.

It seemed as though *his* life had fled;
  That *all* he called his own,
When her pure spirit took its flight,
  Had with that spirit flown.
She had been all in all to him,
  And deep his heart was riven
With anguish, as he thought what woe
  He her kind heart had given.
But all was passed; she lay in death,
  The last word had been said,
The soul had left its prison-house,
  And up to heaven had fled;
But 't was a joy for him to know
  She smiled on him in love,
And hope did whisper in his heart,
  "She 'll guard thee from above."

He sat beneath that old oak tree,
  And children gathered round,
And wondered why he wept, and asked
  What sorrow he had found.
Then told he them this sad, sad tale,
  Which I have told to you;
They asked no more why he did weep,
  For they his sorrow knew.
And soon *their* tears began to fall,
  And men came gathering round,
Till quite a goodly company
  Beneath that tree was found.
The wanderer told his story o'er,
  Unvarnished, true and plain;
And on that night three-score of men
  Did pledge them to abstain.

NATURE'S FAIR DAUGHTER, BEAUTIFUL WATER.

Nature's fair daughter,
Beautiful water!
O, hail it with joy, with echoes of mirth,
Wherever it sparkles or ripples on earth.

Down from the mountain,
Up from the fountain,
Ever it cometh, bright, sparkling and clear,
From the Creator, our pathway to cheer.

Nobly appearing,
O'er cliffs careering,
Pouring impetuously on to the sea,
Chanting, unceasing, the song of the free.

See how it flashes
As onward it dashes
Over the pebbly bed of the brook,
Singing in every sequestered nook.

Now gently falling,
As if 't were calling
Spirits of beauty from forest and dell
To welcome it on to grotto and cell.

Beauteous and bright
Gleams it in light,
Then silently flows beneath the deep glade,
Emblem of life in its sunshine and shade.

Beautiful water!
Nature's fair daughter!
Where'er it sparkles or ripples on earth,
Hail it with joy and with echoes of mirth.

THE TEST OF FRIENDSHIP.

Brightest shine the stars above
  When the night is darkest round us;
Those the friends we dearest love
  Who were near when sorrow bound us.

When no clouds o'ercast our sky,
  When no evil doth attend us,
Then will many gather nigh,
  Ever ready to befriend us.

But when darkness shades our path,
  When misfortune hath its hour,
When we lie beneath its wrath,
  Some will leave us to its power.

Often have we seen at night,
  When the clouds have gathered o'er us,
One lone star send forth its light,
  Marking out the path before us.

Like that star some friendly eye
  Will beam on us in our sorrow;
And, though clouded be our sky,
  We know there 'll be a better morrow.

We know that all will not depart,
  That some will gather round to cheer us:
Know we, in our inmost heart,
  Tried and faithful friends are near us.

Brother, those who do not go
  May be deemèd friends forever;
Love them, trust them, have them know
  Nothing can your friendship sever.

WEEP NOT.

WEEP not, mother,
For another
Tie that bound thyself to earth
Now is sundered,
And is numbered
With those of a heavenly birth.

She hath left thee.
God bereft thee
Of thy dearest earthly friend;
Yet thou 'lt meet her,
Thou wilt greet her
Where reünions have no end

Her life's true sun
Its course did run
From morn unto meridian day;
And now at eve
It takes its leave,
Calmly passing hence away.

Watch the spirit—
'T will inherit
Bliss which mortal cannot tell;
From another
World, my mother,
Angels whisper, "All is well."

'Way with sadness!
There is gladness
In a gathered spirit throng;
She, ascended,
Trials ended,
Joins their ranks and chants their song.

Weep not, mother,
For another
Tie doth bind thyself above;
Doubts are vanished,
Sorrows banished,
She is happy whom you love.

RICH AND POOR.

"GOOD-BY, Ray, good-by," said George Greenville; and the stage wound its way slowly up a steep ascent, and was soon lost to view.

"Well, well, he has gone. Glad of it, heartily glad of it! When will all these paupers be gone?" said the father of George, as he entered the richly-furnished parlor, and seated himself beside an open window.

"Why so glad?" inquired George, who listened with feelings of regret to the remark.

"Why?" resumed the owner of a thousand acres; "ask me no questions; I am glad,—that 's enough. You well know my mind on the subject."

"Father, act not thus. Is this a suitable way to requite his kindness?"

"Kindness!" interrupted the old man; "say not 't was kindness that prompted him to do me a favor; rather say 't was his duty,—and of you should I not expect better things? Did I allow you to visit Lemont but to become acquainted with such a poverty-stricken, pauper-bred youth as Ray Bland?"

Saying this, he arose and left the room.

George seated himself in the chair vacated by his father. He looked across the verdant fields, and mused upon his passionate remarks. "Well," thought he, "I was right; shall I allow the god of Mammon to bind me down? Of what use are riches, unless, whilst we enjoy, we can with them relieve the wants and administer to the necessities of our fellow-men? Shall we hoard them up, or shall we not rather give with a free hand and a willing heart to those who have felt misfortune's scourging rod,— who are crushed, oppressed and trampled upon, by not a few of their more wealthy neighbors?" In such a train of thought he indulged himself till the hour of dinner arrived.

George Greenville had formed an acquaintance with Ray Bland whilst on a visit to a neighboring town. He was a young man, possessing those fine qualities of mind that constitute the true gentleman. His countenance beamed with intelligence, and his sparkling eye betrayed vivacity of mind, the possession of which was a sure passport to the best of society. When the time came that George was to return home to the companionship of his friends, they found that ties of friendship bound them which could not be easily severed, and Ray accepted the invitation of George Greenville to accompany him, and spend a short time at the house of his father. The week had passed away in a pleasant manner. The hour of parting had come and gone. The farewell had been taken, the "good-by" had been repeated, when the conversation above mentioned passed between him and his father.

The family and connections of George were rich; those of Ray were poor. The former lived at ease in the midst of pleasures, and surrounded by all the comforts and conveniences of life; the latter encountered the rough waves of adversity, and was obliged to labor with assiduity, to sustain an equal footing with his neighbors. Thus were the two friends situated; and old Theodore Greenville scorned the idea of having his son associate with a pauper, as he termed all those who were not the possessors of a certain amount of money,— without which, in his opinion, none were worthy to associate with the rich.

"Ray is a person not so much to be hated and sneered at as you would suppose," said George, breaking the silence, and addressing his father at the dinner-table.

"George, I have set my heart against him," was the reply.

"Then," continued the first speaker, "I suppose you are not open to conviction. If I can prove him worthy of your esteem and confidence, will you believe?"

"That cannot be done, perhaps. You may think him to be a worthy young man; but I discard the old saying that poverty is no disgrace! I say that it *is*; and one that can, if its victim choose, be washed away. Ray Bland is a pauper, that 's my only charge against him; and all the thundering eloquence of a Cicero will not alter my opinion, or move me an iota from the stand I have taken,—which is, now and ever, to reject the company of paupers. It is my request that you do the same."

Amelia, the sister of George, now joined in the conversation, inquiring of her father whether it was against his will for *her* to associate with the poor.

"Precisely so," was the brief reply; and the conversation ended. The father left the house for a short walk, as was his custom, whilst George and Amelia retired to the parlor, and conversed, for a long time, upon the rash and unjust decision of their parent. The mutual attachment that existed between George and Ray was not looked upon with indifference by the sister of the former; and she determined upon using all the means in her power to bring the latter into the good will of her father; she resolved, like a noble girl, to cherish a social and friendly feeling toward the friend of her brother. He who knows the warmth of a sister's affection can imagine with what constancy she adhered to this determination. The command of her father not to associate with the poor only served to strengthen her resolution, for she knew with what obstacles her brother would have to contend. She had a kind heart, that would not allow a fellow-being to want, so long as she had, or could obtain, the means to relieve him.

"Do you think father was in earnest in what he said?" inquired Amelia.

"I have no reason to doubt his sincerity," replied George; "but what led you to ask such a question?"

"Because, you know, he often speaks ironically; and, as he left the dinner-room with mother, he smiled, and said something about the poor, and a trick he was about to play."

"True, Amelia," replied George, "he is to play a trick; but it concerns not us. You know poor old Smith is one of father's tenants. Smith has been sick, and has not been able to procure funds with which to pay his rent, and father intends to engage a person to take out all the doors and windows of the house. He hopes Smith will thus be forced to leave. I have been thinking whether we cannot devise some plan to prevent the poor man from being turned thus abruptly from the house."

"I am sure we can," replied Amelia; "yet I had much rather have a trick played upon us than upon poor Smith. Can you not propose some way by which we can prevent father from carrying out his intentions?"

"I will give you the money," replied George, "if you will convey it to Mr. Smith, so that he will be enabled to pay his rent. Recollect it must be carried in the night, and *this* night, as father expects to commence his operations to-morrow or next day. You know that I cannot go, as my time will be fully occupied in attending upon some important business at home." It was not necessary to make this offer more than once. The heart of Amelia bounded with joy, as she anticipated being the bearer of the money to Smith;

and, shortly after dark, being provided with it, she proceeded to his house.

It was a dark night. The moon was obscured by thick clouds, and no twinkling star shone to guide her on her errand of mercy. As she drew near the lonely dwelling of Paul Smith, she perceived no light. She feared that he might be absent. Stealthily along she crept, and, listening at the door, heard the voice of prayer, imploring aid and support during the trials of life, that relief might soon be sent. Amelia silently opened the door, and placed the money on a table, accompanied with a note to Smith, requesting him not to disclose the manner in which he received it, and, as silently withdrawing, wended her way home. As she entered the parlor, she found her father and brother engaged in earnest conversation,— so earnest that she was not at first noticed.

"Confound my tenants!" said Mr. Greenville. "There 's old Paul Smith; if to-morrow's sun does not witness him bringing my just dues, he shall leave,— yes, George, he *shall* leave! I am no more to be trifled with and perplexed by his trivial excuses. All my tenants who do not pay shall toe the same mark. I 'll make them walk up, fodder or no fodder! Ha, ha, ha! old Smith shall know that I have some principle left, if I have passed my sixtieth year — that he shall! Slipnoose, the lawyer, shall have one job."

"You are always visiting your friends, George. It seems as though all are your friends. Yet I don't blame you, for friends are very happy appendages to one's character. I pity the man who lives a friendless life. That 's the reason I have been such a friend to Smith,— but no longer!" As he said this the wealthy landlord left the room.

Amelia related to her brother an account of her adventure, and both were thankful that they been instrumental in relieving the wants of their poor neighbors. The next morning, seated at the table, Mr. Greenville began again to express his opinion respecting poor people in general, and Paul Smith in particular, when a loud rap at the door somewhat startled him. In a few moments a servant entered, and gave information that a person was at the door who wished to see Mr. Greenville. Arriving there, the landlord encountered his tenant, Smith, who immediately told him that by some kind providence he was enabled to pay him his due, and hoped that in future he should be prompt in his payments.

The landlord took the money, and, looking it over, handed him a receipt for the same, and returned to the breakfast-table. Nothing was said about Smith until Mr. Greenville, as he left the room, remarked "that he did not know but that Smith meant well enough."

Nearly a month had elapsed and nothing had been heard of Ray Bland, when, on a certain morning, Mr. Greenville came in and handed George a letter. Upon opening it, George found it to be written by his friend Ray, informing him of his safe arrival home, thanking him for the kind attention he received during his visit, and expressing great pleasure in soon having another opportunity to visit him. George communicated this intelligence to Amelia, and they determined upon using their united efforts in endeavoring to bring over the kind feelings of their father to their young, but poor, friend.

"It 's no use for you to talk," said old Mr. Greenville, after a long conversation with the two; "the die is cast. I have resolved, and all the arguments you can bring forward will not cause me to break my resolution."

"Well," remarked George, "perhaps the day will come when you will deeply regret forming such a resolution. Perhaps the sunshine of prosperity will not always illumine our path."

"Be that as it may," interrupted Mr. Greenville, "we will not allow our imagination to wander forth into the mystical regions of the future, or picture to ourselves scenes of wretchedness, if such await us. Flatter me not with the good intentions of Ray Bland."

Months passed away, and the children of the proud Mr. Greenville forbore to mention in the presence of their father aught concerning their friend Ray Bland, or to excite the anger of the old gentleman by combating his prejudices against the poor.

Months passed away, and again Ray Bland found himself beneath the roof of his former friend. He was received by George and Amelia with the cordiality that had ever marked his intercourse with them; but the father was, if possible, more morose and sullen than usual.

Ray had several times made the attempt to know the cause of this coldness, but as often as he alluded to it George would invariably turn the subject; and he forbore to question further, content with the happiness which he enjoyed in the society of those he held so dear.

It was the evening of a fine day in the early spring, that the three friends sat together. It was the last evening of his visit, and Ray expected not to return for a long time. Alone in his study, the father vented his indignation against paupers, which respect for his daughter's feelings only prevented in the presence of their visitor. He opened the casement. Clouds were gathering in the sky, and now and then a faint flash of lightning illumined the increasing darkness; and the far-off voice of the storm was audible from the distance, each moment increasing in strength and violence. Soon the storm was upon them.

The old gentleman retired to his apartment. Each moment the storm increased in violence, and in vain did he strive to close his eyes in sleep.

At length a flash more vivid, accompanied by a peal of thunder more terrific than any that had preceded it, startled the inmates of the mansion. The wind howled terribly, and the old trees groaned and creaked about the dwelling with a fearful and terrific sound.

Within all was still and quiet. No word was spoken, for it was a fearful night, and in fear and dread they suspended their conversation.

Amelia first broke the silence. "Something must be burning," exclaimed she. In an instant the cry of fire was heard. All started up and rushed to the door; and there, indeed, they were witnesses of a sight which might well appall. The whole upper part of the house was in flames. Instantly the cause flashed upon them. The house had been struck and set on fire by lightning. "My father! O, my father!" shrieked Amelia, and fell fainting to the floor. Quick as the word came the thought of Ray Bland that the aged Mr. Greenville might be in danger; and ere George Greenville had borne his sister to a place of safety, through flame and smoke had Ray Bland reached the chamber which he knew the old gentleman occupied. It was locked. One blow of his foot, with all the force he could muster, and locks and bolts gave way. The room was nearly enveloped in flames, the curtains of the window and bed had been consumed, and now the flames had seized the wood-work and burned with great fury. Upon the floor, prostrate as if dead, lay the proud man, who scorned and detested the poor, and who had boasted of being beyond the reach of adversity. To lift him in his arms and bear him to the street was the work of an instant. He had only been stunned, and the drenching rain through which he was carried soon revived him. Ray bore him to the house of poor Smith, the nearest to his own; and there, with feelings of anguish which cannot be described, surrounded by his children and neighbors, the old man learned a lesson which his whole previous life had not taught, of the dependence which every member of society has upon the whole. While his riches were taking wings to fly away even before his own eyes, he felt how foolish and wicked was his past conduct; and ever after the poor found no warmer friend or more liberal hand than that of old George Greenville.

In the course of a few months a new and spacious building was erected upon the site of the one destroyed; and the neighbors say that the pretty cottage which is being built just over the way is to be the future residence of Ray Bland and the fair Amelia, whose aristocratic father now knows no distinction, save in *merit*, between the *rich* and *poor*.

THE HOMEWARD BOUND.

Slowly he paced the vessel's whitened deck,
While thoughts of hours, and days, and scenes long past,
Brought forth from fountains well-nigh dry a tear:
For in imagination he could see
Himself a tiny boy, in childish sport
Upon a river's bank, quite near his home,
Chasing the butterfly, whose gaudy dress
Lured him away, till, wearied with the chase,
Upon some mossy stone he sat him down;
Or, in some rippling brook, beneath the shade
Of some tall oak, he bathed his parchéd brow;
Then up he sprang, retraced his wandering steps,
Yet heedless ran, and could not leave his play.
And since *that* day what scenes had he passed through,
What trials met, what sights his eyes beheld!

Beneath the burning skies of torrid zones,
On frozen banks of Nova Zembla's coast,
Or the more fertile climes of Italy;
There, where the luscious grape in fulness hangs,
And fields of roses yield a rich perfume;
'Mid orange-groves whence sweetest odors rise,
'Neath branches burdened with their fragrant fruit,
Forth he had wandered.

Mark the semblance now!
For much there is between his childish course
Upon the river's bank and his later
Wanderings. Then, he chased the butterfly. Now,
His inclination led to a pursuit
More bold, adventurous, and far more grand.
Ambition filled his soul. Sometimes he ran

In vain ; and so it was in boyhood's days ;
And thus 't is plainly seen that childhood hours
Are but an index of our future life,
And life an index of that yet to come.

As on the vessel swept, a tear would 'scape
Forth from its hidden cell, and trickle down
The sailor's deeply-furrowed cheek, to bathe
Those recollections with the dew of Thought!

Some deem it weak to weep. Away the thought!
It is not weakness when Affection's fount
O'erflows its borders, and to man displays
The feelings that its powers cannot conceal.
It is not weakness when our feeble words
Find utterance only in our flowing tears.
Call not *such* language "weakness"! Worlds may laugh,
Yet know no joy like that which often flows
In silent tears.

As nearer drew the seaman to his home,
As in the distance first he saw the spot
Where childhood's hours in happiness were spent,
His slow pace quickened to a faster walk,
And, had he had the power, he 'd walked the waves,
And bravely dashed the intrusive spray aside,
To reach the much-loved spot more rapidly
Than wind and tide urged on his noble bark.

THE POOR OF EARTH.

I 've often wondered, as I 've sat
  Within mine own loved home,
And thought of those, my fellow-men,
  Who houseless, homeless, roam ;

That one upon this earth is found
  Whose heart good promptings smother;
And will not share his wealth with him
  Who is his poorer brother!

I 've often wondered, as I 've walked
  Amid life's busy throng,
And seen my fellows who have been
  By Fortune helped along,
That they who bask in its bright rays
  No tear of pity shed
On him who doth no "fortune" seek,
  But asks a crust of bread!

I 've seen the gilded temple raised,
  The aspirant of fame
Ascend the altar's sacred steps,
  To preach a Saviour's name,
And wondered, as I stood and gazed
  At those rich-cushioned pews,
Where he who bears the poor man's fate
  Might hear Salvation's news.

I 've walked within the church-yard's walls,
  With holy dread and fear,
And on its marble tablets read
  "None but the rich lie here."
I 've wandered till I came upon
  A heap of moss-grown stones,
And some one whispered in mine ear,
  "Here rest the poor man's bones."

My spirit wandered on, until
  It left the scenes of earth;
Until I stood with those who 'd passed
  Through death, the second birth.
And I inquired, with holy awe,
  "Who are they within this fold,
Who seem to be Heaven's favorites,
  And wear those crowns of gold?"

Then a being came unto me,
  One of angelic birth,
And in most heavenly accents said,
  "Those were the poor of earth."
Then from my dream I woke, but
  Will ne'er forget its worth;
For ever since that vision
  I have loved "the poor of earth."

And when I see them toiling on
  To earn their daily bread,
And dire oppression crush them down,
  Till every joy hath fled, —
I mind me of that better world,
  And of that heavenly fold,
Where every crown of thorns gives place
  Unto a crown of gold.

IF I DON'T, OTHERS WILL.

"If I don't make it, others will;
So I 'll keep up my death-drugged still.
Come, Zip, my boy, pile on the wood,
And make it blaze as blaze it should;
For I do heartily love to see
The flames dance round it merrily!

"Hogsheads, you want? — well, order them made;
The maker will take his pay in trade.
If, at the first, he will not consent,
Treat him with wine till his wits are spent;
Then, when his reason is gone, you know
Whate'er we want from his hands will flow!

"Ah, what do you say? — 'that won't be fair'?
You 're conscientious, I do declare!
I thought so once, when I was a boy,
But since I have been in this employ

I 've practised it, and many a trick,
By the advice of my friend, Old Nick.
I thought 't was wrong till he hushed my fears
With derisive looks, and taunts, and jeers,
And solemnly said to me, 'My Bill,
If you don't do it, some others will!'

"If I don't sell it, some others will;
So bottles, and pitchers, and mugs I 'll fill.
When trembling child, who is sent, shall come,
Shivering with cold, and ask for rum
(Yet fearing to raise its wet eyes up),
I 'll measure it out in its broken cup!

"Ah! what do you say?—'the child wants bread'?
Well, 't is n't *my* duty to see it fed;
If the parents *will* send to me to buy,
Do you think I 'd let the chance go by
To get me gain? O, I 'm no such fool;
That is not taught in the world's wide school!

"When the old man comes with nervous gait,
Loving, yet cursing his hapless fate,
Though children and wife and friends may meet,
And me with tears and with sighs entreat
Not to sell him that which will be his death,
I 'll hear what the man with money saith;
If he asks for rum and shows the gold,
I 'll deal it forth, and it *shall* be sold!

"Ah! do you say, 'I should heed the cries
Of weeping friends that around me rise'?
May be *you* think so; I tell you what,—
I 've a rule which proves that I should not;
For, know you, though the poison kill,
If I don't sell it, some others will!"

A strange fatality came on all men,
Who met upon a mountain's rocky side;
They had been sane and happy until then,
But then on earth they wished not to abide.

The sun shone brightly, but it had no charm ;
  The soft winds blew, but them did not elate ;
They seemed to think all joined to do them harm,
  And urge them onward to a dreadful fate.
I did say "all men," yet there were a few
  Who kept their reason well,—yet, weak, what could they do?

The men rushed onward to the jagged rocks,
  Then plunged like madmen in their madness o'er ;
From peak to peak they scared the feathered flocks,
  And far below lay weltering in their gore.
The sane men wondered, trembled, and they strove
  To stay the furies ; but they could not do it.
Whate'er they did, however fenced the drove,
  The men would spring the bounds or else break through it,
And o'er the frightful precipice they leaped,
  Till rock and tree seemed in their red blood steeped.

One of the sane men was a great distiller
  And one sold liquors in a famous city ;
And, by the way, one was an honest miller,
  Who looked on both their trades in wrath and pity.
This good "Honestus" spoke to them, and said,
  "*You 'd better jump ; if you don't, others will.*"
Each took his meaning, yet each shook his head.
  "That is no reason we ourselves should kill,"
Said they, while very stupid-brained they seemed,
  As though they of the miller's meaning never dreamed.

NOT MADE FOR AN EDITOR.

BEING A TRUE ACCOUNT OF AN INCIDENT IN THE HISTORY OF THE STUBBS FAMILY.

MR. and MRS. STUBBS were seated at the side of a red-hot cylinder stove. On one side, upon the floor, a small black-and-white dog lay very composedly baking himself; on the other, an old brown cat was, in as undisturbed a manner, doing the same. The warmth that existed between them was proof positive that they had not grown cold towards each other, though the distance between them might lead one to suppose they had.

In one corner of the room was the bust of a man, whose only existence was in the imagination of a miserable ship-carver, who, in his endeavors to breathe life into his block, came near breathing life out of himself, by sitting up late at night at his task. In the other hung a crook-necked squash, festooned with wreaths of spider-webs. Above the mantelpiece was suspended a painting representing a feat performed by a certain dog, of destroying one hundred rats in eight minutes. The frame in which this gem of art was placed was once gilt, but, at the time to which we refer, was covered with the dust of ages.

Mr. Stubbs poked the fire. Mrs. Stubbs poked the dog, when suddenly the door flew open, and their son entered with blackened eyes, bloody hands, bruised face and dirty clothes, the most belligerent-looking creature this side of the "Rio Grande."

"My voice a'nt *still* for war, it 's *loud* for war," he said, as, with a braggadocia sort of air, he threw his cap at the dog, who clenched it between his teeth, shook it nearly to tatters, and then passed it over to the cat.

"What 's the matter now, Jake?" said Mrs. Stubbs. "Always in trouble,—fights and broils seem to be your element. I don't know, Jake, what will become of you, if you go on at this rate. What say you, father?"

Mr. Stubbs threw down the poker, and casting a glance first at his hopeful son, and then at his hoping wife, replied that Jake was an ignorant, pugnacious, good-for-nothing scamp, and never would come to anything, unless to a rope's end.

"O, how *can* you talk so?" said his wife. "You know it 's nat'ral."

"Nat'ral!" shouted the father; "then it 's ten times worse — the harder then to rid him of his quarrelsome habits. But I 've an idea," said he, his face brightening up at the thought, as though he had clenched and made it fast and sure.

The mother started as by an electric shock. The boy, who had retired into one corner in a sullen mood, freshened up, and looked at his father. The ship-carver's fancy sketch brightened up also; but not of its own free will, for the force with which Mr. Stubbs brought his hand in contact with the table caused the dirty veil to fall from the *bust*-er's face.

"What is it?" inquired Mrs. Stubbs, with much animation.

"Why, my dear woman, as we can do nothing with him, *we 'll make him an editor.*"

The old lady inquired what that was; and, being informed, expressed doubts as to his ability.

"Why," said she, "he cannot write distinctly."

"What of that? — let him write with the scissors and paste-pot. Let him learn; many know a great deal more after having learned."

"But he must have some originality in his paper," said Mrs. Stubbs, who, it seemed, did not fall in with the general opinion that "any one can edit a paper."

"Never fear that," said Mr. Stubbs; "he 'll conduct anything he takes hold of, rather than have that conduct him. I 'll tell you what, old woman, Jake *shall* be an editor, whether he can write a line of editorial or not. Jake, come here."

Jake, who had nearly forgotten his fight, was elated at the proposition of his father, and, being asked whether, in his opinion, he could conduct a paper with ability, originality and success, replied, in the slang phrase of the day, that he "could n't do anything else," at the same time clenching his fist, as though to convince his sire that he *could* do something else, notwithstanding.

"As I have never asked you any question relative to public affairs, and as the people of this generation are getting to be wise, I deem it right that I should ask you a few questions before endeavoring to obtain a situation. Now, Jake, who is the President of the United States?"

"General George Washington," replied the intelligent lad, or rather young man; for, though he indulged in many boyish tricks, he was about twenty years of age, a short, dull-looking member of the "great unwashed." The father intimated that he was mistaken; the son persisted in saying that he was not.

"Never mind the catechizer," said Jake; "I 'll conduct a newspaper, I will, for Mr. and Mrs. Stubbs never see the day I could n't conduct anything."

"That 's bright," said Mrs. Stubbs; "he possesses more talent than I was aware of; he 'll make an editor."

"An' he *shall*," said the father, resolutely.

The clock struck nine, which was the signal for Mr. and Mrs. Stubbs to retire, and they did so. No sooner had they left than their dutiful son mounted the table, and, taking down the fancy bust, pulled the dog by the tail to awake him, and set him barking at it. The cat must have her part in the tragedy, so Jake thought; and, pulling her by the tail, she was soon on the field of action.

"Now, sist-a-boy, Tozer; give her an editorial," said he; and, as dog and cat had been through the same performance before, they acted their parts in manner suiting. The dog barked, the cat snapped and snarled, and Jake Stubbs stood by rubbing his hands in a perfect ecstasy of delight.

It is needless for us to relate the many curious adventures Mr. Stubbs met with whilst searching for a situation for Jake.

His endeavors to find a situation such as he wanted were, for a long time, ineffectual. At length he blundered into a small printing-office, where three men and a boy were testing the merits of half a dozen doughnuts, and a bottle of root beer.

Mr. Stubbs was *very* sorry to disturb them. When he mentioned his errand, one of the men — a tall fellow, with check shirt and green apron — said that he had, for a long time, contemplated starting a paper, but, as he was not capable of editing one, he had not carried out his intention. The principal reason why he had not published was, he was poor; business had not prospered in his hands, and an outlay of two thousand dollars would be needed to commence and continue the paper.

"Very well," replied Mr. Stubbs, "that is a large sum; but, if there is no doubt of its being returned, I might think of loaning it to you, for the sake of getting my talented son into business."

"Not the least doubt, not the least," replied Mr. Pica; and he so inflamed the imagination of Mr. Stubbs, that, strange as it may seem to the cautious reader, he wrote a check for the amount, merely taking the unendorsed note of Mr. Pica as security; then, hastening home, he told Mrs. Stubbs to brush up the boy, for he *was an editor*.

* * * * *

Behold, now, Mr. Jake Stubbs in a little room up three pair of stairs, preparing "copy" for the first number of "The Peg Top, or the Buzz of the Nation." He has n't got black eyes now; all the blackness of his person, if not of his character, has settled in his fingers, and they are black with ink. Not all settled, for a few daubs of the "blood of the world," as the dark fluid has been called, were to be seen on his forehead, having passed there from his fingers, when leaning upon them in a pensive mood, vainly endeavoring to bring up thoughts from the mighty depths of his intellect,—so *mighty*, in fact, that his thoughts were kept there, and refused to come up.

Mr. Jake Stubbs had been cutting and pasting all day, when, thinking it a little too severe to inflict further duty upon the assistant editor, he took his pen in hand, resolved upon writing a masterly article as a *leader*.

A sheet of blank paper had lain on the table before him for nearly an hour. He would sit and think. Some idea would pop into his head, then with a dash would the pen go into the ink, but before he could get his pen out the idea had flown, and the world was the loser. Then he threw himself back into his chair,—thought, thought, thought. At length Jake obtained the mastery, as patience and perseverance always will, and the pen became his willing slave, though his mind, being the slave-driver, did not hurry it on very fast. He was able to pen a few words, and wrote "The war with Mexico —"

Well, he had got so far; that was very original, and if he never wrote anything else, would stamp him a man of talent. Into the ink, on the paper, and his pen wrote the little word *are.* "The war with Mexico are." Ten minutes more of steady thought, and three more words brought him to a full stop. "The war with Mexico are a indisputable fact." That last but one was a long word, and a close observer could have seen his head expand with the effort.

"Copy, sir, copy!" shouted the printer's boy, as he stood with his arms daubed with ink, and a straw hat upon his head that had seen service, and looked old enough to retire and live on a pension.

"Copy what?" inquired the editor, who began to feel indignant, imagining that the publisher had seen his labor to write an article, and had sent him word to *copy* from some paper.

"Here," said he, "take this to Mr. Pica, and tell him 't is original, and gives an account of the war with Mexico, with news up to this date."

The boy took it, trudged up stairs with two lines of MS., and the editor arose and walked his office, as though his labors were o'er, and he might rest and see some mighty spirit engrave his name upon the scroll of fame.

He had crossed the floor half a dozen times, when in came the same youth, shouting "Copy, sir, copy!"

"Copy what?" shouted Jake, laying hold of the boy's shirt-sleeve. "Tell me what you want copied! tell me, sir, or I will shake your interiors out of you —"

The boy was small, but spunky. His education had been received at the corners of the streets. He had never taken lessons of a professor, but he had practised upon a number of urchins smaller than himself, and had become a thoroughly proficient and expert pugilist.

It was not for Bill Bite to be roughly handled by any one, not even by an editor. So he pushed him from him, and said,

"I want copy; that 's a civil question,—I want a civil answer."

Jake's organ of combativeness became enlarged. He sprang at the boy, grasped him by the waist, and would have thrown him down stairs, had not a movement the boy made prevented him.

Bill's arms were loose, and, nearing the table, he took the inkstand and dashed the contents into the face of his assailant.

"Murder!" shouted the editor.

"Copy!" shouted the boy; and such a rumpus was created, that up came Mr. Pica, saying that the building was so shaken that an article in type on the subject of "Health and Diet" suddenly transformed itself into "pi."

The two belligerents were parted; the editor and Master Bill Bite stood at extremes. At this crisis who should enter but Mr. Stubbs, senior, who, seeing his son's face blackened with ink, inquired the cause rather indignantly; at which Mr. Pica, not recognizing in the indignant inquirer the father of the "talented editor," turned suddenly about and struck him a blow in the face, that displaced his spectacles, knocked off his white hat into a pond of ink, and made the old fellow see stars amid the cobwebs and dust of the ceiling.

The son, seeing himself again at liberty, flew at the boy, and gave him "copy" of a very impressive kind.

Down from the shelves came dusty papers and empty bottles, whilst up from the printing-office came the inmates, to learn the cause of the disturbance.

A couple of police-officers passing at the time, hearing the noise, entered, and one of them taking Mr. Stubbs, senior, and the other Mr. Stubbs, junior, bore them off to the lock-up.

This affair put a sudden stop to "The Buzz of the Nation." The first number never made its appearance.

Mr. Pica, having obtained the amount of the check, went into the country for his health, and has not been heard from since.

Elder Stubbs and Stubbs the younger paid a fine of five dollars each; and when they reached home and related to Mrs. Stubbs the facts in the case, she took off her spectacles, and, after a few moments' sober thought, came to the sage conclusion that her son Jake was not made for an editor.

HERE'S TO THE HEART THAT'S EVER BRIGHT.

HERE 's to a heart that 's ever bright,
  Whatever may betide it,
Though fortune may not smile aright,
  And evil is beside it;
That lets the world go smiling on,
  But, when it leans to sadness,
Will cheer the heart of every one
  With its bright smile of gladness!

A fig for those who always sigh
  And fear an ill to-morrow;
Who, when they have no troubles nigh,
  Will countless evils borrow;
Who poison every cup of joy,
  By throwing in a bramble;
And every hour of time employ
  In a vexatious scramble.

What though the heart be sometimes sad!
  'T is better not to show it;
'T will only chill a heart that 's glad,
  If it should chance to know it.
So, cheer thee up if evil 's nigh,
  Droop not beneath thy sadness;
If sorrow finds thou wilt not sigh,
  'T will leave thy heart to gladness.

MORNING BEAUTY.

Brightly now on every hill
  The sun's first rays are beaming,
And dew-drops on each blade of grass
  Are in their beauty gleaming.
O'er every hill and every vale
  The huntsman's horn is sounding,
And gayly o'er each brook and fence
  His noble steed is bounding.

There 's beauty in the glorious sun
  When high mid heaven 't is shining,
There 's beauty in the forest oak
  When vines are round it twining ;
There 's beauty in each flower that blooms,
  Each star whose light is glancing
From heaven to earth, as on apace
  'T is noiselessly advancing.

Beauties are all around thy path,
  And gloriously they 're shining ;
Nature hath placed them everywhere,
  To guard men from repining.
Yet 'mong them all there 's naught more fair,
  This beauteous earth adorning,
Than the bright beauty gathering round
  The early hours of morning.

THE RECOMPENSE OF GOODNESS.

When our hours shall all be numbered,
  And the time shall come to die,
When the tear that long hath slumbered
  Sparkles in the watcher's eye,

Shall we not look back with pleasure
  To the hour when some lone heart,
Of our soul's abundant treasure,
  From our bounty took a part?

When the hand of death is resting
  On the friend we most do love,
And the spirit fast is hasting
  To its holy home above,
Then the memory of each favor
  We have given will to us be
Like a full and holy savor,
  Bearing blessings rich and free.

O, then, brother, let thy labor
  Be to do good while you live,
And to every friend and neighbor
  Some kind word and sweet smile give.
Do it, all thy soul revealing,
  And within your soul you 'll know
How one look of kindly feeling
  Cause the tides of love to flow.

BRIDAL SONGS.

TO THE WIFE.

Let a smile illume thy face,
  In thy joyous hours;
Look of sympathy be thine,
  When the darkness lowers.

He thou lovest movest where
  Many trials meet him;
Waiting be when he returns,
  Lovingly to greet him.

Though without the world be cold,
  Be it thy endeavor
That within thy home is known
  Happiness forever.

TO THE HUSBAND.

WHATSOEVER trials rise,
  Tempting thee to falter,
Ne'er forget the solemn vows
  Taken at the altar.

In thy hours of direst grief,
  As in those of gladness,
Minister to her you love,
  Dissipate her sadness.

Be to cheer, to bless, to love,
  Always your endeavor;
Write upon your heart of hearts
  Faithfulness forever.

THE JUG AFLOAT.

"WHAT I tell thee, captain, is sober truth. If thee wishes to prosper, thee must not allow thy sailors grog, lest, when at sea, they become tipsy, and thy ship, running upon hidden rocks, shall be lost; or else, when at the mast-head, giddiness come upon them, and, falling, thy crew shall number one less."

Thus spake a good old Quaker, a native of the city of Penn. Captain Marlin had been for many days and nights considering whether it were best to carry a complement of wine for himself and friends, and grog for his crew. He had that morning met Simon Prim, and asked his opinion, which he gave as above; yet Captain Marlin seemed undetermined. He felt it to be an important question, and he desired to come to a right conclusion.

They had been passing up Broadway; had reached the Trinity, crossing over towards Wall-street. Simon, with his usual gravity, raised his hand, and, pointing to the towering steeple of the splendid edifice, said:

"If thou, neighbor, desired to ascend yonder spire, thinkest thou thou wouldst first drink of thy wine, or thy grog?"

"Certainly not," replied Captain Marlin.

"Then," continued the Quaker, "do not take it to sea with thee; for thou or thy men mayest be called to a spot as high as yonder pinnacle, when thee little thinkest of it."

The two walked down Wall-street without a word from either, till, reaching a shipping-office, Captain Marlin remarked that he had business within. The Quaker very politely bowed, and bade him take heed to good counsel, and good-day.

The owner of the vessel was seated in an arm-chair, reading the shipping news in the *Journal.*

"Did you know," said he, as his captain entered, "that Parvalance & Co. have lost their ship, 'The Dey of Algiers,' and none were saved but the cabin-boy, and he half dead when found?"

"Indeed not; when — where — how happened it?" inquired Captain Marlin, in some haste.

"On a voyage from Canton, with a rich cargo of silks, satins, teas, &c. The *boy* says that the men had drank rather too much, and were stupidly drunk,— but fudge! Captain Marlin, you know enough to know that no man would drink too much at sea. He would be sure to keep at a good distance from a state of intoxication, being aware that much was intrusted to his care which he could not well manage whilst in such a state."

"Perhaps so," said Captain Marlin, doubtingly. "Mr. Granton, this touches a question I have been for days considering. It is, whether I shall allow my men grog."

"Of course, of course!" answered the ship-owner; "nothing so good for them round the Cape. You know the winds there, rather tough gales and heavy seas. Cold water there, Mr. Marlin! Why, rather give them hot coffee with ice crumbled in it, or carry out a cask of ice-cream to refresh them! Man alive, do you think they could live on *such* vapor? You talk like one who never went to sea, unless to see a cattle-show."

Captain Marlin could not refrain from laughing at such reasoning, yet was more than half inclined to favor it. He was fond of his wine, and being, as such folks generally are, of a good disposition, he wished to see all men enjoy themselves, especially when at sea. He wished evil to no man, and had he thought that liquor might injure any of his crew, he would not that morning, in that office, have come to the conclusion to have it on board the "Tangus."

CHAPTER II.

On a bright, clear morning, a deeply-freighted ship started from a New York slip; a fair wind bore it swiftly down the bay, and a few minutes' sail found it far from sight of the metropolis of the Union. Friends had taken the last glimpse of friends, the last interchange of kindly feelings had passed, and deep waters now separated them. It was the "Tangus," Robert Marlin captain, with a picked crew, and bound for the coast of Sumatra. Simon Prim shook his head, as he with others turned and walked home. "'T is a pity men will not see evil and flee from it," said he, and he pulled his straight coat-collar up, and thrust his hands more deeply than ever into his pockets. He was a little startled by a light tap upon the shoulder, and quite a happy voice exclaiming, "Why, Mr. Prim, how are you?"

"Verily, neighbor, thou didst move me; but I was thinking so deeply of Captain Marlin and his success, that no wonder thy light touch should do so."

"But what of him, Prim?"

"His ship, the Tangus, has just left, bound on a long voyage, and with a quantity of deadly poison on board, with which to *refresh* the crew. I tell thee, neighbor, I have fears for the result. The jug may possibly stand still when on land, but when it 's afloat it 's rather unsteady."

"Very true, but you seem to express unusual anxiety in regard to Captain Marlin and his good ship; thousands have been just as imprudent."

"But not in these days of light and knowledge, friend. There have been enough sad examples to warn men not to trifle on such subjects. Twenty years ago I drank. We had our whiskey at our funerals and our weddings. I have seen chief mourners staggering over the grave, and the bridegroom half drunk at the altar; but times are changed now, and thank God for the good that has been effected by this reformation!"

"You speak true, Simon; and I wonder Captain Marlin could, if he considered the evils brought about by intoxicating drink, carry it to sea with him."

"I told him all as I tell it to thee, friend Jones. He asked my opinion, and I gave it him, yet it seems he thought little of it. Good-day, neighbor; I have business with a friend at the 'Croton,' good-day;" and, saying this, Mr. Prim walked up a bye street.

Jones walked on, and thought considerable of the Quaker's last words. His mind that day continually ran upon the subject. Indeed, he seemed unable to think of anything else but of a jug afloat, and at night spoke of it to his wife.

The wife of Captain Marlin had that day called upon Mrs. Jones, and, although her husband had scarcely got out of sight, looked with pleasure to the day of his return, and already anticipated the joyous occasion. There is as much pleasure in anticipation as in realization, it is often said, and there is much truth in the saying. We enjoy the thought of the near approach of some wished for day, but when it arrives we seem to have enjoyed it all before it came.

Mrs. Jones was far from thinking it wrong in Captain Marlin that he carried liquor with him on his voyage, and gave it as her opinion that the vessel was as safe as it could possibly be without it.

"Remember what I say, that is a doomed ship," said Mr. Jones, after some conversation on the subject.

"You are no prophet, my dear," said his wife, "neither am I a prophetess; but I will predict a pleasant voyage and safe return to the Tangus." With such opposite sentiments expressed, they retired.

CHAPTER III.

Insensible to all that is beautiful in nature, and grand and majestic in the works of creation, must the heart of that man be who can see no beauty, grandeur, or majesty, in the mighty abyss of waters, rolling on in their strength — now towering like some vast mountain, and piling wave upon wave, till, like pyramids dancing on pyramids, their tops seem to reach the sky; then sinking as deep as it had before risen, and again mounting up to heaven. There 's beauty in such a scene, and no less when, calm and unruffled, the setting sun sinks beneath the horizon, and for miles and miles leaves its long, glistening track upon the unmoved waters.

'T was so when the crew of the "Tangus" were assembled upon the deck of that noble ship. The day previous had been one of hard labor; the vessel had bravely withstood the storm, and seemed now to be resting after the contest. Not a ripple was to be seen. Far as the eye could reach, was seen the same beautiful stillness. So with the crew; they were resting, though not in drowsy slumberings.

"I say what, Bill," remarked one, "'An honest man 's the noblest work of God,' somebody says, and that 's our captain, every inch, from stem to stern, as honest as Quaker Prim, of Gotham."

"Ay, ay, Jack," said another; "and did you hear how that same Prim tried to induce Captain Marlin to deprive us of our rights?"

"Grog, you mean?"

"Ay, ay."

"No; but how was it?"

"Arrah, the dirty spalpeen he was, if he was afther a trying for to do that — the divil — "

"Will Mr. McFusee wait? By the way, Jack, he, Prim, got him by the button, and began to pour into his ears a long tirade against a man's enjoying himself, and, by the aid of thee, thy, and thou, half convinced the old fellow that he must give up all, and live on ice-water and ship-bread."

"Did?"

"Ay, ay, you know. Captain Marlin. He always looks at both sides, then balances both, as it were, on the point of a needle, and decides, as Squire Saltfish used to say, 'cording to law and evidence."

"By the powers, he 's a man, ivery inch, from the crown of his hat to the soles of his shoes, he is."

"Mr. McFusee, *will* you keep still?" said Mr. Boyden, the narrator. Mr. McFusee signified that he would.

"Well, he balanced this question, and the evidence against flew up as 't were a feather; but down went the evidence for, and he concluded to deal every man his grog in due season."

"That 's the captain, all over," remarked Jack.

As we before said, their labors the day previous were great, and, as a dead calm had set in, and the vessel did not even float lazily along, but remained almost motionless,— not like a thing of life, but like a thing lifeless,— the captain ordered the crew each a can of liquor, and now they sat, each with his measure of grog, relating stories of the past, and surmises of the future.

"I tell you what," said Jack Paragon, "these temperance folks are the most foolish set of reformers myself in particular, and the United States, Texas, and the Gulf of Mexico, in general, ever saw."

"Even so," remarked Mr. Boyden, "but they do some good. 'Give the devil his due,' is an old saw, but none the less true for that. There 's Peter Porper, once a regular soaker, always said his 'plaints were roomattic, — rum-attic, I reckon, however, for he used to live up twelve pairs of stairs,— he and the man in the moon were next-door neighbors; they used to smoke together, and the jolly times they passed were never recorded, for there were no newpapers in those dark ages, and the people were as ignorant as crows. Well, one of these temperance folks got hold of him, and the next I saw of him he was the pet of the nation; loved by the men, caressed by the women — silver pitchers given him by the former, and broadcloth cloaks by the latter."

"No selfish motives in keeping temperate!" said Jack Rowlin, ironically.

"Can't say; but liquor never did me harm. When I find it does, I will leave off."

"That 's the doctrine of Father Neptune — drink and enjoy life."

"Every man to his post!" shouted the captain, as he approached from the quarter-deck. Quick to obey, they were where they were commanded in an instant, each with his tin can half filled with liquor. Captain Marlin, seeing this, ordered them to drink their grog or throw it overboard; they chose the former mode of disposing of it, and threw their empty cans at the cook.

In the distance a small black speck was descried.

CHAPTER IV.

The sun had set in clouds. The heavens were hung in darkness. Ever and anon a peal of thunder echoed above, a flash of vivid lightning illumed the waters, and far as eye could see the waters tossed high their whitened crests. The winds blew stormy, and now heavy drops of rain fell upon the deck of the "Tangus." "Every man to his duty!" shouted the captain; but the captain's voice was not obeyed.

Objects at two feet distance could not be seen. Louder that voice was heard. "Every man to his duty,—save the ship!"

"Captain, what is my duty?" inquired the cook.

"I appoint you under officer. Search for the men, and, if they are not all washed over, tell them I order them to work. If they do not know it, tell them the ship's in danger, and they must work."

The storm was fast increasing, till, at length, instead of blackness, one sheet of livid flame clothed the heavens above. Now all could be seen, and the captain busied himself. But two of the crew were to be seen, and they lay as senseless as logs. They heeded not the rage of the storm. The terrific peals of thunder awoke them not — they were dead drunk!

By the time the storm commenced, the liquor they had drank began to have its effect. Four of the crew, who were usually wide awake — that is, uncommonly lively — when intoxicated, had unfortunately fell overboard, and were lost.

The captain had now food for reflection, but the time and place were not for such musings.

He endeavored to arouse them, but in vain; so, with the aid of the only sober man aboard besides himself, he conveyed them to a place of safety. In the mean time the ship strained in every joint, and he momentarily expected to find himself standing on its wreck.

The waves washed the deck, and everything movable, cook-house and all, went by the board. The only hope of safety was in cutting away the masts, and to this task they diligently applied themselves. All night the captain and cook worked hard, and when morning came they found the storm abating. Soon the sun shone in its brightness; but what a scene did its light reveal! The once stately ship dismasted; four men, including the mate of the vessel, lost, and two lying insensible in the cabin.

It was not strange that the question came home to the mind of Captain Marlin, with force, "Is it right to carry liquor for a ship's crew?" He need ask the opinion of no one; he could find an answer in the scene around him.

CHAPTER V.

"Then thy ship has put in for repairs?" said Simon Prim, as he entered Granton & Co.'s office, on Wall-street.

"What?" exclaimed Mr. Granton, who had heard nothing of the matter. Simon, pulling a paper from his pocket, read:

"LOSS OF LIFE AT SEA.—By a passenger in the 'Sultan,' from ——, we are informed that the ship 'Tangus,' from this port, bound to Sumatra, and owned by Messrs. Granton & Co., of this city, put in at that place in a dismasted condition.

"The 'Tangus' had been three weeks out, when, in a gale, four men were washed overboard. The remainder of her crew being insensible, and the whole duty falling upon the captain and cook, they with great difficulty managed the ship. It is rumored that all were intoxicated. This is the seventh case of loss at sea, caused by intemperance, within four months. When will men become wise, and awake to their own interests on this topic?"

The ship-owner rapidly paced his office. "Can it be?" said he to himself. "Can it be?"

"Give thyself no trouble, friend," said Prim; "what is done is done, and can't be undone. Thy ship is not lost, and things are not so bad as they might be. Look to the future, and mourn not over the past; and remember that it is very dangerous to have a jug afloat."

These few words somewhat quieted him, yet not wholly.

At this moment the wife of Captain Marlin entered. Having heard of the news, she came to learn all that was known respecting it.

"Madam," said he, after relating all he knew, "my mind is changed on the question we some time since discussed. Yes, madam, my mind is changed, and from this hour I will do all I can to exterminate the practice of carrying grog to sea for the crew. And I tell thee what," he continued, turning to friend Prim, who stood near by, "I tell thee what, thee was right in thy predictions; and, though it has been a dear lesson to me, I have learned from it that it is poor policy that puts a jug afloat."

GIVE, AND STAY THEIR MISERY.

Would ye who live in palace halls,
  With servants round to wait,
Know aught of him who, craving, falls
  Before thine outer gate?
Come with me when the piercing blast
  Is whistling wild and free,
When muffled forms are hurrying past,
  And then his portion see.

Come with me through the narrow lanes
  To dwellings dark and damp,
Where poor men strive to ease their pains;
  Where, by a feeble lamp,
The wearied, widowed mother long
  Doth busy needle ply,
Whilst at her feet her children throng,
  And for a morsel cry.

Come with me thou in such an hour,
  To such a place, and see
That He who gave thee wealth gave power
  To stay such misery!
Come with me, — nor with empty hand
  Ope thou the poor man's door;
Come with the produce of thy land,
  And thou shalt gather more.

THE SPIRIT OF MAN.

Ye cannot bind the spirit down;
It is a thing as free
As the albatross-bird that wings
Its wild course o'er the sea.

Go, bind the lightning, guide the sun,
Chain comets, if you can;
But seek not with thy puny strength
To bind the soul of man.

Though all the powers of earth combine,
And all their strength enroll,
To bind man's body as they will,
They cannot bind his soul.

No power on earth can hold it down,
Or bid it hither stay,
As up to heaven with rapid course
It tireless wings its way.

Time is too limited for it,
And earth is not its clime;
It cannot live where sound the words,
"There is an end to time."

It seeks an endless, boundless sphere,
In which to freely roam;
Eternity its course of life,
Infinity its home.

There, there will it forever live;
And there, a spirit free,
'T will range, though earth may pass away,
And Time no longer be.

PAUSE AND THINK.

O! HOW many souls are sorrowing
In this sunlit world, to-day,
Because Wrong, heaven's livery borrowing,
Leadeth trusting souls astray;
Because men, all thoughtless rushing,
Dance along on Error's brink,
And, the voice of conscience hushing,
Will not for a moment think!

'T is the lack of thought that bringeth
Man to where he needs relief;
'T is the lack of thought that wringeth
All his inner self with grief.
Would he give a moment's thinking
Ere his every step is made,
He would not from light be shrinking,
Groping on in Error's shade!

Think, immortal! thou art treading
On a path laid thick with snares,
Where mischievous minds are spreading
Nets to catch thee unawares.
Pause and think! the next step taken
May be that which leads to death;
Rouse thee! let thy spirit waken;
List to, heed the word it saith!

Think, ere thou consent to squander
Aught of time in useless mirth;
Think, ere thou consent to wander,
Disregarding heaven-winged truth.
When the wine in beauty shineth,
When the tempter bids thee drink,
Ere to touch thy hand inclineth,
Be thou cautious — pause and think!

Think, whatever act thou doest;
  Think, whatever word is spoke;
Else the heart of friend the truest
  May be by thee, thoughtless, broke.
How much grief had been prevented,
  If man ne'er had sought to shrink
From the right: — to naught consented,
  Until he had paused to think!

LITTLE NELLY.

MATILDA was a fashionable girl,— a young lady, perhaps, would be the more respectable name by which to call her. She had been reared in affluence. She had never known a want. She had had wants, but she did not know it. She had wanted many things that make a lady's life indeed a life. But Matilda never dreamt of such things.

It was n't fashionable to love the outcast, and therefore she bestowed no pitying look on them. It was n't fashionable to give a few pennies even to a poor, lame orphan girl in the street. So she pretended not to have noticed the plea of little Nelly, who had accosted her during her morning rambles.

"Little Nelly." I remember how she looked when at twilight she sat down on a curb-stone to count the money. She looked sorrowful. She was, indeed, worthy of pity; but little she got. The crowd went hurrying, hustling on; few thoughts came down to little Nelly, on the curb-stone. It had been a gala day. Red flags had flaunted on high poles, and there had been a great noise of drums and fifes, and everybody had seemed happy. Why, then, should sorrow come, with its dark lantern, and look in the face of this little girl?

I will tell you.

There was a poor woman whose husband had been killed in Mexico. She lived in one small room in a secluded part of the city, and by means of her needle, and such assistance

PAGE 314.

as was given to her daughter, who diligently walked the streets, selling apples, she managed to live in a style which she denominated "comfortable." Thus, for upwards of one year, she toiled and lived, and was thankful for all her many blessings.

But sickness came; not severe, but of that kind that bears its victim along slowly to rest. She was unable to do much. She did not wish to do much; but she sat day by day, yea, night by night often, and diligently pursued the avocation that brought her daily bread.

Weeks passed, and yet she was ill. One morning, she called her daughter to her side, and, taking her hand in her own, said:

"Little Nelly, 't is Independence day, to-day. You heard the guns fire, and the bells ring, and the shouts of the happy children, this morning, before you arose. I watched you as you lay listening to all these, and I asked myself, Will my little Nelly be happy? and I thought I heard my mother's voice; — she died long, long ago, but I thought I heard her voice right at my side, saying, 'We shall all be happy soon;' and I wept, for I could not help it.

"But I 've called you now, Nelly, to tell you that I 'm much better this morning, and that, if you can get twenty-five cents to-day, we will have a happy time to-night."

Little Nelly looked happy for a moment, but soon a shadow came over her face; for she could not comprehend the meaning of her mother when she said she was "better," for she looked more feeble than she had ever seen her since the news of how her father was shot in the face at Monterey was told her.

But she tried to be cheerful. She tried to smile, but, O, it was very hard; and she got her mother's breakfast, and, having cleared the things away, took her little basket, and her mother's purse, and went out.

It was, indeed, a happy day without. There was joy depicted on every countenance, and the general happiness infused some of its spirit into the heart of our little trader.

She seemed almost lost in the great crowd; and there were so many dealers about, and so many that presented greater attractions in the display of their stock, that few bought of little Nelly.

It was late in the afternoon, and she had sold but a little, when she encountered a young lady gayly dressed, in whose hand was prominently displayed a bead purse, through the interstices of which the gold and silver glistened.

Nelly held out her humble purse, in which no beads were wrought, through which no coin glistened,—she held it up, and ventured to ask, in pleasant tones, a few pennies of the lady. But not a penny for little Nelly. Not even a look recognized her appeal, but costly, flowing robes rushed by, and nearly prostrated her; they did force her from the sidewalk into the gutter.

Go on, ye proud and selfish one! Go, bend the knee to Fashion's altar, and ask a blessing of its presiding spirit! Bestow no pitying glance on honest poverty; no helping hand to the weak and falling! There is a law which God hath written on all his works, proclaiming justice, and giving unto all as they shall ask of him. Pass on, and heed not that little praying hand; but remember you cannot do so without asking of that law its just requital.

Nelly walked on. She mingled again with the great mass, and twilight came. It was then that she sat down, as I have before stated, to count her money. She had but thirteen cents. All day she had sought to dispose of her stock, that she might carry to her mother the sum named, with which to have a happy time at home. And now the day had gone; the night was drawing its great shadowy cloak about the earth, and Nelly had but about one half of the required sum. What should she do?

It was at this moment I met her. I stooped down, and she told me all her story; — told me all her sorrow, — a great sorrow for a little breast like hers. I made up the trifling amount, and, taking her by the hand, we went together towards her home.

Reaching the house, we entered, and were met on the stairs by an old lady, who whispered in my ear, "Walk softly." I suspected in a moment the reason why she asked me thus to walk. She then led the way. She tried to keep back the little girl, but she could not. She hurried up the stairs, and through a long, dark entry, to a door, which she quickly opened.

Nelly sprang to the bed on which lay her mother. I heard a sigh — a sob. It was from the child. The mother spoke in a tone so joyous that I was at first surprised to hear it from one who, it was supposed, was near her end. But I soon found it was no matter of surprise.

How clear and fair was that face! How pleading and eloquent those eyes, as they turned, in all their full-orbed brightness, upon me, as I approached the bedside of the mother of Nelly! There were needed no words to convey to my mind the thoughts that dwelt within that soul, whose strength seemed to increase as that of the body diminished.

With one of her pale hands she took mine; with the other, that of her daughter.

"Blessings on you both!" she said. "Nelly, my dear Nelly, my faithful, loving Nelly, I am *much* better than I was; I shall soon be well, and what a happy time we will have to-night! I hear that voice again to-night, Nelly. Don't you hear it? It says, 'We shall all be happy soon.' I see a bright star above your head, my child; and now I see my mother. She is all bright and radiant, and there is a beauty around her that I cannot describe. Nelly, I am better. Why, I feel quite well."

She sprang forward, and, with her hands yet clasping Nelly's and my own, she stretched her arms upward. There was a bright glow of indescribable joy upon her features. She spoke calmly, sweetly spoke. "We shall all be happy soon — happy soon — happy ——" then fell back on the pillow, and moved no more — spoke not again.

She was indeed happy. But, Nelly — she was sad. For a long time she kept her hand in that of her mother. She at length removed it, and fell upon the floor, beneath the weight of her new sorrow. Yet it was but for a moment. Suddenly she sprang up, as if imbued with angelic hope and peace. We were surprised to see the change, and to behold her face beam with so much joy, and hear her voice lose its sadness. We looked forth with that inner sight which, on such occasions, seems quickened to our sense, and could see that mother, and that mother's mother, bending over that child, and raising her up to strength and hope, and a living peace and joy.

Nelly's little purse lay on the floor, where she had dropped it when she came in. The old nurse picked it up, and laid it on a stand beside the bed. A tear stole out from beneath the eyelids of the child as she beheld it, and thought how all day she had worked and walked to get the little sum with which her mother and she were to be made happy on that Independence night. I called her to me. We sat down and talked over the past, the present and the future, and I was astonished to hear the language which her pure and gentle, patient soul poured forth.

"Well, sir," she said, "we are happy to-night, though you think, perhaps, there is greater cause for sorrow. But mother has gone from all these toiling scenes. She will work no more all the long day, and the night, to earn a shilling, with which to buy our daily bread. She has gone where they have food that we know not of; and she 's happy to-night, and, sir, we shall all be happy soon. We shall all go up there to live amid realities. These are but shadows here of those great, real things that exist there; and I sometimes think, when sitting amid these shadows, that it will be a happy time when we leave them, and walk amid more substantial things."

Thus she talked for some time.

Having rendered such assistance as I could, I left. The next day there was a funeral, and little Nelly was what they called "the chief mourner;" yet it seemed a very inappropriate name for one whose sorrow was so cheerful. There were but few of us who followed; and, when we reached the grave, and the face of the earthly form was exposed to the sunlight for the last time, little Nelly sung the following lines, which I had hastily penned for the occasion:

WE SHALL ALL BE HAPPY SOON.

Dry our tears and wipe our eyes!
Angel friends beyond the skies
Open wide heaven's shining portal,
Welcome us to joys immortal.
Fear not, weep not, ours the boon;
We shall all be happy soon!

Hark! a voice is whispering near us;
'T is an angel-voice to cheer us;
It entreats us not to weep,
Fresh and green our souls to keep;
And it sings, in cheerful tune,
We shall all be happy soon.

Thus through life, though grief and care
May be given us to bear,

Though all dense and dark the cloud
That our weary forms enshroud,
Night will pass, and come the noon,
We shall all be happy soon.

When the last line of each verse was sung, it was no fancy thought in us, in Nelly more than all others, that suggested the union of other voices with our own; neither was it an illusion that pictured a great thing with harps, repeating the words, "We shall all be happy soon."

The sexton even, he who was so used to grave-yard scenes, was doubly interested; and, when the last look was taken, and Nelly seemed to look less in the dark grave and more up to the bright sky above her than those in her situation usually do, I saw him watch her, and a tear trickled down his wrinkled face.

As we turned to leave, I asked him why he wept. His features brightened up. "For joy, for joy," said he. "I have put away the dead here for forty long years; but I never beheld so happy a burial as this. It seems as though the angels were with that child She looks so heavenly."

Perhaps they were. And why say "perhaps"? Do we not *know* they are ever round us, and very near to such a one as Nelly, at such a time?

REÜNION.

When we muse o'er days departed,
  Lights that shone but shine no more,
Friends of ours who long since started
  O'er the sea without a shore;
Journeying on and journeying ever,
  Their freed spirits wing their flight,
Ceasing in their progress never
  Towards the fountain-head of light;
Oft we wish that they were near us,—
  We might see the friends we love,—
Then there come these words to cheer us,
  "Ye shall meet them all above."

When the sun's first ray approacheth,
  Ushering in the noonday light;
When the noise of day encroacheth
  On the silence of the night;
When the dreams depart that blest us
  In the hours forever fled,—
In which friends long gone carest us,
  Friends we number with the dead,—
Comes this thought, Ye ne'er shall hear them,
  Ne'er shall see the friends ye love;
Voices say, "Ye shall be near them,
  With them in the world above."

When within the grave's enclosure
  Ye do drop the silent tear,
Tremble not at its disclosure,
  Myriad spirits hover near.

Hark! they whisper, do ye hear not,
Mingling with your rising sighs,
Words that bid you hope, and fear not,
Angel-voices from the skies?
And as dust to dust returneth, —
That which held the gem you love, —
Thine afflicted spirit learneth
It will meet that gem above.

Thus whene'er a friend departeth
In my soul I know 't is right;
And, although the warm tear starteth,
As he passes from my sight,
I do know that him I cherish
Here on earth shall never die;
That, though all things else shall perish,
He shall live and reign on high.
And, that when a few hours more
Shall have passed, then those I love,
Who have journeyed on before,
I shall meet and greet above.

THE VILLAGE MYSTERY.

About fifty miles from a southern city, about five years ago, a most mysterious personage seemed to fall from the clouds into the midst of a circle of young ladies, whose hours and days were thenceforth busily employed in quizzing, guessing, pondering and wondering.

He was a tall, graceful-formed gentleman, wearing a professional-looking cloak, and buff pants, tightly strapped over boots of delicate make, polished up to the very highest capabilities of Day and Martin. He had no baggage; which fact led some wise-headed old ladies to report him to be a gentleman of leisure, a literary millionaire, it might be, who was travelling through "the States" for the purpose of picking up items for a book on "Ameriky." The old men wagged their heads, and looked most impenetrably mysterious. The young men became jealous. To be sure he was not superlatively handsome, but he had a foreign air, which was considerable among the girls; and his appearance indicated wealth, for his dress was of the first quality and cut. He had half a dozen glistening rings on his hands; he wore a breast-pin of dazzling brilliance; and every time he moved a chained lion could not have made more noise, and clatter, and show with his fetters, than he did with a massive double-linked chain, that danced and flirted upon his crimson vest.

Abby and Nelly, the belles of the place, had each had an eye upon the new comer, since he passed by the splendid mansion of their abode, casting a sly glance up to the open window at which they stood.

In a week, our foreign friend had made the circuit of all the fashionable society of Greendale. He had drank tea with the "Commissioners," and walked out with their amiable daughters. He had visited the pastor, and had evinced great interest in the prosperity of the church. He had even exhorted in the conference-meeting, and had become so popular that some few, taking it for granted that so devout a man *must* be a clergyman, had serious thoughts of asking the old parson to leave, and the stranger to accept the pulpit,—four hundred and eighty-two dollars a year, and a donation-party's offerings. He had attended the sewing-circle, and made himself perfectly at home with everybody and everything. The young men's society for ameliorating the condition of the Esquimauxs and Hottentots had been favored with his presence; and, likewise, with a speech of five minutes long, which speech had, in an astonishingly short time, been printed on pink satin and handsomely framed.

The lower class of people, for whom the stranger talked so much, and shed so many tears, and gave vent to so many pitiful exclamations, but with whom, however, he did not deign to associate, were filled with a prodigious amount of wonder at the lion and his adventures. They gathered at Squire Brim's tavern, and at the store on the corner, and wondered and talked over the matter. The questions with them were, Who is he?—where did he come, and where is he going to? They would not believe all they had heard conjectured about him, and some few were so far independent as to hint of the possibility of imposition.

There were two who determined to find out, at all hazards, the name, history, come from and go to, of the mysterious guest; and, to accomplish their purpose, they found it necessary for them to go to Baltimore early the subsequent morning.

The morning came. After taking a measurement of the height, breadth and bulk of the foreigner, as also a mental daguerreotype of his personal appearance, they departed.

Having been very politely invited, it is no strange matter of fact that, just as the sun has turned the meridian, on the fifth of March, a young man is seen walking slowly upon the shady side of Butternut-street, Greendale. To him all eyes are directed. Boys stop their plays, and turn their inquisitive eyes towards the pedestrian. The loungers at Brim's tavern flock to the door, and gaze earnestly at him; while Bridget the house-maid, and Dennis the hostler, hold a short confab on the back stairs, each equally wondering whose "bairn" he can be.

As he continues on his way, he meets a couple of sociable old ladies, with whom he formed an acquaintance at the sewing-circle. They shake hands most cordially.

"Abby and Nelly are waiting for you; they 're expecting you," says one of the ladies, as she breathes a blessing and bids him good-by, with a hope that he will have a pleasant time at the deacon's.

Let us now take a few steps in advance, and enter the hospitable mansion to which our mysterious personage, who has given his name as Sir Charles Nepod, is passing.

Up these beautiful white steps walk with dainty tread. At this highly-polished door ring with gentle hand.

A stout serving-man answers our call, and a tittering serving-girl scampers away and conceals herself behind the staircase, as we enter. What, think you, can be going on? A wedding, forsooth,—perhaps a dinner-party.

A brace of charming girls, the deacon's only daughters, are seated in the front parlor. We are introduced, and soon learn that they are waiting the arrival of the talented, the benevolent Sir Charles; and, as a matter of form and courtesy, rather than of sincerity and hospitality, we are invited to remain and meet him in the dining-room. We decline; bid them good-by, and leave. As we pass out, we are hailed in a loud whisper by the man who first met us, who glibly runs on with his talk as he leads the way, walking sideways all the time to the door.

"An' sirs,—sirs, dus yers know what the young Misthresses is afther? Well, sirs, they 's goin' fur to hev' a greath dinner with the furriner. Yes, sirs, with the furriner as come frum a furrin land, and was n't born in this at all a' tall."

As we reach the door, he steps up, whispers in our ears,

"An' I tells yer what, sirs, Kate,—that 's the gal yer sees, sirs,—me and she 's goin' to see all frum the little winder beyant. This is conveniently private to you, sirs, an' I hopes ye 'll say nothing to no one about it, sirs; 't is a private sacret, sirs."

What should induce this man to give us this information, we cannnot conceive. However, we have no reason to doubt what he tells us, and therefore understand that a dinner-party is to come off, with a wedding in perspective.

As we pass into the street, we meet Nepod.

As he ascends the steps, the two girls, forgetting all rules of etiquette, spring to the door, completely bewildering honest Mike, who is at hand, and welcome the man of the age.

"Mother and aunty have just gone out," says Nelly;—"they thought we young folks would enjoy our dinner much better by ourselves alone."

"How considerate!" replies the guest. "I met the good old ladies on the street. How kind in them to be so thoughtful! How pleasantly will pass the hours of to-day! This day will be the happiest of my life."

The three pass to the dining-room. Though early in March, the weather is quite warm. In the haste of the moment, and somewhat confused by his warm welcome, our hero has taken his hat and cloak and laid them on a lounge near an open window. Seated at the table, the company discourse on a variety of subjects, and the two sisters vie with each other in doing the agreeable.

Down town all was excitement, and a great crowd was gathered at the tavern. The investigating committee had returned from the city, and with the committee three men of mysterious look. To the uninitiated the mystery that had puzzled them for so long a time grew yet more mysterious. Nothing could be learned from the two who had returned, respecting Sir Charles, or the additional strangers. Only dark and mysterious hints were thrown out, rendering the whole affair more completely befogged than before.

Mr. Brim, the keeper of the tavern, silently conducted the new comers out by a back passage, and soon they were seen in the same path which Sir Charles had followed.

One of the men quietly opened the front door of the deacon's home, and, entering, knocked upon the door of the dining-room. A voice said, "Come in;" and he proceeded to do so.

In an instant, as if struck by an electric shock, the distinguished guest sprang from the table, and leaped through the open window, leaving his hat and cloak behind. But the leap did not injure him, for he fell into the arms of a man who stood ready to embrace him; and, mystery on mystery, they placed hand-cuffs on his wrists!

Judge, if you can, of the astonishment and mortification of the deacon's girls, when they were told that he who had been their guest was a bold highwayman, who had escaped from the penitentiary.

There was great ado in Greendale that afternoon and evening. Those who had been unable to gain his attention said they knew all the time he was a rogue. The young men's society voted to sell the frame and destroy the printed speech; and the next Sabbath the good pastor preached about a roaring lion that went about seeking whom he might devour.

THE WAYSIDE DEATH.

Not many years since, an old man, who had for a long time sat by the wayside depending upon the charity of those who passed by for his daily bread, died a few moments after receiving an ill-mannered reply to his request for alms. Subsequent inquiries proved that he had been a soldier in the American Revolution.

When Freedom's call rang o'er the land,
To bring its bold defenders nigh,
Young Alfred took a foremost stand,
Resolved to gain the day or die.
And well he fought, and won the trust;
When the day's conflicts had been braved,
The foe's proud ensigns lay in dust,
While Freedom's banner victor waved.

But now he is a poor old man,
And they who with him, side by side,
Fought bravely in that little van,
Have left him, one by one, — have died.
And now to no one can he tell,
Though touched with patriot fire his tongue,
The story of those days which well
Deserve to be by freemen sung,
And cherished long as life shall last;
To childhood told, that it may know
Who braved the storm when came the blast,
And vanquished Freedom's direst foe.

He sits there on the curb-stone now,
That brave old man of years gone by;
His head 'neath age and care would bow,
But yet he raiseth it on high,

And, stretching out his feeble hands,
He asks a penny from man's purse,
Food for himself from off that land
He fought to save. Yet, but a curse
Falls from their lips to greet his ear;
And he, despairing, turns and sighs,
And bows his head, — there falls *one* tear,
It is the last — he dies.

* * * * * *

Now men do rudely lift his hat,
To gaze upon his furrowed face,
And say, "It is the man who sat
Here for so long a foul disgrace."
Crowds gather round the spot to see,
And then pass idly on, and say,
To those who ask who it can be,
"'T is but a vagrant of the way."

Thus he who fought and bled to gain
The blessings which are round us strewn,
For one he asked, besought in vain,
Received man's curse, and died — unknown.

O, my own country! shall it be
That they who through thy struggle passed,
And bore thy banner manfully,
Shall thus neglected die at last?
O, shall it be no help shall come
From thy o'erflowing wealth to bless?
Wilt thou be blind, wilt thou be dumb,
To pleas like theirs in wretchedness?

Answer! and let your answer be
A helping hand lowered down to raise
From want and woe those who for thee
Won all thy honor, all thy praise,
And made thee what thou art to-day,
A refuge and a hope for man;
Speak! ere the last one wings away;
Act! act while yet to-day you can.

BEAUTY AND INNOCENCE.

[FOR AN ENGRAVING OF COTTAGE GIRL AND LAMB.]

O, MAIDEN, standing in the open field,
  On pasture sparkling with the morning dew !
What joy thou findest Nature now to yield
  To hearts developed right, — hearts that are true !

Above is beauty, as along the sky
  The dawn of light sends forth its herald ray
To arch the heavens, and myriad leagues on high
  Proclaim the coming of the god of day.

Beneath is beauty ; see the glistening gems
  Around thy feet in rich profusion strewn ;
Such as ne'er glows in kingly diadems,
  Such as man's handiwork hath never shown.

Around is beauty ; on each vale and hill,
  In open field and in the shady wood,
A voice is whispering, soft, and low, and still,
  " All, all is beautiful, for God is good."

Thou, too, art beautiful, O, maiden fair,
  While Innocence within thine arms doth rest ;
And thou wilt e'er be thus, no grief thou 'lt share,
  If such a blessing dwell within thy breast
As that whose emblem now lies gently there.

NIGHT.

I 'VE watched the sun go down, and evening draw
Its twilight mantle o'er the passive earth,
And hang its robe of blue, all gemmed with stars,
High over all for mortal eyes to gaze at.
And now I come to tread this sodded earth,
To walk alone in Nature's vaulted hall;
Yet, not alone; — I hear the rustling leaf,
The cricket's note, the night-bird's early lay;
I feel the cool breeze as it fans my brow,
And scent the fragrance of the untainted air.

I love the night. There 's something in its shade
That sends a soothing influence o'er the soul,
And fits it for reflection, sober thought.
It comes bearing a balm to weary ones,
A something undefinable, yet felt
By souls that feel the want of something real.

And now 't is night, and well it is that I
Am here. I stand, my hand on this old tree,
Pressing its mossy side, with no one near
I can call fellow in the human strife,
The great, unfinished drama of this life.
Alone, alone, with Nature and its God,
I 'll sit me down, and for a moment muse
On busy scenes, and, like some warrior chief,
Behold, yet mingle not in earth's great acts.

To-night how various are the states of men!
Some, bowed by sickness, press their sleepless couch,
Wishing while day doth last that night would come,
And now that night is with them wish for day.
Remorse holds some in its unyielding grasp;
Despair, more cruel yet, haunts some men's souls;
Both, ministers of justice conscience sends
To do its fearful bidding in those breasts
Which have rebelled and disavowed its rule.

Perchance, a maiden happy as a queen
To-night doth fix her destiny. A happy throng
Gather around, and envy her her bliss.
They little know what magic power lies low
In the filled wine-cup as they pass it round;
They little think it plants a venomed dart
In the glad soul of her whose lips do press
Its dancing sparkles.

Sorrow's nucleus!
Round that cup shall twine memories so dark
That night were noonday to them, to their gloom.
Dash it aside! See you not how laughs
Within the chalice brim an evil eye?
Each sparkling ray that from its depth comes up
Is the foul tempter's hand outstretched to grasp
The thoughtless that may venture in his reach.

How to-night the throng press on to bend
The knee to Baal, and to place a crown
On Magog's princely head! Dollars and dimes,
A purse well-filled, a soul that pants for more;
An eye that sees a farthing in the dust,
And in its glitter plenitude of joy,
Yet sees no beauty in the stars above,
No cause for gladness in the light of day, —
A hand that grasps the wealth of earth, and yields
For sake of it the richer stores of heaven;
A soul that loves the perishing of earth,
And hates that wealth which rust can ne'er corrupt.
How many such! How many bar their souls
'Gainst every good, yet ope it wide to wrong!
This night they 're all in arms. They watch and wait;
Now that the sun hath fled, and evening's shade
Doth follow in its path, they put in play
The plans which they in daylight have devised,
Entrapping thoughtless feet, and leading down
The flower-strewn path a daughter or a son,
On whose fair, white brow, the warm, warm moisture
Of a parent's kiss seems yet to linger.
Stay! daughter, son, O, heed a friend's advice,

Rush not in thoughtless gayety along!
Beware of pit-falls. Listen and you 'll hear
From some deep pit a warning voice to thee;
For thousands low have fallen, who once had
Hopes, prospects, fair as thine; they listened, fell!
And from the depths of their deep misery call
On thee to *think*. O, follow not, but reach
A helping hand to raise them from their woe!

Clouds hide the moon; how now doth wrong prevail!
Wrong holdeth carnival, and death is near.
O, what a sight were it for man to see,
Should there on this dark, shrouded hour
Burst in an instant forth a noonday light!
How many who are deemèd righteous men,
And bear a fair exterior by day,
Would now be seen in fellowship with sin!
Laughing, and sending forth their jibes and jeers,
And doing deeds which Infamy might own.

But not alone to wrong and base intrigue
Do minister these shades of night; for Love
Holds high her beacon Charity to guide
To deeds that angels might be proud to own.
Beneath the shadows that these clouds do cast,
Hath many a willing hand bestowed a gift
Its modest worth in secret would confer.
No human eye beheld the welcome purse
Dropped at the poor man's humble cottage door;
But angels saw the act, and they have made
A lasting record of it on the scroll
That bears the register of human life.

Many a patient sufferer watches now
The passing hours, and counts them as they flee.
Many a watcher with a sleepless eye
Keeps record of the sick man's every breath.
Many a mother bends above her child
In deep solicitude, in deathless love.

Night wears away, and up the eastern sky
The dawn approaches. So shall life depart,—

This life of ours on earth, — and a new birth
Approach to greet us with immortal joys,
So gently on our inner life shall come
The light of heaven.

Time moveth on, and I must join again
The busy toil of life ; and I must go.
And yet I would not. I would rather stay
And talk with these green woods, — for woods *can* talk.
Didst ever hear their voice? In spring they speak
Of early love and youth, and ardent hope ;
In summer, of the noon of wedded life,
All buds and blossoms and sweet-smelling flowers ;
In autumn, of domestic bliss with all its fund
Of ripe enjoyments, and then winter hears
The leafless trees sing mysterious hymns,
And point their long lean arms to homes above.
Yes, the old woods talk, and I might hold
A sweet communion here with them to-night.
Farewell to Night ; farewell these thoughts of mine,
For day hath come.

NOT DEAD, BUT CHANGED.

I SAT and mused o'er all the years gone by ;
Of friends departed, and of others going ;
And dwelt upon their memories with a sigh,
Till floods of tears, their hidden springs o'erflowing,
Betrayed my grief. Soon, a bright light above me,
Voices saying, "We're near thee yet to love thee,"
Dispelled my tears. I raised my drooping head,
And asked, "Who, who, — the dead?"
When the angelic host around me ranged
Whispered within my ear, "*Not dead, but changed.*"

THE DISINHERITED.

My next door neighbor's name was Jotham Jenks. This was all I knew about him, until the circumstance I am about to tell you occurred.

One evening I had seated myself by my fire, and had taken up an evening paper with which to occupy my time, until an acquaintance of mine, who I momentarily expected, should arrive. It was December,—cold, blustering, and by no means an agreeable time to be out of doors, or away from a good fire. Such being the state of affairs, as far as weather was concerned, I began to think I should not see my friend that night, when a smart rap upon the outer door, half a dozen times repeated, prevented me from further speculation.

Why did n't he ring?—there was a bell. It must have been a stranger, else he would have used it.

Presently a servant came with the information that a stranger was at the door with a carriage, and wished my immediate presence.

"Request him to walk in," said I.

"He cannot wait a moment," answered the servant;—"he wishes you to put on your hat and coat, and go with him."

"Where?"

"He did not say."

This was a strange interruption,—strange that a man, a stranger, in fact, should call for me to go out with him on *such* a night; but I mustered courage, and went out to meet him. I don't know what induced me so readily to grant his request; but out I went, hatted, coated and booted. As I approached, I heard the falling of steps, and the voice of the coachman requesting me to hurry. Reaching the carriage, I looked in and beheld Jotham Jenks. In I jumped, and before I was seated the carriage was moving.

The whip snapped, the wheels whirled round, and we passed through the lighted streets with almost incredible speed. I ventured to make an inquiry, and the reply was,

"You are doing a good deed. My name is Jotham Jenks. Ask no questions now."

Thus was a veto put upon the movements of my tongue for the time being. I, however, recognized the voice of Mr. Jenks; and though I knew but little respecting him, I judged from his appearance that he was a quiet, unoffending man; and such I afterwards found him.

For thirty minutes the horses raced along, causing the water, ice and snow, to take to themselves wings and fly upon pedestrians, windows, and sundry other animate and inanimate objects of creation. For myself, I began to experience some misgiving, for thus exposing myself to what, I did not know.

At length the carriage turned down a dark, narrow street, leading to one of the wharves, upon which we finally found ourselves. The driver jumped from his seat, opened the carriage-door, threw down the steps, and we got out.

Matters had reached a crisis. Was I to be thrown into the water? The assurance of my companion that I was doing a good deed seemed to disfavor this supposition, as what possible good could that do myself or any one else? Yet, for what was I taken from a warm room, on such a cold, dismal, dark night, and hurried to the wharf?

"Now," said I to the stranger, "I *must* know the meaning of all this,—the why and the wherefore."

He took my hand in his. It was quite dark. I could not see, yet I could tell by his voice that he wept, as he said,

"In a berth in the cabin of that vessel lies a young man, far from his home, among strangers,—sick, perhaps dying. No relative, other than those of the great brotherhood of mankind, is near to minister to his wants, or to speak comfort to his troubled heart. He had been here about two days, when I was informed of his situation by a friend who came in the same vessel. I have brought you here that you might listen to his statements, and assist me in assisting him. There is much of romance in his narrative, and, as you are preparing a volume of life-sketches, as found in town and country, I have thought that what falls from his lips might fill a few pages with interest and profit to your readers."

I thanked him for his thoughtfulness. My suspicions and fears were all allayed; I asked no more questions, but followed my friend as he passed to the vessel, and descended the narrow stairway to the cabin.

A small lamp hung from the ceiling, and shed a sort of gloomy light around. I had been in chambers of sickness, but never in a room where more neatness was discernible, or more sufficiency for its tenant, than in the cabin in which I then was. A sailor boy seated by a berth indicated to me the spot where the sick man lay. We were informed that he had just fallen into a sleep, and we were careful not to awake him.

But, notwithstanding all our care, our movements awoke him. He gazed around as one often does after a deep sleep; but a consciousness of his situation, and a recognition of my companion, soon dispelled his vacant looks, and his features were illumed with as expressive a smile as it has ever been my fortune to behold.

I was introduced to the invalid, and soon we were as familiar as old acquaintances. His name was Egbert Lawrence, and his age I should judge from appearances to be about twenty-five.

"It is possible that my dear, good friend, Mr. Jenks, has given you some account of my circumstances," he remarked, addressing me.

I replied that he had not, any further than to state that he was friendless. He started, as I said this, and exclaimed,

"Friendless! His own modesty, that sure mark of true merit, induced him to say that; but, dear sir, I have a friend in him, greater than in any other on earth now. I had a friend, but, alas! she 's gone."

I corrected his impression; remarked that I only intended to convey the fact that he was in a strange country, among a strange people, and that Mr. Jenks had told me he was worthy of assistance, and that a sketch of his life would interest me.

"Then you would like to hear of my past, would you?"

"Most certainly," I replied; "and should consider it a favor should you consent to give it to me."

To this he at once consented.

"I was born in the west of England," he began, "and can well remember what a charming little village it was in which I passed my earliest days. My mother was a woman of the finest sensibilities,—too fine, in fact, for the rough winds of this world. Her heart beat too strongly in sympathy with the poor and oppressed, the weary-footed and troubled ones, to live among and not have the weight of their sorrows and cares bear also upon her, and gradually wear out the earth tenement of her spirit.

"As far as a fine, sensitive feeling was hers, so far it was mine. I inherited it. But I would not flatter myself so much as to say that I, in like manner, partook of her heavenly, loving nature, or that I in any of her noble traits was worthy of being her son.

"Many times have I been the bearer of her secret charities. Many times have I heard the poor bless the unknown hand that placed bounties at their door. Many times have I seen my mother weep while I told her of what I heard the recipients of her benevolence tell their neighbors, and the many conjectures in their minds as to who the donor could be. And, O, there *was* joy sparkling in her eyes when I told her of what I had seen and heard! The grateful poor, concluding, after all their surmising, that, as they could not tell for a certainty who it was who gave them food and clothing, they would kneel down and thank God; for, said they, in their honest, simple manner, He knows. The benevolent hand cannot hide itself from his presence, or escape his reward.

"My father was quite a different person. How it was they met and loved, I could not for a long time determine. But one evening my mother told me all about it, and said he was not the man of her choice, but of her parents' choice; and that she had never loved him with that deep and earnest love that alone can bind two hearts in one embrace. But she said she had endeavored to do her duty towards him. Good woman! I knew that. 'T was her very nature to do that. 'T was a law of her being, and she could not evade it.

"My father was a rough, coarse-minded man. He held an office under the government, and, from being accustomed to the exercise of some little authority without doors, became habituated to a morose, ill-natured manner of words and behavior within our home. I remember how I changed my tone of voice, and my mode of action, when at night he came home. With my mother I talked and laughed, and played merrily in her presence, and rather liked to have her look on my sports; but when my father came I never smiled. I sat up on my chair in one corner as stiff and upright as the elm-tree in front of our house. I never played in his presence. I seldom heard a kind word from him. My mother used to call me 'Berty, my dear,' when she wished me; but my father always shouted, sternly, 'Egbert, come here, sir!' and I would tremblingly respond, 'Sir.'

"Few persons seemed to love him; those who did, did so with an eye to business. It was policy in them to flatter the man who could favor them pecuniarily, and they hesitated not to do so. One time, when my father's vote and influence were worth five thousand pounds to his party, and he exhibited symptoms of withholding them, he had rich presents sent him, and every night some half a dozen or more would call in and sit and talk with him, and tell him how admirably all the schemes he had started for the good of the town had succeeded, and in all manner of ways would flatter the old gentleman, so that he would be quite pleasant all the next day. At this time handsome carriages came to take him to ride, and gentlemen proposed an afternoon's shooting or fishing, or sport of some kind, and my father always accepted and was always delighted. The simple man, he could n't see through the gauze bags they were drawing over his head! He did not notice the nets with which they were entangling his feet. When election came, he gave his vote, and did not keep back his influence.

"My father was not benevolent to any great degree. He gave, it is true. He gave to missionary societies, to education and tract societies, and his name was always found printed in their monthly reports; but he never gave, as my mother did, to the poor around us, unseen, unknown. Not even he knew of my mother's charitable acts; but all the town knew of his, and he was looked upon by the great mass of public mind to be the most benevolent. But it was not so. Far from it. One shilling from my mother, given with the heart, with sympathy, given for the sake of doing good, not for the sake of popularity, was a greater gift than a hundred pounds from my father's hand, given as he always gave it.

"I attended school but little. My mother wished me to have a good education, but my father said if I could 'figure' well it was enough. I was taken from school and put in a store,—a place which I abhorred. I was put there to sell tape, and pins, and thread, and yarn; and I was kept behind the counter from early morn until late at night.

"I had one brother, but his mind was nothing like mine. He partook of my father's nature. We seldom agreed upon any matter, and I always chose to be alone rather than with him. I do not think I was wrong in this, for our minds were of different casts. Neither of us made our minds or our dispositions. There was, therefore, no blame upon any one, if, on account of the difference in our mental organizations, our affinities led us apart. It was a perfectly natural result of a natural cause.

"I will not weary you with more detail of my life to-night; but to-morrow, if you have any interest in what I have begun to tell you, I will tell you more."

I had noticed that he began to be exhausted with his effort, and was about to propose that a future time be allotted to what more he chose to relate.

I assured him of an increased interest in him, and suggested removing him to a good boarding-house. He at first declined, but upon further urging he accepted, and, having seen that all his wants were for that night attended to, we left, with the understanding that a carriage should convey him to more commodious quarters on the morrow, if the weather permitted.

I had no fears of my companion as we rode up the wharf and drove through the streets, the storm beating down furiously around us. I reached my home, and Mr. Jenks thanked me for my kindness in blindly following him, and I in return thanked him for the pleasant adventure to which he had introduced me.

CHAPTER II.

The next morning the weather was clear and the air invigorating, as is often the case after a severe storm. With my neighbor Jenks I procured a good home for the wanderer, and in a short time he was located in it.

I was soon seated by his side, and he continued his narrative.

"I told you last evening of my parents, and of my entrance upon business life. About that time a great sorrow visited me. My mother was taken sick, rapidly declined, and in a fortnight left this state of existence. Beyond this world it seemed all dark to me then; but now it is brighter there than here, and there is no uncertainty in my mind respecting that coming state.

"I have not told you she died. She did not die. There is no such word as death in my vocabulary. She did not sleep even. She passed from a crumbling, falling building into an enduring and beautiful temple, not made with hands. But to me, then, as I have told you, it was all dark; and it was not a wonder that I was sad, and that it was indeed a heavy sorrow that rested on my spirit. Even with the faith that she had, the thought of being left with a man such as my father was would have made me sad. You will wonder, perhaps, that I had not learned from such a mother as mine a clearer faith than that which possessed my mind at the time of her departure; but I had not. It was impossible for me to accept a truth with that amount of evidence which satisfied her mind, and I doubted, at times, a future existence. But I do not doubt it now. I have had proof,— abundant proof; and, O, the joy that fills my soul is unfathomable.

"My father now became more tyrannical than ever, and everything tended to destroy whatever there was of my mother's disposition in my character. But nothing could force it from me. I was sensitive as ever to the remarks and the looks of all with whom I came in contact, and the severe and unmerited reprimands of my father almost crushed me.

"Several years passed by. I wasted them in a retail store. It was, however, not a complete loss to me, for there I formed an acquaintance with a young lady, the daughter of a poor collier. Our friendship ripened to mutual love, and we were happy only when in each other's presence. Our interviews were frequent, and unknown to any one but ourselves for a long time. At length my father became acquainted with the facts. He called me to his room one night, and scolded me, threatened to disinherit me, and treated me as though I had been guilty of the most heinous crime.

"'You miserable, good-for-nothing scamp!' said he. 'Why do you seek to lower yourself in the estimation of every man, and bring disgrace on the name and fame of my family, by associating with the poor daughter of a worthless laborer?'

"This fired my brain; but I was timid and dare not speak my thoughts in his presence. I listened. He showered upon me all the evil epithets his tongue could dispense, and, raving like a madman, he pushed me to the door, and told me to cease my visits upon Evelina or leave his house forever and change my name, for he would not shelter me, or own any relationship to me.

"Poor girl! She little thought how much I that night endured for her, or how much I was willing to bear. She was a beautiful being,—so much like my mother, so gentle, and loving, and benevolent! We were one. True, no earthly law recognized us as such; but God's law did,—a law written with his hand on our beating hearts. We had been joined far, far back, ages gone by, when our souls first had their birth,—long ere they became enshrined in earth forms. The church might have passed its ceremonial bond about us, but that would have been mere form—that would have been a union which man might have put asunder, and often does. But of a true union of souls it is useless to say 'what God has joined let no man put asunder;' for he cannot any more than he can annul any other of his great laws.

"My father's reprimands and threatenings could not, therefore, dissolve that bond which united me to Evelina, and she to me. So, as soon as I left his room, I sought her presence. I told her all, and she wept to think of what she had caused, as she said. But I tried to convince her, and succeeded in doing so finally, that it was not she who had caused it. She had not made her soul or its attributes. God had made them, and if they were in unison with mine, or if they had attractions that drew my soul to hers, the law under which they came together and would not be separated was God's law, and we could not escape it.

"That night we walked down by the river's side, and we talked of those great principles that govern us. We studied, there in the clear moonlight, God's works, and I asked her whether in loving the beautiful and the good we did not love God.

"Her mind opened a bright effulgence of light to my spirit. 'Yes,' said she, 'it is even so. God is a spirit. He fills immensity,—and if so, then he imbues this little flower with his own life, for he is the life of all things. It is as he made it, and as we love it we love him. When we love a being for his goodness, we love God; for that goodness is of God."

"'Yes,' I remarked; 'I see it is so. I do not love you as a material being. It is not your flesh and bones merely that I love, but it is the goodness dwelling in you. As that goodness is more abundant in you than in others, in like degree does God dwell in you more than in them. If, therefore, I love you more than I love them, I love God more than I should did my supreme love find its highest object in them. In loving you, therefore, I love God so far as you possess the characteristics by which we personify that being. It is not wrong, therefore, to love you or the flower; for goodness exists in one, and beauty in the other, and they both are of God, and in loving them we love God.'

"We parted at a late hour. I went with her to the door of the little cottage in which she dwelt with her father. Her mother had died, as they call it, long years before; and, as I kissed her, and pressed her hand and bade her good-by, I felt more strongly than ever a determination to bear any privation, endure any suffering, for her sake.

"I reached my home. I found the doors fastened and all quiet. The moon shone very clear, and it was nearly as light as at noon-day. I tried the windows, and fortunately found one of them unfastened. I raised it very carefully, and crept in, and up to my room. The next morning at breakfast my father spoke not a word, but I knew by his manner that he was aware of my disregard of his command, and I thought that all that prevented him from talking to me was a want of language strong enough to express the passionate feelings that ran riot in his soul.

"I judged rightly. For at night his passion found vent in words, and such a copious torrent of abuse that I shuddered. Nevertheless, I yielded not one position of my heart, and was conscious that I had a strength of purpose that would ever defend the right, and could not be swayed by mere words.

"There was no limit to my father's abuse when it became known to a few of his friends that I had been seen in company with the collier's daughter. I endured all, and was willing to endure more. He seemed to have a peculiar dislike of Evelina's father, as also to her. This I could not account for.

"At length I became of age, and on my birthday my father called me to him, and, in his usual stern, uncompromising way, asked me if I persisted in paying attention to Evelina. I answered promptly that I did. I had had so many conflicts that I had lost much of my timidity, and I now defined my position clear, and maintained it resolutely.

"'Then leave my house at once!' said my father. 'I throw you from me as I would a reptile from my clothes; and go, go with my curse upon you! Take your penniless girl, and build yourself a name if you can; for you have lost the one you might have held with honor to yourself and to me. I had chosen for you a wife, a rich and fashionable lady, the daughter of a nobleman, and one of whom to be proud; but you have thought best to be your own judge in such matters, and you made a fool of yourself. But you shall not stamp my family with such folly, or wed its name to dishonor.'

"I endeavored to reply; but he would hear no word from my lips. He sprang from his seat, walked the room in the greatest rage, and whenever I opened my mouth to speak would shout, 'Stop your noise, you ungrateful, heartless wretch!'

"He was determined to carry out his threat. That night he locked me out of the house, and took special pains to make the windows fast. In the papers of the next day he advertised me as disinherited and cast off, and warned the world against me. He also circulated false reports respecting me, and spared neither money nor effort to injure me. He prejudiced my employers, so that they at once discharged me, without a moment's warning. And all this from a father! O, how often I thought of that loving, sympathizing mother! How often I recognized her presence in my silent hours of thought! Dear, sainted friend! she *was* with me often, unseen but not unfelt.

"Evelina faltered not. She bore all the opprobrium of false friends with a brave heart, and rested on my promises as the dove rests its weary head beneath its downy wing. Her father had confidence in me.

"It was astonishing how changed all things were. The day previous, I was the son of a wealthy and influential man. I was respected, apparently, by all. Very many professed a friendship for me, and told me how much they valued my company. Young ladies politely recognized me as I passed through the streets; and old ladies singled me out as an example for their sons to follow. But on that day no one knew me. Not one of those who had professed such friendship for me came and took me by the hand when I needed their friendly grasp the most! Young ladies, when we met, cast their glances on the earth, on the sky, anywhere but on me. Old ladies scandalized me, and warned the objects of their paternal consideration against a course like mine.

"And why all this? It was because I loved Evelina,—a poor man's only child!"

CHAPTER III.

Egbert's health seemed to improve now that he was in more comfortable quarters, and had sympathizing friends to whom he could narrate the story of his life. In the course of a few days he rode out a short distance. After a rest of a week, during which his strength had increased, he continued his narrative, in which we had become deeply interested.

"I found a home at the cottage of Evelina. We made arrangements to be married according to law, and in due time I applied to the minister of the town to perform the ceremonies. I was surprised when he refused; yet I well knew what inducements led him to act thus. My father was the leading man in his church. The minister looked to him as one of the chief pillars of support to his society, and consequently to his means of livelihood. There was no one in the town upon whom the public eye, religious or political, rested with more hope than upon my father. He exhorted in the meetings with an earnestness worthy of the most devoted follower of Cromwell; and was as strict and rigid in the performance of his public religious duties as the most precise Puritan of the old school could wish. Did the chapel need repairs, my father was consulted. Was it proposed to make a donation to the pastor, my father was expected to head the list with a large subscription, and he did. Was it strange, then, that he gave such a decided refusal to my simple request, knowing, as he did, and everybody did, my circumstances? It seems not. Perhaps it was foolish for me to ask a favor of such a man; but I did, and he had an opportunity of exhibiting his allegiance to public opinion, and his disregard of the voice within, that must have commanded him to do right, and to adhere to truth and justice in the face of all opposition.

"It was soon noised abroad that I had endeavored to get married and had failed. There was great rejoicing, and one old lady took the trouble to send her man-servant to me with the message that she was glad to know that her good pastor had indignantly refused to place his seal on my bond of iniquity.

"The dark cloud that all this time overshadowed my path rested also on the path of Evelina's father. This was all that troubled me. He, good man, had more true religion in his soul than the pastor and all the people in theirs; yet he was scorned and ill-treated. All this was not new to him. He had lived in that town four-and-forty years, and had always been frowned upon by the boasting descendants of proud families, and had received but little good from their hands. The church looked upon him as a poor, incorrigible sinner. No one spoke to him, unless it was to ask him to perform some hard job. It was not strange that, judging from the works of the people who called themselves Christians, he had a dislike to their forms. He chose a living Christianity; and theirs, with all its rites, with all its pretensions, with all its heralded faith, was but a mockery to him. It was but a shadow of a substantial reality. He chose the substance; he rejected the shadow, and men called him 'infidel' who had not a tithe of vital religion in their own souls, while his was filled to repletion with that heavenly boon.

"For a time the war of persecution raged without, and slander and base innuendoes the weapons were employed against us. But within all was peace and quiet, and our home was indeed a heaven,—for we judged that heaven is no locality, no ideal country staked off so many leagues this way, and so many that; but that it is in our own souls, and we could have our heaven here as well as beyond the grave. We thought Christ meant so when he said 'the kingdom of heaven is within you'! We pitied those who were always saying that when they reached heaven there would be an end of all sorrow, and wished they could see as we did that heaven was to reach them, not they to reach it. We feared that the saying of Pope,

> 'Man never *is*, but always *to be* blest,'

might prove true of them, and that even when they had passed the boundary which they fancied divided them from heaven, they would yet be looking on to some future state for the anticipated bliss.

"What cared we, in our home, for the jibes and sneers and falsehoods without? Those who are conscious of being in the right have no fear of the goal to which their feet are tending. I heard from my father often, but never met him. By some means he always evaded me. That which troubled him most was the calmness with which I received the results of his course towards me. He knew that I was happy and contented. This was what troubled him. Had I manifested a great sorrow and writhing beneath what he deemed troubles, he would have greatly rejoiced, and so would all his friends.

"I had accumulated a small property, and was prospering, notwithstanding the efforts of many to embarrass me. A few began to see that I was not so bad as I had been represented to be, and they began to sympathize with me. This aroused my father's anger afresh.

"We had been married by a magistrate of another town, and the clouds above our outside or temporary affairs seemed breaking away, when an event occurred that frustrated all our plans.

"One evening I heard the cry of 'fire,' and, on attempting to go out, I found the entry of the house filled with a dense smoke. The smoke poured into the room in which Evelina and her father were seated. I rushed to the window, dashed it out, and, having seen my wife and her father safely deposited without, secured what of the property I could. In a few moments the cottage was enveloped in flames, and it was not long before no vestige of our happy home remained, except the smoking embers and a heap of ashes. We were now, indeed, poor in gold and lands; but it seemed to each of us that what had been taken from our purse had been put in our hearts, for we loved each other more than ever before, if such a love were possible; and, though we received but little sympathy from without, we had a fund of sympathy within, that made us forget our seeming sorrows, and rejoice in bliss unspeakable.

"It was reported that I had fired the cottage. I well knew with whom this charge originated, and I had good reasons for believing that the match that fired our house came from the same source.

"Our condition was such that we concluded to leave the place where so much had been endured, and those who had strewn our path with what they intended for thorns and brambles.

"We left. We journeyed to Liverpool, and engaged a passage in a New York packet for the United States. It was a beautiful morning when we set sail, and everything seemed reviving in the possessing of life. Our ship's flags looked like smiling guardians as they fluttered above us, and all on board the 'White Wing' were happy. There were about three hundred passengers. There were old and young; some travelling on business, some for a place they might call their home, some for pleasure, and a few for the improvement of their health. There were entire families, and, in some cases, those of three generations. How varied were the hopes that filled their souls! how different the objects that led them forth over the deep and trackless sea, exposing themselves to countless perils!

"Evelina and myself mused thus as we sat on the deck at twilight of the first day out, and watched the movements, and listened to the various expressions that fell from the lips of the crowded passengers.

"She always had a bright gleam of religious, philosophical thought, with which to illumine every hour of our existence, and radiate, with heavenly joy, our every conversation. 'There are not more dangers here than on land,' said she; 'to be true to our inner consciousness, we must say that wherever we are we are exposed to peril, and wherever we are we are protected from evil. I have known a man to cross the ocean a hundred times, and fall at last at his own door, and by it become maimed for life. There is no such a thing as an accident. Every result has a legitimate cause. Everything acts in obedience to undeviating laws of God. We complain when we fall, but the same law that causes us to fall guides planets in their course, and regulates every motion of every object. It is only when we disobey these laws that evil comes, and every transgression receives its own penalty. It is impossible that it should be otherwise.'

"We soon became acquainted with a number of the passengers, and passed very many pleasant and profitable hours together. Evelina was the light of every circle, and the days flew by on rapid wings. The ship had made a rapid passage, and we were fast nearing our destined haven.

"One Sabbath evening a storm commenced. The wind blew a hurricane. Everything on deck was lashed, and the sea rolled and pitched our vessel about as though it had been but a feather on its surface. We had all day expected the storm, and were prepared for it. As night advanced the storm increased. The rain fell in torrents, and the darkness was most intense. After a while, the lightning came, and the thunder reverberated with terrific peals over us. There were shrieks and wailings aboard our vessel, and many a brave heart quailed beneath the terror upon us.

"I cared not for myself. My chief concern was for my

dear wife and her father. We kept our state-room for a long time, but at length deemed it prudent to leave it. As we did so, we heard an awful crash, and many a shriek and hurried prayer. I myself began to fear, as the mast and flying rigging went by us; but Evelina, even in such an hour, had words to cheer us all. She seemed, indeed, more of heaven than earth; and I cared not for my fate, provided we both met the same.

"The captain ordered the boats to be got in readiness, and it was quickly done. Soon another crash, and another mast fell, bearing to the raging abyss of waters another company of helpless men, women and children.

"I clasped my wife in my arms, and, amid the wreck and frantic crowd of passengers, sprang to a boat. I placed Evelina in it, and was just about to assist her father to the same boat, when a large wave dashed over the ship and bore me alone over the wide waters. I remembered no more until I opened my eyes, and the sun was shining brightly all around me, and a young man was bathing my head, and brushing back my wet hair, while some were standing by expressing great joy.

"I soon became conscious of my situation, and I asked for Evelina. What a sadness filled my soul when I was told she was not there,—that they had not heard of any such person! Human language is weak with which to express the sorrow I then felt. Through all my varied life I had had nothing that so crushed my spirit, and filled it with a sense of loneliness which it is impossible to describe. I ascertained that I was on board of a vessel bound to Boston; that I was found holding on a raft, almost insensible when found, and quite so a few moments afterwards. For a long time no one expected that I would recover my consciousness, but the constant efforts of the passengers and crew were finally crowned with success, and I opened my eyes.

"I gave all the information I could respecting the fate of the vessel, but thoughts of my wife, and surmisings as to her fate and that of her father, often choked my utterance, and my words gave way for my tears.

"The next morning I was delirious, with a fever. My anxiety for my wife, and the exposure I had suffered, brought my body and mind into a very critical state. For several days I talked wildly. At the close of the fifth, I became sane in mind. I was yet quite ill. That night the ship entered Boston harbor. It anchored in the stream, and the next morning it hauled up to a wharf.

CHAPTER IV.

"I was a perfect stranger. The captain was attentive to my wants, and made me as comfortable as he could. You will remember how neat and quiet all appeared when, with my friend Jenks, you called on me. All of the passengers took an interest in my welfare, and made up a purse for me; but they could not remain long with me. They had been long absent from home, and were desirous of seeing their families and friends, or else they had business in this or some other place. One of them introduced my friend Jenks to me; and, O, sir, he has been, indeed, a good friend to one having so few claims on his attention. He told me one night of you, and, agreeable to his promise, he brought you to the cabin of the vessel. The rest you know."

Egbert had regained his strength to a great degree, and gave me the close of his narrative while we were having a pleasant drive through the country. A month had passed since we first met, and though many of the passengers had been heard from, the names of Evelina and her father had not been reported.

When we reached our home, from our afternoon's drive, I took up an evening paper, and the first paragraph I read was the following:

"MORE FROM THE WHITE WING. — The Orion, which arrived at this port this morning, brought fifteen passengers, rescued from the boats of the 'White Wing.'"

Among the names mentioned in the above notice were these: "Mrs. Evelina Lawrence and her father, of England;" and, at the conclusion, was the following item:

"The case of Mrs. Lawrence and her father is one of those that loudly call for a bestowal of public sympathy and aid in her behalf. She has lost a beloved husband,— one who, judging from the heavy sorrow that oppresses her, and the sighs and tears that break her recital of the events of their last hours together, was bound with the closest bonds of soul affinity to her own spirit. They must have been one, and are, indeed, one now, though to mortal eyes separated. We commend her to the kind charities of those who would follow the golden rule of doing unto others as they, in like circumstances, would have others do unto them."

Egbert noticed my interest in that which I was reading; indeed, it would have been strange if he had not; for I could not suppress my joy, and it found expression in an occasional exclamation.

At length, I handed him the paper.

"My God! my wife!" he exclaimed, and he actually danced with joy and thankfulness. He would have rushed into the street, and by sudden exposure have caused a relapse of disease, had not I taken him by the hand, and forcibly, for a few moments, restrained him. So excessive was his happiness that, for a short time, he was delirious with joy. He laughed and wept by turns: at one moment extending his arms, and folding them as if clasping a beloved form; the next, trembling as if in some fearful danger. But this did not long continue. He soon became calm and rational, and we called a carriage for the purpose of going to the vessel on board of which he expected to greet his wife and her father.

My neighbor Jenks accompanied us, and, as we rode hastily along, my mind reverted to the night when first I met Egbert. That eventful evening came more vividly to mind as we found ourselves on the same wharf, and the carriage door was opened, and we alighted on nearly the same spot that we did at that time.

Egbert leaped from the carriage, and at one bound was on the vessel's deck. He flew to the cabin, and in a moment I heard the loud exclamations on either side, "My Evelina!" "My Egbert!" Mr. Jenks and myself followed below. An old gentleman met us, and, though a stranger, he grasped a hand of ours in each of his, and wept with joy as he bade us welcome. The cabin was witness of a scene which a painter well might covet for a study. In close embrace Egbert and Evelina mingled joys that seldom are known on earth. The old man held our hands, his face raised, eyes turned upward, while tears of happiness, such as he had never before known, coursed down his features. The officers of the ship came hurrying in, and the crew darkened the gangway with their presence. What a joyous time was that! The evening was passed in recounting the adventures of each; and even I had something to add to the general recital. It appeared that the boat in which Egbert had placed his charge was safely cleared of the wreck, and, after being floated about two days, was met by an English ship bound to London. They, together with about twenty others who were in the boat, were soon comfortably cared for. At the expiration of a few weeks, they reached London, and were there placed on board a vessel bound to Boston, at which place they in due season arrived. The grief of Mrs. L. during all this time I will not attempt to describe. The mind of my reader can better depict it than I can with pen. Hope buoyed her up. And, though she had seen him swept from her side into the waters where waves towered up to the skies and sank again many fathoms below, yet she did hope she might see him again on earth.

In the silent hour of night, as she lay and mused of those things, she thought she could hear a sweet voice whispering in her ear, "Berty lives, and you will meet him once again." And, as if in response to the voice, she said in her own mind, "I know he lives; but it may be in that bright world where, unencumbered with these mortal frames, we roam amid ever-enduring scenes." The voice again said, "On earth, on earth."

But now they had met. It was no mere vision now, and the truth flashed upon her mind that that voice she had heard and thought a dream was not all a dream. And then she mused on as she was wont to do, and, after relating to us the incident, she said, "May it not be that much of our life that we have thought passed in dreamland, and therefore among unreal things, has been spent with actual existences? For what *is* an 'unreal thing'? It would not be a 'thing' had it no existence; and what is the 'it' that we speak of? Can we not then conclude that there is nothing but what *is* and *must* have an existence, though not so tangible to our senses as to enable us to handle it or see it? What we call 'imagination' may be, after all, more real than the hard stones beneath our feet — less indestructible than they."

Thus she spake, and her theory seemed very plausible to me, though my friend Jenks, who was an exceedingly precise, matter-of-fact man, could not see any foundation for the theory.

It was a late hour when Mr. Jenks and myself passed to our homes. The next day Evelina and her father were coseyly quartered at the house in which Egbert had boarded.

In the course of a a few weeks they arranged to go to the west, and locate in a flourishing town on the banks of the Ohio, not many miles above Cincinnati.

Mr. Jenks and myself accompanied them to the cars; and, amid our best wishes for their success, and their countless expressions of gratitude to us, the train started, and in a few moments the Disinherited was going to an inheritance which God had provided, and which lay in rich profusion awaiting their possession.

Our hearts went with them. We could truly say they were worthy God's blessing; yet we had not need ask him to bestow it upon them; for their very existence was a proof that he gave it to them.

THE SEASONS ALL ARE BEAUTIFUL.

THE seasons all are beautiful,
  There is not one that 's sad, —
Not one that does not give to thee
  A thought to make thee glad.
I have heard a mournful cadence
  Fall on my listening ear, —
'T was some one whispering, mournfully,
  "The Autumn days are here."

But Autumn is not sorrowful, —
  O, full of joy is it;
I love at twilight hour to watch
  The shadows as they flit, —
The shadows of the falling leaves,
  Upon their forest bed,
And hear the rustling music tones
  Beneath the maiden's tread.

The falling leaf! Say, what has it
  To sadden human thought?
For are not all its hours of life
  With dancing beauty fraught?
And, having danced and sang its joy,
  It seeketh now its rest, —
Is there a better place for it
  Than on its parent's breast?

Ye think it dies. So they of old
  Thought of the soul of man.
But, ah, ye know not all its course
  Since first its life began,
And ye know not what future waits,
  Or what essential part

That fallen leaf has yet to fill,
In God's great work of art.

Count years and years, then multiply
The whole till ages crowd
Upon your mind, and even then
Ye shall not see its shroud.
But ye may see, — if look you can
Upon that fallen leaf, —
A higher life for it than now
The life you deem so brief.

And so shall we to higher life
And purer joys ascend ;
And, passing on, and on, and on,
Be further from our end.
This is the truth that Autumn brings, —
Is aught of sorrow here ?
If not, then deem it beautiful,
Keep back the intrusive tear.

Spring surely you 'll call beautiful,
With its early buds and flowers,
Its bubbling brooks, its gushing streams,
And gentle twilight hours.
And Summer, that is beautiful,
With fragrance on each breeze,
And myriad warblers that give
Free concerts 'mong the trees.

I 've told you of the Autumn days, —
Ye cannot call *them* sad,
With such a lesson as *they* teach,
To make the spirit glad.
And Winter comes ; how clear and cold,
In dazzling brilliance drest ! —
Say, is not Winter beautiful,
With jewels on his crest ?

Thus are all seasons beautiful ;
They all have joy for thee,
And gladness for each living soul
Comes from them full and free.

SPRING.

It is early spring-time. The winter has passed with reluctant step, and even now the traces of its footsteps are discernible on every side. At noon of these bright days the sun looks down smilingly upon the soil it seeks to bless with its cheerful, cheering rays. The tiny grass-blades peep out, and stretch forth their graceful forms, as if to thank the unknown source from which their enjoyments spring. "Unknown," I said. Is it "fancy" that makes my soul withdraw that word, and suggest that it may be that even that blade of grass recognizes the hand that ministers to all its wants? I think not. I think that what we term "fancy" and "imagination" are the most real and enduring portions of existence. They are of that immortal part that will live after crumbling column and the adamantine foundations of earth have passed away, and lost their present identity in countless forms of a higher existence. Are not all the forces of nature unseen, yet are they not real? Most assuredly they are. But I am talking of spring. I hinted at winter's tardy withdrawal. Look you how that little pile of snow hides itself in yonder shady nook,—right there where the sun's rays never come; right there, as if ashamed, like a man out of place,—pity that it lingers. Here and there, at the side of the brook, a little ice is waiting to be dissolved, that it may bound away, bright and sparkling, over the glistening pebbles.

The farmer opens his barn doors that the warm, fresh

breeze may ramble amid its rafters. The cattle snuff the refreshing winds, that bear tidings of green fields. The housewife opens door and windows, and begins to live more without than within.

Let us to the woods. How the old leaves rustle beneath our tread! Winter hides his cold, wet hand underneath these leaves, and occasionally we feel his chilling touch as we pass along. But from above the pleasant sunshine comes trickling down between the branches, and the warm south wind blows cheeringly among the trees.

> "Didst thou not hear yon swallow sing,
> Chirp, chirp? — In every note he seemed to say,
> 'T is spring, 't is spring."

Yes, 't is spring; bright, glorious season, when nature awakes to new life and forest-concerts begin.

Up with the window, throw open the closed shutter, let the fresh air in, and let the housed captive breathe the invigorating elixir of life; better by far than all your pills and cordials, and more strengthening than all the poor-man's plasters that have been or ever will be spread.

The hale and hearty youth, whose clear and boisterous laugh did the old man good, as he heard it ring forth on the clear air of a winter's night, has become satiated with the pleasures of sleigh-rides and merry frolics, and welcomes the spring-time of year as a man greeteth the return of an old friend from a long journey. How his bright eye flashes with the joyous soul within him, as he treads the earth, and beholds the trees put forth their buds, and hears the warblings of the birds once again, where a few weeks since winter brooded in silence!

In town and country the coming of spring changes the general appearance of affairs. Not only nature, but men change. There is no longer the cold and frigid countenance. Men do not walk with quick and measured tread, but pass carelessly, easily along, as though it was a luxury and not a task to walk. Children are seen in little companies, plucking the flowers and forcing the buds from their stems, as though to punish them for their tardiness.

The very beasts of burden and of the field partake of the general joy; as Thomson says,

> "Nor undelighted by the boundless spring
> Are the broad monsters of the foaming deep;
> From the deep ooze and gelid cavern roused,
> They flounce and tumble in unwieldy joy."

In the town storekeepers obtain fresh supplies of goods; the mechanic contracts new jobs; the merchant repairs his vessel, and sends it forth, deeply freighted with the productions of our own clime, to far distant lands; and the people generally brush up, and have the appearance of being a number of years younger than they were a month since.

In the country, the farmer is full of work. The ploughs are brought forth from their winter quarters, the earth is opened, that the warm sun and refreshing rains may prepare it for use; old fences are repaired, and new ones made; the housewife brushes up inside and out, and with the aid of the whitewash every old fence and shed is made clean and pleasing to the eye.

Welcome spring, a hearty welcome to thee! Touch the cheek of the maiden, and make it as bright as the rose; with thy fresh air give health to the sick and joy to the downcast. Thou bringest with thee sweet-smelling flowers, and the birds of the woods carol forth thy welcome.

A TEXT FOR A LIFETIME.

ONE word for humanity. One word for those who dwell in want around us. O, ye who know not what it is to hunger, and have naught to meet your desire; ye who never are cold, with naught to warm your chilled blood, forget not those who endure all these things. They are your brethren. They are of the same family as yourself, and have a claim upon your love, your sympathy, your kindness.

Live not for yourselves. The world needs to learn this lesson. Mankind have to learn that only as they bless others are they themselves blest. It was the fine thought of the good Indian, *Wah-pan-nah*, that man should not pile up his dollars,— they may fall down and crush him,— but spread them out.

"There be dark spot on you brother's path,— go lay dollar there and make it bright," said he.

And since that suggestion came we have thought it over and over, and have found it a text for a lifetime of goodness. Go place the bright dollar in the poor man's hand, and the good you do will be reflected in rays of gratitude from a smiling face, and fall on you like the warm sunshine, to cheer and refresh and strengthen your own soul.

There are in this world too many dollars "piled up," and on the surface we see but the brightness of one. Were these all spread out, what a wide field of radiant beauty would greet our vision! Instead of being a useless encumbrance, a care, a constant source of perplexity to one man, this wealth would make every man comfortable and happy. It would perform its legitimate work, were it not chained by avarice, — that canker-worm that destroys the fairest portions of our social system.

And there is a joy in doing good, and in dispensing the bounties with which we are blest, that hath no equal in the household of man. To know that we have fed the hungry, clothed the naked, wiped away one tear, bathed in the sunlight of hope one desponding spirit, gives to us a happiness that hoarded wealth, though broad as earth and high as heaven, cannot impart.

This is the *true* wealth. This the wealth that rust cannot corrupt. There is no other real wealth in the universe. Gold and silver, houses and lands, are not wealth to the longing, aspiring soul of man. The joy of the spirit, which is the reward of a good deed, comes a gift from God, a treasure worthy of being garnered into the storehouse of an immortal being.

There was one spot on earth where joy reigned. It was not in marble palace; but in a low cot, beneath a roof of thatch.

There was an indwelling sense of duty done; a feeling somewhat akin to that which we might suppose angels to feel, when a poor, earth-wearied traveller is relieved by them.

That was a subject fit for a Raphael's pencil, as she, of form and feature more angelic than human, sat beside that cottage door, and her mild blue eye gazed steadfastly up to heaven, and the light of the moon disclosed to mortal view her calm and beautiful features.

Two hours previous, over a sick and languishing child a mother bowed with maternal fondness. She pressed her lips to his chilled forehead, and wiped the cold sweat from his aching brow.

"Be patient, my child," said she; "God will provide." And why did she bid him "be patient"? None could have been more so; for through the long hours of that long summer day he had lain there, suffered and endured all; yet not one sigh had arisen from his breast, not one complaint had passed his parched lips.

"I know it," said he. And the mother kissed him again, and again said,

"God will provide."

Mother and son! the one sick, the other crushed down with poverty and sorrow. Yet in this her hour of adversity her trust in the God of her fathers wavered not; she firmly relied on Him for support, whom she had never found forgetful of her. The widow and the fatherless were in that low tenement, and above was the God who had promised to protect them.

Again she whispered in the lad's ear, "God will provide."

The light of that day's sun had not rested upon food in that dwelling. Heavily the hours passed by. Each seemed longer than that which had preceded it.

A rap at the door was heard. She arose and hastened to it. No person was in sight; but in the moon's bright rays stood a basket, on which lay a card, stating that it and its contents were for her and her child, and that on the morrow a nurse and every comfort they might want would be provided.

She bowed herself beside it, and thanked God for the gift. Then with a joyful heart she carried it within, and her child's eye sparkled as he heard the glad news, that He who watcheth the sparrows had not forgotten them.

Let us return now to that thatched cottage. She, whose mild eye gazeth up to heaven, whilst passing the door of the famishing mother and child an hour previous, had heard the words with which that mother had encouraged her dying son.

With speed the maiden hastened to her home, and from

her own limited store carried forth that basket, and heaven-like bestowed the gift unseen and unknown, save by Him who seeth and who rewardeth. The deed of mercy accomplished, she hastened to her home; and now, as she looks upward, how her eye beams with joy, and her heart breaks forth in songs of gratitude to Him who made her the instrument of so much good!

Gold, with all its power, cannot bring joy unless dealt forth with a willing heart like hers. The king in his palace, whose sceptre's sway extends over vast dominions, hath no pleasures capable of rivalling that which, by an act of charity, was brought to the soul of that young cottage girl.

Reader, whatever your condition, you can possess a joy like hers. If you have not what men call wealth, with which to help the weak and desponding, you have a smile of sympathy, a look of kindness, a word of love. Give those, and you shall know what a blessed thing is Charity.

NOW CLOSE THE BOOK.

Now close the book. Each page hath done its part,
Each thought hath left its impress on the heart.
O, may it be that naught hath here been traced
That after years may wish to have effaced!
O, may it be Humanity hath won
Some slight bestowment by the task now done!

If struggling Right hath found one cheering word,
If Hope hath in desponding heart been stirred,
If Sorrow hath from one lone soul been driven
By one kind word of Sympathy here given,
Then in my soul a living joy shall dwell,
Brighter than art can paint or language tell.

Yes, close the book: the story and the song
Have each been said, and sung. I see the throng
Of gentle ministrants who 've led my pen
Withdraw their aid. I hear the word, Amen.
And now to you, who have been with me through
The "Town and Country," I must bid adieu.

THE LADY'S TOKEN; OR, GIFT OF FRIENDSHIP. Edited by COTESWORTH PINCKNEY. 32mo, cloth, gilt.

GOLDEN LEAFLETS; A SELECTION OF POETRY. Designed as a Present Book for all Seasons. Edited by J. M. FLETCHER. 32mo, cloth, gilt.

GEMS OF WISDOM. A Collection of Gems from the best Authors of all Nations and Times. 32mo, cloth, gilt.

AMERICAN ETIQUETTE. 32mo, cloth, gilt.

CHILD'S WREATH; OR, POEMS FOR CHILDREN. Edited by S. C. C. 32mo, cloth, gilt.

One of the best Juvenile gift books published.

GIFT OF REMEMBRANCE. 32mo, cloth, gilt.

THE MEMENTO. 32mo, cloth, gilt.

GIFT OF LOVE. 32mo, cloth, gilt.

*** The following series of demi-miniature Gift Books have had, and continue to have, a very extensive sale. Upwards of *two hundred thousand* have been sold within a short period. They are printed on fine, white paper, neatly bound in cloth, emblematically embossed, gilt edge, and put up in packages of one dozen each.

THE OFFERING.	WEDDING RING.
BIBLE GEMS.	THE SEASONS.
VASE OF FLOWERS.	FLORAL WREATH.
GIFT OF PIETY	FRIENDSHIP'S JEWEL.
SACRED GIFT.	CRYSTAL GEM.
GOLDEN VASE.	DAILY FOOD.

J. B. would call the attention of dealers to his large and varied stock of

STATIONERY,

including Letter, Note, and Bill Papers, Envelopes, Blank Books, Steel Pens, Pencils, Inks, and articles usually wanted by New England jobbers, all of which will be furnished at the very lowest prices.